Ulrich Beck

Since the 1980s, Ulrich Beck has worked extensively on his theories of second modernity and the risk society. In *Ulrich Beck*, Mads P. Sørensen and Allan Christiansen provide an extensive and thorough introduction to the German sociologist's collected works. The book covers his sociology of work, his theories of individualization, globalization and subpolitics, his world-famous theory of the risk society and second modernity as well as his latest work on cosmopolitanism.

Focusing on the theory outlined in Beck's chief work, *Risk Society,* and on his theory of second modernity, Sørensen and Christiansen explain the sociologist's ideas and writing in a clear and accessible way. Largely concerned with the last 25 years of Beck's authorship, the book nevertheless takes a retrospective look at his works from the late 1970s and early 1980s, and reviews the critique that has been raised against Beck's sociology through the years. Each chapter of *Ulrich Beck* comes with a list of suggested further reading, as well as explanations of core terms. The book also includes a biography of Beck, and full bibliographies of his work in both English and German.

This comprehensive introduction will be of interest to all students of sociology, contemporary social theory, globalization theory, environmental studies, politics, geography and risk studies.

Mads P. Sørensen is Senior Researcher at the Danish Centre for Studies in Research and Research Policy, Aarhus University. He is author and co-author of several books, book chapters and journal articles on – among others – Ulrich Beck, subpolitics, political consumerism, Karl Marx and Adam Smith.

Allan Christiansen is Head of Development and Coaching in a major Danish industrial group and is also part-time lecturer at the Department of Business Communication, Aarhus University, Business and Social Science.

Routledge Advances in Sociology

Ulrich Beck

An introduction to the
theory of second modernity
and the risk society

**Mads P. Sørensen and
Allan Christiansen**

Routledge
Taylor & Francis Group

LONDON AND NEW YORK

First published 2013
by Routledge
2 Park Square, Milton Park, Abingdon, Oxon, OX14 4RN

Simultaneously published in the USA and Canada
by Routledge
711 Third Avenue, New York, NY 10017

Routledge is an imprint of the Taylor & Francis Group, an informa business

British Library Cataloguing in Publication Data
A catalogue record for this book is available from the British Library

Library of Congress Cataloging in Publication Data
Sørensen, Mads Peter.
Ulrich Beck: an introduction to the theory of second modernity and the risk society / Mads P. Sørensen and Allan Christiansen. – 1st ed.
p. cm. – (Routledge advances in sociology; 74)
Includes bibliographical references and index.
1. Social change. 2. Civilization, Modern. 3. Risk perception. 4. Risk-taking (Psychology) 5. Social sciences–Philosophy. 6. Beck, Ulrich, 1944– Political and social views. I. Christiansen, Allan. II. Title.
HM831.S667 2012
303.4–dc23
2012001668

ISBN: 978-0-415-69369-1 (hbk)
ISBN: 978-0-203-10792-8 (ebk)

Typeset in Times New Roman by Prepress Projects Ltd, Perth, UK

Contents

Figures

Tables

Preface

Ulrich Beck is one the world's most influential contemporary sociologists. His authorship is as impressive as it is well established, as made abundantly clear by the bibliography at the back of this book. He has authored more than 40 books and over 250 articles and he remains ferociously productive to this day. His chief work – *Risk Society*, from 1986 (first translated to English in 1992) – is already considered a classic, and over the last many years he has, time and time again, proven his ability to propel new and interesting topics onto the stage and into the discursive and investigative spotlights of international sociology. His works have been translated into more than 30 different languages, and his theory of the risk society has garnered him a solid reputation throughout most of the world. Today, a professor emeritus at the University of Munich, Beck remains a highly active researcher and critical intellectual, as well as a recurring visiting professor at the London School of Economics. He is the editor in chief of the journal *Soziale Welt* as well as editor of the series 'Edition Zweite Moderne', which is regularly published by the large German publishing house Suhrkamp (the name of the series is a direct reference to his own theory of how we all, today, live in a new kind of modernity: the second modernity). Furthermore, Ulrich Beck is also a highly requested speaker and visiting professor, with a record of appearances that spans most of the globe, ranging from such highly esteemed universities as Harvard to an array of prestigious political and ethical forums, one of the most recent examples being German Chancellor Angela Merkel's 'commission for a secure energy supply' in which he participated in 2011.

Ulrich Beck, in other words, is simply sociologically famous. Yet, despite his status and work in the field, curiously few attempts have been made towards presenting a comprehensive introduction to his work. Certain particular elements of his sociology have, of course – as we will cover in this book – seen fairly extensive coverage already; this is especially true of his theory of the risk society. However, the fact is that, to the best of our knowledge (and apart from the book that we ourselves published in Danish with Aarhus University Press in 2006, *Ulrich Beck: Risikosamfundet og det andet moderne*), no comprehensive introduction to his collected works has ever been readily available, until now. Monographs and articles have been written which may serve as specialized introductions to particular parts and aspects of his theoretical system, but so far no attempt has been made, by any book, towards presenting a thorough, coherent account of all parts of his writings.

Because of this, we now present our introduction to the work of Ulrich Beck in a new, rewritten and expanded English edition which we hope may serve as a complete introduction to Beck's writings. The book is meant to provide an insight to Beck's collected sociology and function as an accessible introduction into the various theories and concepts/terms he has formed. This book should not be considered a critical introduction and we do not aim to problematize or critically discuss Beck's work as we present it. Instead we have opted for a faithful presentation of Beck's sociology which is as straightforward as possible. We will, none the less, offer our own brief assessment of his theories in the final chapter of the book along with a resume of the prevalent strands of the criticism which has been made of his theories through the years.

This book is for readers wholly unfamiliar with Beck, as well as readers who have tried their hand at tackling and understanding his writings on their own, but who now find themselves in want of an overview of his authorship. Fully understanding Beck's many theories and his use of specific terms and concepts can be a difficult venture and one might well, reading his work, find oneself in need of clarification. This is understandable, as Ulrich Beck is not always an easy read. It can be difficult to completely grasp his theories and terms, which is why we will be making a sustained effort, throughout the book, to explain his theories and concepts. Tables and figures will be supplied throughout the book, which are meant to contain and represent his main arguments. In addition to this, we will also be providing lists of definitions which should help to further elucidate Beck's main terms and concepts. Furthermore, each individual chapter will be followed by an overview of the most important further reading. In an effort to make the book as reader-friendly and accessible as possible, we have striven to keep the number of notes throughout the book to an absolute minimum. We have sought, as well, to reduce the number of references but have opted to provide references to the original works as we discuss them, in order to allow the reader easy access to Beck's own treatment of the particular topics in question. Any italicized passages in quotes are thus in the original sources, unless clearly marked otherwise.

We would like to make use of this preface to extend our thanks to Ulrich Beck, who, years ago, welcomed us to Munich as visiting fellow and student, respectively, at the Institute of Sociology of Ludwig-Maximilians University. It was a great experience for us both – and meeting this sympathetic, worldly and highly engaged sociologist was an enriching experience, both personally and professionally. We would furthermore like to express our gratitude for the multitude of interviews and conversations he has agreed to have with us throughout the years. We would also like to thank his secretary, Almut Kleine, for her friendliness and helpfulness in providing us with material for the previous Danish edition of this book – material which has been reused in this new edition. We owe our thanks, as well, to Aarhus University Press and its general manager, Carsten Fenger-Grøndahl, for their permission to let us use our Danish book as a starting point for this new, rewritten and heavily expanded English version. We would also like to thank the current director, Niels Mejlgaard, as well as the previous director, Ebbe Krogh Graversen, at the Danish Centre for Studies in Research and Research Policy at Aarhus University, for their support and encouragement during the project. We would like to thank Stefan K. Larsen for translating our work from Danish into fluent and reader-friendly English, for handling the manuscript's formatting, figures, tables and indexing and for locating, updating, cross-checking and cross-referencing quotes, bibliographies and translations for us. We would like to thank the Aarhus University Foundation for economically supporting the project and Ida Lundorff Haugen for helping us procure research articles and other relevant written material. Finally, we would like to thank Emily Briggs, Jennifer Dodd and Gerhard Boomgaarden at Routledge for their work on the book.

Mads P. Sørensen and Allan Christiansen
Aarhus, December 2011

1 Introduction and a short biography

One afternoon, during his first year as a law student, as Ulrich Beck was walking around the south German university town of Freiburg and contemplating the nature of reality, he was suddenly struck by the realization that it was not actually the nature of reality *as such* that he was attempting to grasp at all. Rather, it was his own view or notion of what he believed reality *to be*. Reality as such, it dawned on him, he could not really know anything about. This sudden realization came as quite a shock to him – as did, in its wake, the exhilarating vertiginous feeling that he might, in fact, be the first person ever to think, ever to have *reached*, this particular thought. A fellow student, however, later eased his mind by letting him know that the very same notion had already been entertained a couple of centuries previously, by the German philosopher Immanuel Kant. Still, this did little to change the gravity with which Beck perceived the significance of his metaphysical insights. It was because of this particular epiphanic moment (of which Beck today speaks with a marvellous amount of self-deprecation) that he was led away from his law studies and towards philosophy. So what he did, plain and simply, was to quit his law studies and start reading Kant. However, perhaps his realization led to more than a mere change of educational trajectories. This would seem to be the case, at least, as the fundamental problem of *reality* has kept him occupied ever since. It was this same problem which was responsible for his later abandonment of philosophy in favour of sociology when philosophy, under close scrutiny, turned out to be much more occupied with its own concepts than with reality – a tendency which Beck also believes persists in certain parts of sociology; particularly with respect to the system theories of Niklas Luhmann and Talcott Parsons; theories which Beck, consequently, has never cared much for.

Beck has always, he says of himself, felt a keen sense of responsibility towards his own concepts and for making sure that they correspond as closely to reality as they possibly can, without making false claims of actual representation. Beck realized early on exactly how harmful poor, bad and stale concepts and theories can be and how much their application can distort reality around them. As he was working on his dissertation (Beck, 1974), he became increasingly aware of how vital the values and notions which sociology entertains about the world – the same values and notions on which it bases so many of its questions and so much of its research – really were. Should the basic notions and values of sociology and research turn out to be wrong, they would render all subsequent answers and research futile and useless. The results would resemble nothing more than a distorted mirage, a funhouse mirror representation of reality in itself. Beck, therefore, has adamantly insisted that it is an imperative, core responsibility for sociologists to make sure their theories correspond closely with the reality they intend to describe. Thus, when Beck today takes such sharp issue with what he calls the methodological nationalism – that is sociological theory's tendency to assume that the world can be divided into 'nation-state containers' with each container holding its respective people, territory and society within it – he does so because it is exactly the kind of notion that presents a distorted version of reality (see Chapter 6 below). We can simply no longer coherently view the world as something to be divided into containers of nation-states. It is not reality. Societies today are interconnected across national borders and – as we will examine in Chapter 5 – it is one of Beck's main points of argument that the society of today is a world risk society. In his view, then, methodological nationalism is simply working from a distorted view of reality: the national borders no longer exist in reality; they exist purely in our minds. This realization must, necessarily, serve as a starting point for all further research into the matter. Should the researchers instead choose to cling to methodological nationalism, they will inevitably end up reproducing traditional representations of a false reality. It is this same line of thought which is behind Beck's work with the theory of risk society and second modernity. Reality has shifted, and so now, in order for us to be able to grasp reality at all, we must create new concepts and theories for our approach. What we need now, in other words, is a *new sociology* which is prepared to approach and reason about reality, *as it is*.

This, in short, is the project of Ulrich Beck. He wishes to create a sociology which functions in accordance with the reality we all live in and experience daily. He calls his own sociology a *science of reality*. Note that most sociologists will, all things considered, probably want to claim that they, too, are conducting a kind of science of reality but the fact is that many of them are really, according to Beck, merely conducting a particular kind of fruitless *zombie science* (or the 'science of unreality', as he would probably prefer to call it today; e.g. Beck, 2006: 21). This is the case for the sociologists in whose works the antiquated sociological preconceptions and ideas still – much like zombies – remain active after death; a science in which distorted beliefs and notions about what constitutes the real world remain on their feet, shuffling about and causing all kinds of intellectual havoc, long after their actual demise. Needless to say these kinds of picturesque characterizations have not exactly contributed in any particularly positive way to Beck's popularity amongst his fellow sociologists. His sociology in general, as we shall discuss further, later on in this book, has also been surrounded by much debate. However, Beck is nonetheless widely considered part of the absolute world elite of contemporary sociology. His books – first and foremost *Risk Society* – have been translated into more than 30 different languages and have seen large print runs throughout most of the world. Beck is without a doubt one of the most productive and innovative sociologists of our time. He has not halted his continuous production of books and articles, in spite of recently becoming professor emeritus, and he is still writing articles, editorials and comments for newspapers and journals worldwide. Throughout the last 25–30 years he has, several times, proven himself able to produce new, thought-provoking theory drafts which have then gone on to set the sociological agenda, changing how the broad social sciences have understood and discussed various topics. This began as early as the 1970s when he helped introduce a new, subject-oriented perspective into the field of sociology as a science; momentum really started to gather throughout the 1980s and 1990s as Beck engaged himself in his theory of individualization, globalization and risk society, propelling each field to a point where it went on to receive widespread public recognition and debate. Beck has continued his productivity throughout the late 1990s and into the 2000s, which have seen his critique of the methodological nationalism of the social sciences and his cosmopolitan project of reenlightenment.

From Slupsk to sociological world fame: a short biography

Born in Slupsk in the Pomeranian province of Poland in 1944, the son of a nurse and a German naval officer, and being the youngest out of five siblings, Ulrich Beck did not seem immediately destined to eventually go on to become one of the most influential sociologists of our time. His father never returned home from the Second World War and the rest of the family had no choice but to flee westwards as a consequence of the new political rumblings and demarcations that were being drawn throughout and across Europe at the time. The family found a new home in Hanover, where Ulrich Beck grew up and spent his childhood. One of Beck's best friends from his time in Hanover is the painter Jobst Günther, who today resides in Berlin and, in various works, has drawn inspiration from, and commented upon, Beck's sociology and writings. The one year of his youth he spent attending an American high school also remains one of Beck's fond memories. In 1966, having served two years of military service, Beck moved to Freiburg and enrolled in law school. He had ambitions of one day becoming a fiction writer and had decided that practising law would provide the means necessary for supporting a writing career.

It was not long, however, before Beck gave up on his law studies, as well as on his notion of writing fiction. His literary ambitions, however, still run like a vein through his books to this day. Beck has been called a poet of modernization, a pet name which can easily be seen as an approving nod towards his unorthodox prose, his fluid style of writing and his use of metaphors, which are often as whimsical as they are thought provoking. It is clear to see, then, that Beck, in his writings, has drawn much inspiration from the essays of Gottfried Benn, as well as from the sheer power of language in the writings of Friedrich Nietzsche. In 1967, having broken his bonds with law school once and for all, Beck turned to philosophy. He wished for yet another fresh start in a new place, and this time he chose Munich. He based his choice primarily on the fact that the philosophical milieu in Munich at the time was the most attractive. Once in Munich, Beck dedicated himself wholly to philosophy, both analytical and continental. His main interest, however, was German idealism and his preferred philosophers were Kant and Fichte. He also followed additional courses in psychology, social studies and sociology. Beck recalls with particular fondness two teachers of philosophy: Andreas Konrad, who tutored Beck in logics and analytical philosophy, and the Fichte scholar Reinhardt Lauth, whose lectures on Fichte thrilled Beck greatly. The relationship between Lauth and Beck, however, would eventually be ruined by a disagreement about – what else? – *reality*, as Lauth, much to Beck's dismay, refused to relate to or concern himself with the questions of student politics that were being discussed at the time and opted to stick with the theoretical world and philosophical concepts of Fichte. Beck, on the other hand, saw Lauth's behaviour – his refusal to relate to the *real* world – as a symptom of the state of philosophy in general, of a more general kind of ailment. Philosophy, Beck believed, was much too occupied with its own concepts and terms. It had a tendency only rarely to allow reality even so much as to enter its highly theoretical domain. Increasingly, Beck began to focus on what had initially started out as one of his minor elective courses: sociology. It was here that he found the particular kind of intellectual scrutiny of, and preoccupation with, reality that he sought. Especially responsible for introducing Beck to the world of sociology, for drawing him in, as it were, was the professor of sociology, Karl Martin Bolte, the one person who may well have had the single largest impact on Beck's career and work.

Beck and Bolte first met during Bolte's office hours, the week before that year's courses were scheduled to begin. Beck, then a second-semester sociology student, had sought out Bolte to let him know exactly how poorly he felt Bolte's upcoming teaching schedule had been planned out. Bolte listened politely to the complaints of the young student and then, once Beck finally fell silent, asked him to make a personal appearance at one of the courses, where he would be given the opportunity to deliver a presentation and expand on his criticisms. Beck showed up, delivered his presentation and received a devastating barrage of criticism from the other students following the course. However, Bolte, as Beck was leaving the room, grabbed the young disenfranchised student by the elbow, pulled him aside and told him that he himself had very much liked the presentation and thought Beck perhaps ought to consider following the course from that point on. Beck did so and, in the years to come, Bolte became his mentor. They kept working together long after Beck's time as a student had come to an end. After Beck finished his dissertation studying with Bolte in 1972, Bolte hired him to work on research project SFB 101, titled 'Theoretische Grundlagen sozialwissenschaftlicher Berufs- und Arbeitskräfteforschung' (roughly 'Theoretical framework for labour market and workforce research in the social sciences'). Here Beck eventually ended up working with Michael Brater, with whom he went on to develop a fruitful cooperative relationship throughout the 1970s. The two of them shared an interest in exploring the relations between different aspects of the construction of identity and the choice of vocation and occupation, that is of working in certain lines of work or holding particular jobs. It was during this period that Beck took the first steps towards his later thoughts of individualization. Beck worked under

Bolte up until 1979, when he submitted his dissertation on the construction of reality through vocation to the faculty of social sciences at Ludwig-Maximilian University in Munich. It only barely passed and it has never been published. The conservative faculty council did not at all care for what they felt were clearly the neo-Marxist tendencies of the dissertation. However, Bolte came to Beck's aid and, thanks to Bolte's intervention and defence, Beck's work was accepted after all. Beck never did turn completely Marxist during his student years, although many of his peers eventually did. His theoretical role model during those years was Jürgen Habermas, whereas the older parts of the Frankfurt School did not really have much of an impact on him. What fascinated Beck about Habermas was his ability to bridge the gap between philosophy and sociology.

During his student years at the Institute of Sociology in Munich, Beck met Elisabeth Gernsheim, who is today also an internationally renowned sociologist. They married in 1975 and in 1979 they were both hired at the University of Münster. Here, in 1980, he was appointed co-editor of the journal *Soziale Welt*, which he still edits to this day. However, the cooperative atmosphere between Ulrich Beck and Heinz Hartmann, who was the leader of the Institute of Sociology at Münster, soured after a couple of years, prompting Beck to seek new challenges elsewhere. These turned out to come in the shape of a position as professor with the relatively new University of Bamberg, where Beck, along with two colleagues, were given the responsibility for establishing an Institute of Sociology from the ground up. During his time as a professor in Bamberg, such people as Christoph Lau and Wolfgang Bonß were among his assistants. Beck arrived at Bamberg in 1981 and stayed there until 1992, when he applied for and received a professorship of sociology at his old university in Munich. It is from here that he is today a professor emeritus. The chair he occupied until 2009, which is still called the *Lehrstuhl Beck* (Beck Chair), is presently held by Professor Heike Kahlert. Additionally, Ulrich Beck was also, during his time as a professor in Munich, head of the large research project on reflexive modernization called SFB 536, which started in 1999 and continued until 2009. SFB 536 – financed by the German Research Council and other research foundations – saw continuous participation from a large number of researchers from both German and foreign universities, including five universities from the general Munich area: LMU (Ludwig-Maximillians-Universität), Bundeswehr University Munich, University of Augsburg, Institut für Sozialwissenschaftliche Forschung e. V. and Technical University of Munich. Today, Beck is affiliated with the London School of Economics and Political Science (LSE), serving as *British Journal of Sociology* Visiting Centennial Professor, a professorship he has held since 1997 and which entails him spending some weeks in London every semester, teaching and conducting research, working at the same institute as such people as Richard Sennett, Nikolas Rose and Saskia Sassen. At the LSE, Beck has also collaborated closely with his good friend and colleague Anthony Giddens, who for a number of years served as Director of the LSE.

All things considered then, Beck is part of the elite of contemporary, international sociology. As is apparent from the bibliography at the back of this book, he has not come to his status by a stroke of luck or simple good fortune. He has, throughout the years, remained a highly active sociologist. His productions span more than 40 books and over 250 research articles. In addition to this, he is a stalwart contributor to various European newspapers. Over the years, he has been a visiting fellow at a number of universities in and outside Germany (Essen, Berlin, Cardiff and Harvard among others) and has received honorary doctorates from three universities: University of Jyväskyla in Finland (1996), University of Macerata in Italy (2006) and University UNED Madrid in Spain (2007). He has received a number of awards for his work and his involvement as intellectual commentator – such as *Kultureller Ehrenpreis der Stadt München* (Cultural Honorary Award of the City of Munich) (1997), *Cicero-Preis für öffentliche Reden* (Cicero award for public speaking) (1999), *German–British Forum Awards für besondere Verdienste um deutsch–britische Beziehungen* (German–British Forum awards for contributions to German–British relations) (1999), *Preis der Gesellschaft für Soziologie (DGS) für herausragende Leistungen auf dem Gebiet der öffentlichen Wirksamkeit der Soziologie* (German Society of Sociology award for outstanding achievements in the field of the public effects of sociology) (2004) and *Schader-Preis der Schader-Stiftung für Geisteswissenschaftler* (Schader Foundation award for the humanities) in 2005. Ulrich Beck has, throughout the years, been a member of various think tanks and a participant in different state commissions. In 2010, he was appointed senior fellow at the American think tank The Breakthrough Institute. He is a past member of the *Kommission für Zukunftsfragen der Freistaaten Bayern und Sachsen* (Commission for questions about the future of Bavaria and Saxony) in which he served from 1995 to 1997. And in 2011 – curiously, the year of the twenty-fifth anniversary of his book *Risk Society*, which was first published in 1986, a book in which it is the danger of radioactive leaks from nuclear power plants, more than anything else, that serves as a symbol of the emergent risk society – Beck was appointed to serve in German Chancellor Angela Merkel's 'ethical commission for a safe energy supply', which was formed in the wake of the nuclear disaster at the Fukushima plant in Japan. With its final report of May 2011, the commission was amongst those to recommend the swift and complete phasing-out of nuclear power in Germany, which the government and Reichstag initiated that same year.

This book and its contents

In this book we present an introduction to Beck's extensive body of work. Our main focus will be on the particular theory that has influenced almost all of his writing since his chief work, *Risk Society*, and runs through most of his work like a clear red thread, namely *the theory of second modernity*. We will, of course, also be taking a closer look at his single largest claim to fame, which is the theory of the risk society. Beck has worked extensively on both theories since the mid 1980s. Although we will, then, be preoccupied largely with the last 25 years of his authorship, we will also make sure to leave room for a retrospective look at his works from the late 1970s and early 1980s. This book is, all things considered, meant to provide a collected introduction to the sociology of Ulrich Beck. We will be starting off our exposition of Beck's sociology in Chapter 2, by providing an in-depth view of the theory of the *risk society*. As we shall see, Beck believes that we have left classic industrial society and that we instead now find ourselves living in the industrial risk society. In Chapter 3 we shall illustrate how this kind of transition from industry to risk society might be understood within a larger theoretical framework, by utilizing a more encompassing theory of our contemporary world, namely *the theory of second modernity*. According to Beck the social transition from a society of industry to one of risk coincides with a larger and more encompassing shift of modernity in general: a shift from first modernity to second modernity. Beck believes that five specific processes of change are responsible for this development:

•   a multidimensional *globalization process*;
•   a radicalized and intensified *individualization process*;
•   a global *environmental crisis*;
•   a *gender revolution*;
•   a *third industrial revolution*.

These five processes of change will be commented upon in depth in Chapters 4, 5 and 7 below. In Chapter 4, we offer an account of the new, *radicalized individualization process* – including the *gender revolution*, which is directly linked with the individualization process. In Chapter 5, we deal with the *multidimensional globalization process* and cover its influence on life and society today. As will be made apparent, the *global environmental crisis* is also one major dimension to be considered part of the current globalization process. Additionally in that chapter we take a look at Beck's current thoughts and writing, which have been occupied mainly with the cosmopolitanism. Finally, we spend Chapter 7 covering the last of the five change processes, namely the *third industrial revolution* and its influence on working life. In that chapter, we also offer a retrospect on Beck's labour market sociology of the 1970s. The transition from first, simple modernity to a new and reflexive second modernity brings with it an array of new challenges and changes, for both the political world as well as sociology and the sciences in general. These challenges and changes will be scrutinized in closer detail in Chapter 6. Finally, we conclude the book in Chapter 8, by offering a critical view of the theory of second modernity. This chapter will feature both an overview of the kind of critiques others have mounted against Beck's theories and, along with it, our own assessment of his theories about the risk society and the coming of second modernity. Furthermore, the book offers a collected bibliography of Ulrich Beck's publications, books and research articles, in both German and English.

2 Risk society
The return of uncertainty

On Friday 11 March 2011, at 14:46 local time, Japan was struck by the most powerful earthquake in the country's history. The epicentre of the quake was located some 130 kilometres east of the city of Sendai, 70 kilometres off the coast of the Tohoku region. The suboceanic tremors of the violent quake, measured at 9.0 on the Moment Magnitude Scale, then caused a destructive tsunami that hit the coast roughly 40 minutes after the main quake. The waves, exceeding heights of 12–14 metres, caused massive amounts of destruction and loss of life, as it travelled more than 10 kilometres inland. Buildings and bridges collapsed, entire trains filled with passengers were buried under the avalanche of mud and water and entire cities were eradicated. The losses were staggering: more than 15,000 people lost their lives in the flood itself, another 5,000 were injured and more than 4,500 people are still, to this day, reported missing. With regard to sheer material damages, more than 250,000 buildings were completely or partially destroyed by the water.[1] However, the full ramifications of the tragedy in Japan would prove to be much more frightening, as another serious consequence of the tsunami turned out to be the subsequent failure of several Japanese nuclear power plants. Several nuclear facilities were flooded following the earthquake. Fukushima 1, a six-reactor facility – which had been built, supposedly, to withstand tsunamis – was hardest hit, and, although protective safety walls had been erected all around the facility, these were built to withstand waves up to only six metres in height. The wave which hit Fukushima 1, however, exceeded 13 metres in height before it broke and rolled back; by then, all six reactors had been flooded. Three out of the six reactors had been shut down for routine maintenance before the tsunami hit. Reactor 4 had been de-fuelled but 5 and 6 still held active fuel supplies when the wave struck them. Meanwhile, the other reactors shut down automatically and emergency backup generators were engaged the moment the tremors from the quake had first registered on sensors in the plant's emergency system. The flooding of the reactors, however, disabled every backup generator except one and caused the plant to be cut off from the regular power grid as well. Fukushima staff were able, using the one functional generator, to keep reactors 5 and 6 in a sufficiently cooled, shut-down state. However, the fuel basin with discarded fuel rods, along with reactors 1, 2 and 3, was left entirely without power and thus without cooling. This caused the fuel rods to overheat and resulted in at least one confirmed meltdown and possibly several others. Explosions and fires destroyed large parts of the reactor buildings, leaking large amounts of radioactive material into the surroundings. In the days to follow, ocean water was pumped into the reactors, in an attempt to regain control and contain the meltdowns and supply the facility with cooling. In order to make room for this large amount of new, massively radiated ocean water that had been used to cool to the failing facility during the meltdown, the plant's water basins – which contained polluted water from the facility's regular cooling procedures – had to be drained out into the ocean, releasing large quantities of radioactive water back into the environment. The IAEA (International Atomic Energy Agency) classified the incident as the worst kind of nuclear disaster – a so-called level 7 or 'Major Accident' on the International Nuclear and Radiological Event Scale (INES).[2] The world has witnessed only one such level 7 nuclear disaster prior to the one in Fukushima. In 1986, the Soviet nuclear power plant at Chernobyl lost control of its reactor 4 during a routine shutdown. The reactor was supposed to be turned off, in order to allow for a series of tests on new security procedures and protocols, but something went wrong during shutdown and a violent explosion tore a hole in the roof of reactor 4, releasing a cloud of radioactive material into the plant's surroundings. Thousands of people were directly affected by the incident, with many Russians succumbing to radioactive exposure, others falling severely ill in the days to follow and even more still being forcibly evicted from their homes (Chernobyl Forum 2003–2006, 2006). Meanwhile, the citizens of Ukraine, Belarus and the rest of Europe found themselves at the mercy of the weather, unable to do anything but wait and hope, literally, for the wind not to blow the wrong way or take a turn that would bring the radioactive cloud into their areas.

That same year, Ulrich Beck was working by the idyllic lake Sternberger See, a little south of Munich, at the foot of the Alps, in his summer residence, putting the finishing touches to his now world-famous book *Risk Society: Towards a New Modernity*. The book came out in German that same year and Beck, in the preface, wrote that much of its content – which he had fought to bring about by way of argument and theory – had already been made to resemble merely a timid description of reality, thanks to the recent Chernobyl accident.

A new society

To Beck, the kind of nuclear disasters that occurred at Fukushima and Chernobyl, although decidedly terrible occurrences, are also potent symbols of our transition from industrial society to what he calls *risk society*. In the risk society we experience, suddenly, the unwelcome return of frightening uncertainties – exactly the same uncertainty which modernity sought to rid itself of by means of science and rationality to begin with. Ironically, it is because of the complete success of the project of modernity – the sheer technological and scientific progress of industrial society – that the transition from industrial society to risk society has even occurred. The harnessing of the atom and the technological gains in nuclear power, for example, stand in many ways as a pinnacle of human creation, technological effort and scientific endurance through history; it is an expression of people's ability to completely tame and contain the most fundamental parts of nature and capacity to control them for our own purposes. With the rise of nuclear power and other advanced technology, humanity has once and for all emancipated itself from the bonds of nature. However, this sort of emancipation does not come without a price. Chernobyl and Fukushima are clear illustrations of this. In the wake of the Chernobyl disaster in 1986, many sought to downplay the general seriousness of the event, of the hazards and dangers of nuclear power and the risk of another radioactive leak, by pointing out that the Chernobyl plant had been built with old-fashioned technology, that it was more or less derelict and poorly maintained and that it was *these* factors, rather than any inherent dangers of nuclear power *itself*, which caused the accident; this effectively helped absolve other, newer plants from scrutiny and from guilt by general association.

Indeed, the Bavarian prime minister, Franz Josef Strauß of the Christian Social Union, for example, spoke of the incident as being a specifically 'communist' kind of catastrophe (i.e. one that could not have happened in the capitalist western world). However, this argument fell, says Beck, with Fukushima: an accident which occurred in exactly the kind of capitalist, tip-top high-tech – and very security-minded (Zielcke, 2011) – facility and country which Strauß claimed to be safe and, since not a communist regime, basically removed from nuclear risk by virtue of ideology. Beck sees these kinds of accidents as symbols which mark our transition into risk society.

The transition from industrial society to risk society occurs, says Beck, as the new and unintended side effects of industrial society (such as radioactive emissions) – the *new* risks – end up taking a central and previously unpredicted role in the public eye and debate. In other words: once we can no longer ignore the dangers of radioactive emission, global warming and all the other kinds of risks that have followed in the wake of our industrialized way of life (and once we find ourselves invoking these risks as arguments alongside traditional economical and scientific facts during public debate and governance), we have, once and for all, entered the risk society. Beck's reason for describing contemporary society as a risk society, then, is not simply that he thinks that risks are something new or that it is only *now* that we have begun to really *produce* risks on a relevant scale. His justification for using the term *risk society*, rather, is that recent years have seen the rise of a brand new species of risks which are different from our earlier, tangible risks and that we have started to take these new risks to be vital questions for society and its development. The fact that massive air pollution exists, for example, is not enough to call a given society – even though it may experience and suffer from massive air pollution – a risk society. The risk society emerges only once the pollution comes to be, and is perceived as, a problem in and by itself; risk society arises once people start to question whether a particular kind of product or production method can be seen as beneficial and whether the product is *worth* the pollution it causes, with the knowledge that to put a complete stop to the production of this particular product or production method might entail significant economic drawbacks.

In other words: industrial society has always polluted the environment – that is a part of the proverbial package – but it is only once the matter of pollution *itself* obtains the status of a problem in the minds of the population – once pollution becomes a prominent matter of public debate – that the transition from industrial society to risk society occurs.

A trademark symptom of the risk society, then, is the multitude of political deals, efforts and agreements which aim to abolish or regulate certain kinds of production and pollution or at least limit their impact and prevalence in the grand scheme of society. Such agreements tacitly acknowledge the fact that we are continually facing self-inflicted risks that occur as *side effects* of certain production methods and of our industrialized way of life in general. A good example of this kind of acknowledgement, which has led to several political agreements and specific changes to products and production methods, can be found in the case of chlorofluorocarbon (CFC) gases. These gases were once used as refrigerants, as propellants in spray cans and as industrial strength solvents; indeed, from the 1930s on, CFCs replaced liquid ammonia as a refrigerant in fridges all over the world. Over the course of the 1970s, however, increasing amount of evidence came to be gathered in support of the claim that CFC emissions were harmful to the ozone layer. In the 1980s, as scientists were able to prove that a dramatic thinning in the ozone layer over the Antarctica had taken place – and that several large holes in the layer had significantly increased human exposure to the harmful ultraviolet rays of the sun – it quickly resulted in several political agreements aimed at abolishing the use of CFC gases altogether. Starting with the United Nations (UN) summit in Vienna in 1985 and followed up with the Montreal summit in 1987, agreements were made to start phasing out the use of the gases. Several more meetings followed from 1990 on, each time with the purpose of introducing further sanctions, addendums and restrictions to the Montreal Protocol. A total of 196 countries have ratified the Montreal Protocol on phasing out the use of CFC gases and, as a result, the production and use of certain CFC gases are today entirely abolished, with the remaining CFC gases set to be completely phased out in the western world by 2020 and in developing countries by 2040.[3]

The complete success of this particular effort, however, remains fairly singular. Although recent years have seen widening international recognition of the fact that global warming is man-made, very little political action has been taken towards lowering carbon dioxide (CO_2) emissions worldwide. By signing the Kyoto Protocol of 1997, the participating countries agreed to work towards lowering the emission of greenhouse gases by roughly 5 per cent from the emission levels of 1990 (United Nations, 1998) but, in effect, only a few countries have made good on their promises. The climate summit in Copenhagen, December 2009 (COP 15), came and went without leaving any real results to show for itself. In this light then, the most impressive part of the successful phase-out of CFCs was not that the international community simply managed to *recognize* that the thinning of the ozone layer was a man-made problem, but that it actually, by a singular effort, managed to formulate and implement the necessary political measures for handling and alleviating the actual problem in an effective manner.

Although global political action still seems to be lacking with regard to climate problems, Ulrich Beck takes both cases as examples of our transition away from industrial society – in which side effects were either ignored or unknown – and into the risk society, in which these side effects take up more and more space in the public debate.

The end of industrial society

Ulrich Beck is far from the first sociologist to claim that we can no longer really coherently refer to our society as an industrial one. Since the late 1950s, people have doubted whether or not industrial society is really a fitting term to attach to the kind of society in which they have found themselves to be living. New suggestions started to come up throughout the 1950s; for example, attempting to pin a new name on society and the times, John Kenneth Galbraith suggested in 1958 that we should use the term *affluent society*, whereas David Riesman, Fritz Machlup and Joffre Dumazedier in the early 1960s argued that notion of *industry* was no longer a trademark characteristic of their time, opting instead to rely on terms such as *service*, *knowledge* and *leisure* for their descriptions of society. Others opted for claiming that they now lived in a *post-industrial society* rather than an industrial one. This particular diagnostic term was first used by Alan Touraine in 1969, later to be adopted in 1973 by Daniel Bell, who also coined the term *information society* (Bell, 1973).

The introduction of these new diagnostic terms for society marked the start of a new and massive flood of more or less conflicting and competing descriptions of society in general (see Table 2.1). Since the early 1980s the debate and discussion which surrounded the tradition of social diagnostics had become increasingly tied up with the discussion of the concept of modernity itself. This discussion came to characterize sociology as a field from the mid 1980s on. Throughout the 1990s – as a sort of reaction to all the talk of the 1980s about postmodern society and the like – came a slew of social terms that aimed to underline and support modernity in order to illustrate that it was still a prevalent trait of society which needed discussion and a coherent, elaborate vocabulary backing it; that modernity was still relevant enough, influential enough, to merit the continued work on – and additions to – its terminology. As illustrated in the next chapter, Beck's theory of the risk society is meant to operate within the boundaries of this larger debate about modernity in itself. Throughout the last two decades, Ulrich Beck's concept of the risk society has become increasingly prevalent and popular in the social sciences. All things considered, however, Beck is not at all the first to use the term *risk society*, either. As early as 1981, the Israeli sociologist Yair Aharoni published the book *The No-Risk Society* (Aharoni, 1981), in which he argued that we are living in a society which has a large focus on creating and ensuring security for everybody, and that a fundamental part of our security is insurance against the kinds of risks which are side effects of industrialized society itself. Beck's view, five years later, is that it is no longer possible to *provide* this kind of security, given new kinds of incalculable, man-made risks. Uncertainty has made its return to society and we cannot get rid of it. We simply cannot insure ourselves

Table 2.1 Recent decades' diagnostic terms for society

Term	Source
The affluent society	Galbraith (1958)
The service society	Riesman (1961)
The knowledge society	Machlup (1962)
The leisure society	Dumazedier (1962)
The advanced industrial society	Marcuse (1964)
The new industrial society	Galbraith (1967)
The post-industrial society	Touraine (1969), Bell (1973)
The optional society	Dovring and Dovring (1971)
The post-materialistic society	Inglehart (1977)
The postmodern society	Lyotard ([1979] 1984)
The No-Risk society	Aharoni (1981)
The Risk society	Beck (1986)
The information society	Bell (1987)
The late capitalist society	Benhabib and Cornell (1987), for example
The communication society	Münch (1991), for example
The late modern society	Giddens (1991, 1994a)
The post-capitalistic society	Steele (1992), for example
The post-scarcity society	Giddens (1994b)
The network society	Castells (1996)
The post-full employment society	Beck (2000a)
The individualized society	Bauman (2001a)
The hypermodern society	Ziehe (2001)

Note
What is provided here is not meant to be an exhaustive list. Rather, it is an overview of terms which have won prevalence, that is terms that have seen wide use over prolonged periods of time and have garnered a certain extent of acknowledgement and use in academic and/or broader contexts. In addition to these terms, sociologists have used terms such as 'the multicultural society', 'the experience society', 'the media society', 'the disciplinary society', 'the opinion society', 'the dream society', 'the learning society', 'the paradoxical society', 'the postnational society', 'the globalized society' and 'the hyper complex society'.

against the dangers of radioactive emissions, such as those from Chernobyl and Fukushima. Nor can we insure ourselves against the perils of global warming, the holes in the ozone layer or those risks intricately tied to our releasing genetically modified plants and other organisms into nature. Risk society has come to be stark reality, not because of any kind of a relapse or 'reversion' back into the risky conditions of earlier ages, to the world as it looked before industrial society, but rather, paradoxically, as a direct consequence of the sheer success of the industrial project, which turned out to be so very effective at turning society into exactly the kind of *no-risk* society which Aharoni once wrote about (Jacobsen, 2003).

Risk and hazard

The term *risk society* is actually a somewhat misleading one which ought to have been replaced by the term *hazard society* (Sørensen, 2002) or perhaps rather *self-jeopardy society*. However, when Ulrich Beck published *Risk Society* (Beck, 1986, 1992) in Germany in 1986, he was not aware of the theoretical distinction between risks and hazards that was commonly made in sociological risk theory at the time. By this theoretical distinction, risks were perceived to be clearly delimited, predictable uncertainties and secondary consequences of specific human actions. A worker (and only a worker) runs the risk of getting hurt in a workplace accident, a motorist runs the risk of being involved in a traffic accident and a home owner may run the risk of having his or her house broken into or burned down. One can, supported by sufficient evidence in the form of various statistical data, propose highly accurate risk assessments in order to calculate the likelihood of such an event taking place. Once a risk can be calculated, we can insure ourselves against it. Unlike these kinds of risks – which people run on a wholly individualized basis, simply by acting and engaging with their surroundings – hazards are externally caused events which the individual cannot do anything to prevent; nor is it possible to calculate or assess whether or not a given hazard will occur. The German sociologist Niklas Luhmann illustrates the difference between hazards and risks by asking us to consider the differences between second-hand smoking and regular (active) smoking: The smoker runs a risk, but, by doing so, he or she subjects others to the hazards of second-hand smoke:

> It is only to the smokers themselves that cancer is a risk; to anybody else it will always be a hazard. If we are dealing with damages caused by our own decisions, then we are dealing with risks regardless of how these risks may be weighed against our chances and our rational deliberations. In this case, one assumes that the damages would not have occurred if we had made another decision. Hazards, on the other hand, are damages that occur from causes that are out of our own control, such as unavoidable natural disasters or decisions made by other individuals, groups and organizations.
>
> (Luhmann, 1990: 143; our translation)

Unlike risks, hazards – such as natural disasters or epidemics – cannot be contained, kept in, delimited or walled off. They are not prone to affect any certain areas or specific demographics (e.g. workers, motorists, home owners). Everybody is, in principle, as likely to be affected by natural disasters or epidemics as everybody else. Nor are there any such things as completely secure areas or places where natural disasters or disease cannot strike or reach us. Unlike risks, hazards are not a matter of timing or of 'being in the wrong place at the wrong time', either. Whereas the motorist is running the risk of getting involved in a traffic accident only for the time which he or she spends in the vehicle and on the road, the danger of being infected with illness or struck by a natural disaster never quite goes away. This particular distinction, which is a sort of standard distinction that is quite common to sociological risk theory, was not part of Beck's theoretical landscape until after he had published *Risk Society*. Thus, there is little system or pattern to his use of the terms *risk* and *hazard* in this work and both terms seem to be used interchangeably and more or less synonymously with one another. Thus Beck alternates between calling the kind of phenomena he analyses in the book – holes in the ozone layer, nuclear disasters, gene technology and so – kinds of risks and kinds of hazards. This does not, however, mean that Beck thinks that the kinds of risks he is interested in discussing are comparable to workplace accidents or traffic accidents. His point, rather, is that these new risks are strongly related to the kinds of phenomena which sociological risk theory calls hazards, as they are not limited to affect any particular area or demographic. Nor can the perils of these new kinds of risks be confined or expected to occur at a particular moment or in a specific time span. They are threats to which everybody is exposed – at least in principle – for an indefinable period of time. So what the meltdown at Chernobyl and the recent events at Fukushima have shown us all too clearly is that the notion of *uncontrollable uncertainty* has made its return to society.

Three historical epochs

It was not until the book *Gegengifte*, published in Germany in 1988 (Beck, 1988, 1995a) that Beck incorporated the distinction between risk and hazard:

> 'Risks' are understood here (similarly in principle to the prevailing concep-tion) to be determinable, calculable uncertainties; modernity itself produced them in the form of foreseen or unforeseen secondary consequences, for which social responsibility is (or is not) taken through regulatory measures. They can be 'determined' by technical precautions, probability calculations, etc., but (and this is frequently not taken into account) also by social insti-tutions for attribution, liability and by contingency plans. There is, accord-ingly, a consensus in international social-scientific literature that one should distinguish here between pre-industrial hazards, not based on technological-economic decisions, and thus externalizable (onto nature, the gods), and industrial risks, products of social choice, which must be weighed against opportunities and acknowledge, dealt with or simply foisted on individuals.
>
> (Beck, 1995a: 77)

By way of this new distinction between risk and hazard, Beck divided history into three specific epochs, according to the kind of risks and hazards that were/are prevalent and characteristic of their time (see Table 2.2).

Pre-modern society was dominated by the *non-man-made hazards*. The major hazards for humanity during this period were natural disasters and large-scale epidemics, such as cholera and the plague, against which nothing could be done.

In *classic industrial society*, these hazards would come to be gradually replaced and supplemented by *man-made risks*. Unlike the traditional kinds of hazard, these risks were contained and clearly limited in their range. As in the cases of the

Table 2.2 Ulrich Beck's use of the terms 'risk' and 'hazard' (since 1988)

Period	Examples	Term	Cause	Possibility of avoiding harm
Pre-modern society	Natural disasters, epidemics	Hazards	External causes	People are exposed to the events and cannot avoid them
Industrial society	Unemployment, accidents (traffic, work etc.)	Risks	Man-made	People can (in principle) avoid or insure themselves against them
Risk society	Radioactive leaking, gene technology, holes in the ozone layer, global warming, terrorism	Self-jeopardy, man-made disasters	Man-made	People are exposed to the events, cannot avoid them and cannot insure themselves against them

workers, motorists and home owners, risks were particular problems that affected only specific demographic *groups of people* in specific *places* at specific *times* (Beck, 1995a: 78). Since one could so easily identify and characterize the people who were subjected to a specific risk, one could also – at least in principle – do something to alleviate the risk itself. By collecting data from previous mishaps, it was possible to calculate the likelihood that similar accidents might happen again in the future. This made it possible for people to *insure* themselves against that specific kind of event, simply by signing up with private or public insurance initiatives.

Beck's understanding of risks is largely inspired by the French sociologist, and student of Foucault, François Ewald, who has described modern society as an *insurance society* (e.g. Ewald, 1991). The deciding factor for whether or not a given society is a modern one – according to Ewald – is its stance on the principle of insurance, as only a truly modern society is founded on this particular principle. In Ewald's own words, society enters 'into modernity, as soon as insurance turns into a matter of society, as soon as the social contract comes to resemble an insurance contract. Insurance is at the core of modern society' (Ewald, 1991: 288; our translation). The principle of insurance is ultimately founded on transparency and calculability (Bonß, 1995). If we follow Max Weber's process of modernization as one in which mystery and magic are gradually eliminated from the world, we may well come to see the technology of insurance as the high point of this process. Uncertainty – the mystical, enchanted or magical aspects of the world – can finally once and for all be turned into fully rational phenomena and thus done away with by sheer calculation; by means of statistics and raw probability, the odds of any given event happening may be calculated and assessed. Transparency is key to the principle of insurance. A transparent world, then, will no longer be able to surprise us. Or at least one would not think so.

However, uncertainty makes its grim return with the arrival of the risk society. Uncertainty – bringing holes in the ozone layer, global warming, the hazards of radioactive emissions from nuclear power plants, global financial crises, gene technology, fertilizer residue in our food, global terror and all the other frightening phenomena which Beck calls *man-made disasters* (Beck, 1995a) or *new risks* (Beck, 1991a) – has returned to be a part of our society once again.[4] Beck puts it like this:

> Insurance protection (whether private or state-organized) had a twofold function from the perspective of social theory, namely, *neutralizing damage* and thereby *neutralizing fear*. To the extent that the expansion of risk outstrips insurance protection, the latter loses its function of neutralizing fear at both the social and the political level, behind the still intact Potemkin façade of insurance protection. Free-floating fears are being set free.
>
> (Beck, 2009a: 139)

Thus, when Beck discusses the transition from industrial society to risk society, the principle of insurance is a pivotal point of the argument:

> The entry into risk society occurs at the moment at which the manufactured risks undermine or annul the provident state's prevailing risk calculations. Those who ask for a operational criterion for this transition find their answer here: *the absence of private insurance protection.*
>
> (Beck, 2009a: 110)

The new risks are characterized by the fact that we cannot insure ourselves against them fully, if at all. We cannot insure ourselves against them, simply because they are by definition utterly unpredictable (Beck, 2009a: 132–139). It is more or less impossible to determine the likelihood of a radioactive leak from a nuclear power plant or an act of domestic terrorism, and it is equally hard to predict anything about the extent of the potential damages either would cause, were they to occur. The uncertainty is simply too great, the unknown variables too many. Thus, we can only partially insure ourselves against these new risks. Airline companies experienced this at first hand during the aftermath of 11 September 2001, as they realized that it was more or less impossible to purchase any kind of insurance against terrorist attacks; and while insurance premiums skyrocketed – reaching rates that were eight to fifteen times as high as prior to the attack – the actual insurance amounts were cut drastically, severely limiting the compensation an airline company would be able to receive in case of further terrorist attacks (Hundsbæk, 2001).

We may well ask ourselves whether or not we, in the third historical epoch, have been witnessing an actual rise in the number of risks or whether a more likely explanation is simply that we, by now, have come to be much more aware of the new risks that surround us. Beck's answer is that there are two sides to that question, namely:

> the risk itself and *public perception of it.* It is not clear whether it is the risks that have intensified, or our *view* of them. Both sides converge, condition

each other, strengthen each other, and because risks are risks in *knowledge,* perceptions of risks and risks are not different things, but one and the same.

(Beck, 1992: 55)

Ulrich Beck is of the opinion that the three epochs exhibit substantially differ-ent rosters of risks. Thus Beck, in his book *World at Risk* (Beck, 2009a), disagrees with Mary Douglas and Aarond Wildavsky and their claim – much of which is elaborated in their book *Risk and Culture* (Douglas and Wildavsky, 1982) – that there are no real or significant differences between the kind of hazards that we are facing today and the kinds of hazards people used to face in earlier times. According to Beck (2009a: 84), Douglas and Wildavsky understand hazards as culturally perceived and organized in world society, but Beck argues that, when it comes to the new type of risks, they are often a matter of *both* social staging and real physical transformation or destruction. This is the case, for example, when it comes to the problems of climate change which serves as a recurrent example throughout *World at Risk.* According to Beck, however, Douglas and Wildavsky seem to miss or ignore the fact that 'people in the Stone Age did not have the capacity for nuclear and ecological self-destruction and that the threats posed by lurking demons did not exhibit the same political dynamic as the man-made risks of climate change' (Beck, 2009a: 84).[5]

It should be mentioned here that Beck does not take the transition from one historical epoch to mean that society suddenly rids itself of the hazards and risks that already exist. We are still, to this day, very vulnerable to such 'old-fashioned' hazards as natural disasters and epidemics. There have been countless tragic examples of this in recent years. For examples of our continuing vulnerability to natural disasters, one need only think back to the tsunami which struck Indonesia, Sri Lanka, Thailand and other countries in the Indian Ocean in December 2004, to the earthquake that struck China's Sichuan province in 2008 and cost more than 68,000 people their lives or to the earthquake in Haiti in 2010, where more than 300,000 people died.[6] Furthermore, we are still trying to combat workplace accidents and other risks of industrial modernity. Thus Beck's primary point of argument is that different times and societies are defined by – and have their agendas dictated through – different types and kinds of risks and hazards. He also reminds us that natural disasters end up being disasters only because of their overall negative influence on and consequences for humanity and civilization; much depends on the number of people living in an area which is suddenly hit by a natural disaster, on the general readiness of the populace, and on the quality of buildings and engineering in the area. Such factors are largely decisive for the extent and damages of a natural disaster. In an interview following the Fukushima incident, Beck put it this way:

The term *natural disaster* in itself connotes an event[7] which is not caused by people and thus it also indicates that no person can be held responsible for its occurrence, as such. However, this kind of view belongs in a previ-ous century. We can see that the term is deceitful by considering the fact that, to nature itself, natural disasters are simply nothing more than dramatic processes of change. Such changes, such as a tsunami or an earthquake, do not become catastrophic events until they meet human civilization. The current events in Japan illustrate how the things we categorize as nature and the things we categorize as civilization are directly interwoven.

(Zielcke, 2011; our translation)

A new logic of distribution

As new kinds of risks began to register with society they also heralded the coming of a new logic of distribution. In risk societies, the kind of *wealth*-oriented logic of distribution that was prevalent to industrial society is gradually supplemented and replaced by a *risk*-oriented logic of distribution (Beck, 1992: 19–50). Whereas the focus of industrial society was on *obtaining* wealth, the focus of risk society is on *avoiding* risk. Rather than concern themselves with the material needs and problems of contemporary society, as people do in an industrial society, citizens of a risk society concern themselves largely with *future* hazards and risks (Beck, 1992: 51–53). They are concerned with avoiding nuclear war, with reducing the holes in the ozone layer, with putting a stop to global warming, with researching the potential side effects of genetically modified crops, with keeping water supplies free from pollution and residue and so on. They are concerned with *future* problems.

This means that the solid faith and optimism about the future, which had been a trademark of modernity since its beginning in the mid-eighteenth century, is no longer as prevalent or as dominant as it once used to be. Whereas optimistic, progressive and forward-looking thinkers such as Turgot, Adam Smith, Condorcet, Hegel and Marx have always been accompanied and to a certain extent counterpointed by spokesmen of a rival pessimistic tradition – such as Nietzsche, Spengler, Horkheimer and Adorno – the basic *nature* of modernity has always been a positively charged, optimistic one. The goal was always to *arrive at* a certain society and a certain condition, such as the thoroughly rationalized society, bourgeois society, communist society or welfare society. As both the bourgeois and communist revolutions made abundantly clear, there was always a strong sense among people that change was possible and that progress could be and should be made. This faith in progress, however, suffers a serious blow to morale, once we recognize that it is precisely the industrialized way of life in itself that has brought with it the serious environmental problems we are battling today. Again, this is not exactly a novel line of thought; it has appeared a number of times, especially in the wake of the First World War and during the horrors inflicted upon humanity during the Second World War and the Holocaust. However, Beck's main point is that is has been the global environmental crisis which has finally, once and for all, turned our notion of progress pessimistic and made pessimism a fundamental *governing* principle. Consider, for example, the 'caution principle', which is often invoked when we consider matters of the environment and production; no longer do we allow a certain kind of production to take place, until it is clearly specified exactly what kind of effect it will have on the environment. Whereas classic industrial society saw the future as a potential bringer of much-needed progress and wealth, risk society holds a much grimmer view of what lies ahead. To risk society, the future is the home of all *potential* catastrophes and disasters.

Industrial society, according to Beck, had its consciousness determined by its being, whereas risk society has it the other way around. In risk society, Beck says, 'consciousness determines being' (Beck, 1992: 23). What Beck means by this is that, whereas industrial society's most pressing matters were often questions of how to deal with the specific, existing problems of the time (such as poverty and need), present-day political and social agendas are largely occupied with matters of the *future*, of prognoses and predictions about possible future catastrophes and accidents. Thus the word *risk* does not cover the same conceptual space as the term *catastrophe* or *disaster*; risk is 'the anticipation of catastrophe' (Beck, 2009a: 188) with all the political and social implications it may have. The Fukushima incident offered a clear example of the kind of political power that may be harnessed by an appeal to predictions about future disasters and accidents, as nuclear power suddenly became a hot political topic worldwide. This newfound – or rediscovered – awareness of the risks of nuclear power also led to several political resolutions and new measures; in the summer of 2011, for example, Germany initiated a complete phasing-out of nuclear power. Furthermore, these new kinds of risks, and the predictions about future catastrophes and disasters that follow in their wake, have also spawned a new kind of global community because of what Beck calls *the commonality of anxiety*:

> The driving force in the class society can be summarized in the phrase: *I am hungry!* The movement set in motion by the risk society, on the other hand, is expressed in the statement: *I am afraid!* The *commonality of anxiety* takes the place of the *commonality of need*. The type of the risk society marks in this sense a social epoch in which *solidarity from anxiety* arises and becomes a political force.
>
> (Beck, 1992: 49)

Although Beck writes that we have yet to fully realize what opportunities and possibilities this new commonality of anxiety might bring with it, he makes sure to restate adamantly, several times, that it is from this new commonality of anxiety – our shared destiny at the hands of our shared hazards and dangers – that we must somehow manage to extract the recipe for a better world (e.g. Beck, 2005). Unlike the problems people were trying to deal with during the industrial society, our problems of today work in ways that affect everybody in more or less the same way. Nobody is able to really hide from radioactive pollution, from harmful smog particles in the air we breathe or from the consequences of global warming in toto. Beck puts it eloquently, when he says that '*poverty is hierarchic, smog is democratic*' (Beck, 1992: 36). This means that our usual way of distinguishing between 'us' and 'them' more or less collapses or is, at the very least, rapidly losing meaning and significance. We are all, by now, decisively in the same boat. (See Table 2.3.)

Table 2.3 Risk society versus industrial society

Industrial society		Risk society
Production of wealth	→	Production of risks
Elimination of scarcity/need	→	Elimination of risks
Wealth distribution	→	Risk distribution
An aim to achieve	→	An aim to avoid
Combating reality	→	Combating possible futures
Positive focus on the possibilities of the future	→	Negative focus on the future's potential disasters
Being determines consciousness (materialism)	→	Consciousness determines being (idealism)
Poverty	→	Anxiety
I am hungry	→	I am afraid
Us/them distinctions (rich/poor, American/Russian etc.)	→	Us/them distinctions are diluted and lose meaning
Need is hierarchic	→	Smog is democratic
The industrial process is apolitical	→	The industrial process is political (the sources of wealth are also the sources of pollution)

The traditional gaps between, for example, the rich and poor or separate parts of the world, however, still matter – and they gain new meaning and significance with the arrival of the risk society. We will return to these new inequalities in Chapter 5, where we will also be taking a closer look at Beck's analysis of the possibility that human beings may manage to come together and cooperate with each other across national boundaries and class divides, in a joint effort to effectively address the new risks and man-made hazards.

The changed status of nature

The environmental problems which we are already facing – along with those looming on the horizon – cannot simply be attributed to a 'cruel' method or some 'extreme' characteristic of nature in itself. Holes in the ozone layer and crop fertilizer residue in our water supplies may well be located in nature but they are caused by our industrialized way of life. Beck speaks – using a term from Anthony Giddens – of *manufactured risks* and of a new, *manufactured uncertainty* (e.g. Beck, 1994a: 8–13; see for example Giddens, 1994b). Thus, the clear distinction used to separate nature and classic industrial society is dissolved by the risk society (see Table 2.4):

The opposition between nature and society is a construct which belongs in the 19th century and which serves a dual purpose by both dominating *and*

Table 2.4 The understanding of nature in industrial society and risk society

Industrial society	Risk society
Nature as separated from society	Nature as a societal matter
Nature as external phenomenon	Nature as internal phenomenon
Nature as point of origin	Nature as artificial/produced entity

ignoring nature. By the end of the 20th century, nature *has* been dominated and exploited and has thus been transformed from an external factor to an *internal* one, from a presupposed phenomenon to a *produced* one.

(Beck, 1986: 9)[8]

Because of this, Beck is unable to use the German term *Umwelt-Probleme* in his work, as *Umwelt* in German refers to both our environment and that-which-surrounds-us in general. The new risks, however, are not problems that originate in our surroundings; we have caused them ourselves. So Beck instead opts to discuss what he calls '*Innen*welt-Probleme' (Beck, 1986: 10–12).

Side effects

One of the most important terms in Beck's theory of the risk society, is the term *side effect* (*Nebenfolgen* in German). Beck takes the risks of risk society to be side effects of our industrialized way of life. Specifically, the risks are *unintended side effects*: side effects that could not have been planned for, are not wanted or needed and could not have been predicted. They simply appeared wherever industrial society turned out to be prosperous and successful (see Beck, 2009a: ch. 12). While people were busy making as much money as possible, striving after scientific progress, abolishing poverty, the risks quietly and swiftly sneaked in, behind the back of a society that had its attention directed elsewhere. This line of thought is entirely central to Beck's sociology. As we shall see in the chapters to come, the unintended side effects of industrial life are in fact in themselves the very key to Beck's theoretical apparatus, and his adherence to the notion of side effects places him within a tradition of thought that goes a long way back in time. During the 1700s and 1800s the idea of unintended side effects was a commonly used way of explaining the occurrence and nature of any new phenomenon. The notion can be found in the works of the German philosopher G. W. F Hegel, who in his philosophy of history argued that reason and the idea of freedom will ultimately prevail in spite of the fact that every actor and agent in the history of the world seem to have been driven by passion and thus committed acts that lead to all kinds of accidents and misfortunes. This is because reason itself will always end up operating behind the backs of the agents of history, asserting itself and its ways through the *cunning of reason* – 'die List der Vernunft' (Hegel, [1831] 1976: 49) – and thus will make sure that everything turns out to the common good, after all. Similar notions occur earlier throughout German philosophy, especially in the works of Immanuel Kant, but nowhere is the notion of *Nebenfolge* more prevalent than in the works of the Scottish social philosopher Adam Smith, who spends much of his 1776 philosophical–economical magnum opus, *The Wealth of Nations*, discussing and elaborating on this idea, calling it 'the invisible hand'. To Smith, the 'invisible hand' works around and behind the backs of market entrepreneurs and business-men and ensures that the market always benefits the common good, in spite of the fact that each contender in a given market is always in it in order to pursue his or her own private economical interests and gains (Smith, [1776] 1976). Smith was heavily influenced by the Dutch-English doctor and writer Bernard de Mandeville, who in the early 1700s published *The Fable of the Bees*, in which he provoked the middle classes with his idea of 'private vices, public benefits' (Mandeville, [1705–1733] 1957). Mandeville sought to raise public awareness of the positive side effects – in the shape of social wealth – that always followed along whenever individuals acted out their own private vices and desires. The vanity of people resulted in more work for the tailors; the drunken proclivities of people funded the life and trade of the wine merchants; and so on. What all these thinkers and theoreticians have in common is their conviction that some kind of order will always assert itself in favour of the common good of a society, no matter what kinds of egoistical acts and ventures its citizens may undertake; there will always be beneficial, though unintended, societal side effects in the wake of the self-centred and myopic actions of individuals.

Beck considers the idea of unintended side effects in a different light, how-ever. To Beck, the agents and individuals of industrial society were not driven by egoism or self-absorbed interest. On the contrary they had undertaken a pro-ject which was, collectively speaking, a very good and noble one. If anything, industrial society can be described as a gigantic and very effective *cure* against material need and poverty. Seen in this light, industrialization is an attempt to do away with a general state of material scarcity and need. Rather than simply submit to fate, people saw – with the advent of the industrial project – a pos-sibility of acting, of taking matters into their own hands. In the modern indus-trial project which started in the 1700s, people sought to tame nature and make themselves its master. The treatment, obviously, worked very much as planned. However, like most other efficient treatments, this one too turned out to entail an array of *side effects*. Along with the production of wealth and security came new kinds of risks and man-made disasters and hazards. These new risks and man-made hazards are what Beck calls *unintended side effects*, and they are the key to understanding his theory of the risk society. Beck's negative/pessimistic rendition of the notion of unintended side effects, too, has several theoretical precursors and ancestors. Thinkers such as Karl Popper and Friedrich August von Hayek warned us against the *negative* unintended side effects that might follow in the wake of social reformation and changes which were on too large a scale or too drastic (e.g. Popper, [1945] 1993). Beck, along with André Kieserling and Boris Holzer, has attempted to excavate the theoretical roots of the notion of side effects, in the article 'Side Effects as a Problem for the Development of

Sociological Theory' ('Nebenfolgen als Problem soziologischer Theoriebildung'; Beck, Holzer and Kieserling, 2001).

Core terms

Hazard: In the risk literature of Niklas Luhmann, François Ewald and others, the term *hazard* is usually taken to be a counter-term to that of *risk*. A hazard is incalculable, erratic and difficult to delimit. It does not strike a specific group and its causes are external (nature, gods etc.). In Beck's *Risk Society*, the term *hazard* is used almost synonymously with the term *risk*. From 1988 onwards, Beck too makes a specific distinction between the two terms.

Industrial society: Among classical sociologists, *industrial society* is a description of a desired societal disposition. Later on, and especially in the mid-twentieth century, the term came to denote actual society, the thought here being that industry had replaced agriculture as the most important trade factor, in charge of setting the societal agenda. In Beck's work industrial society is a class society as well, exhibiting marked distinctions being made between different people; these distinctions are later erased or stripped of importance in the risk society.

Risk: In the risk literature, *risk* acts as a counter-term to that of *hazard*. A risk, here, is taken to be a distinct, outlined and calculable uncertainty which is a side effect of the actions of particular individuals. Risks are the objects in the world of insurance. It is against risks that we insure ourselves – and not hazards, against which, owing to their erratic nature, we cannot insure ourselves. Although in his book *Risk Society* Beck uses the terms *danger* and *risk* as synonyms, he later on adopts the distinction made by risk literature in general.

Risk society: Ulrich Beck's term for the kind of society which has replaced industrial societies. The transition from industrial society to risk society started approximately 40 years ago. By *risk society*, Beck means a society which is producing a new kind of risks that are different from those produced by industrial society. These are also put at the forefront of political debate and societal development in the risk society.

Self-jeopardy/man-made disasters: Ulrich Beck's terms for the kind of risks that are constituents of the risk society, for example radioactive leaks and emissions, gene technology, holes in the ozone layer, terrorism and contamination of deep groundwater by nitrates from use of fertilizer. These new kinds of risks, or man-made disasters, amalgamate the characteristics of traditional risks and hazards: they are both erratic and uncontainable and, at the same time, they are man-made (i.e. products of our industrial way of life.)

Side effects (*Nebenfolgen* in German): Side effects follow from a given action, but are not the immediately intended core product/consequence of that action. Risk society, according to Beck, has emerged because of the *unintended side effects* of industrial society.

Further reading

Beck, U. (1992) *Risk Society: Towards a New Modernity.* London: Sage Publications.
Beck, U. (1995) *Ecological Politics in an Age of Risk.* Cambridge: Polity Press.
Beck, U. (2009) *World at Risk.* Cambridge: Polity Press.

3   The theory of second modernity
Ulrich Beck's diagnosis of contemporary modernity

Before we go on to take a closer look at the transition from industrial society to risk society and how it affects the individual, community, state, politics and labour market, we will explain how Ulrich Beck views this transition, which, he says, is taking place within the framework of his *theory of second modernity*.

The theory of second modernity is Beck's attempt at solving the problem of social diagnostics with which sociology has been struggling since the 1970s. When the French philosopher Jean-François Lyotard handed in his report on knowledge in highly developed societies – titled *The Postmodern Condition: A Report on Knowledge* (Lyotard, [1979] 1984) – to the Council of Universities, Quebec, nobody could have foreseen the landslide that would come to be set in motion by his short, often quite difficult, piece of writing. Without his intending to do so, the report ended up causing a riotous discussion about how to understand the times we were living in: Were we still part of modernity – that is, were we still part of the era that had been launched with the age of enlightenment of the 1700s – or had modernity, by now, more or less run its course? What Lyotard had pointed out in his report, among other things, was that the grand narrative of progress, science and liberation that had been supporting and providing the basic foundation for the entire modern era, had come to lose its efficiency, status and ability to function as a shared point of social reference. A scientist, for example, could no longer simply hope to argue for the relevance of her research merely by appealing to notions of scientific truth. Performativity, by then, had become the deciding factor. As Lyotard writes in his report:

> The question (overt or implied) now asked by the professionalist student, the State or institutions of higher education is no longer 'is it true?' but 'What use is it?' In the context of mercantilization of knowledge, more often than not this question is equivalent to 'Is it saleable?' And in the context of power-growth: 'Is it efficient?'
>
> (Lyotard, [1979] 1984: 51)

Other philosophers, sociologists and theoreticians of culture were quick to adopt the notion of postmodernity.[1] Over quite a short period of time, the end of modernity became a widely known and accepted cultural fact, and with it came the acceptance that we were now ourselves living in new and postmodern times. Lyotard and the French cultural theoretician Jean Baudrillard were among the most prevalent advocates for postmodernity. During the early 1980s, postmodernism spread like wildfire, heavily influencing the arts. In sociology, the grandest, most disturbing and spectacular farewell to modernity came with the Polish-English sociologist Zygmunt Bauman's 1989 book, *Modernity and the Holocaust*, which argued that the holocaust was a distinctly *modern* genocide; the holocaust, simply put, was a child of modernity itself (Bauman, 1989). Bauman, as a response, had dedicated himself to moving *beyond* modernity.[2] Although the idea and diagnosis of postmodernity was a widely researched sociology topic, very little consensus was established on what the postmodern really *was*. The only thing that the many considerations and definitions of postmodernity really had in common was the notion that it somehow had to do with a *break* with/from modernity. Ulrich Beck developed his theory of the risk society during the peak of the tumultuous debate surrounding the postmodern, which is evident from the preface to his book *Risk Society*. Here, Beck writes that the main purpose of his book is to animate the post-skeletal structure, which is the only thing left standing from the discussion of postmodernity:

> The theme of this book is the unremarkable prefix 'post'. It is the key word of our times. Everything is 'post'. We have become used to *post*-industrialism now for some time, and we can still more or less make sense of it. With *post*-modernism things begin to get blurred. The concept of *post*-Enlightenment is so dark even a cat would hesitate to venture in. It hints at a 'beyond' which it cannot name, and in the substantive elements that it names *and* negates it remains tied to the familiar. *Past plus post* – that is the basic recipe with which we confront a reality that is out of joint. This book is an attempt to track down the word 'post', alternatively called 'late' or 'trans'.
>
> (Beck, 1992: 9)

Beck's theory of second modernity is his attempt at offering a resolution to the debate between the 'modernists' and 'postmodernists' of sociology; between the advocates of the postmodern diagnosis and the advocates of the diagnosis that we still, to this day, are living in modernity. A prevalent member of this latter group is the German philosopher and sociologist Jürgen Habermas, who claimed – and still claims – against the advocates of the postmodern, that we must still regard modernity as an 'incomplete project' (Habermas, [1980] 1981). Beck attempts to place himself somewhere between these two extreme views. Although he acknowledges the *diagnosis* – that, through recent years, society has undergone such radical changes that it no longer makes sense to attempt to understand it from a modern point of view – he also makes an argumentative point out of the fact that distinctly modern ideas, such as human rights, rationality and science, are still very prevalent and still influence many aspects of our society and times, albeit in new ways. Thus modernity, to Beck, is not being phased out so much as *transformed*. It is a matter of both discontinuity and continuity at once, and

Beck – while he rejects the idea of the postmodern – acknowledges that there are breaks and shifts taking place *within* modernity itself.

These days, says Beck, we are in fact experiencing the transition from one phase of modernity to another; from first modernity to *second modernity*:

> All around the world, society is undergoing radical change – radical in the sense that it poses a challenge to Enlightenment-based modernity and opens up a space in which people choose new and unexpected forms of the social and the political . . . Some authors, who lay great stress on the openness of the human project amid new contingencies, complexities and uncertainties, operate with the term 'post-modernity' (Bauman, Lyotard, Harvey, Haraway). However, we reject the idea that so far this is a move from the modern to the postmodern. On theoretical as well as on empirical grounds our conclusion is that all Western societies are still 'modern' societies: there has been no movement beyond the realm of the modern to its opposite, because there has been no clear break with the basic principles of modernity but rather a transformation of basic institutions of modernity (for example, the nation-state and the nuclear family). We would suggest, therefore, that what we are witnessing is a second modernity.
>
> (Beck and Lau, 2005: 525–526)

Industrial society and modernity

Traditionally, sociology has sought to couple modernity with industrial society. Although there exists a wide array of explanations of the nature of modernity, differing in scope, focus and complexity, most theoreticians have tended to agree that modernity is a historical period which began in the age of enlightenment in the early 1700s. Furthermore, there seems to be a wide acceptance of the claim that modernity is founded on the ideals of the time, such as reason, freedom and scientific progress through understanding of and dominion over nature. This, man's fundamental control over nature, was imagined to be obtainable through reason and science. It gained significant momentum with the industrialization of the 1800s. Modernity and industrial society, then, have always gone hand in hand. In the words of the English sociologist Anthony Giddens, modernity can be 'understood as roughly equivalent to "the industrialized world", so long as it be recognized that industrialism is not its only institutional dimension' (Giddens, 1991: 15).[3] In the works of classic sociologists too, such as Émile Durkheim, Max Weber, Ferdinand Tönnies, Georg Simmel and Karl Marx, we find this kind of close interconnection between modernity and industrialism. With Beck's theory of second modernity, modernity is detached from industrialism. According to Beck, we are currently witnessing modernity's detaching from – and development beyond – its roots in industrial society. To Beck, only the society of first modernity can be called industrial, as the transition towards second modernity is actively shifting us towards a new kind of society: the risk society. Thus, second modernity can be illustrated as in Figure 3.1.

Figure 3.1 The continuity of modernity.

Premises of first modern society

What does, in fact, characterize first modernity, apart from its connection with industrial society? With his colleagues Wolfgang Bonß and Christoph Lau, Beck tried in 2001 to explain exactly what first modernity *was*, by identifying a series of premises on which first modernity could be said to rest (Beck, Bonß and Lau, 2003). Their article identified six distinct premises of first modern society, which were universally and naturally true. Historically these six premises – although they can be traced far back in the history of ideas – were only beginning to see gradual naturalization through modernity, culminating in the years following the Second World War. These basic premises, according to Beck, provide the foundation for first modern society; they are explicit and implicit assumptions that are valid on a large, universal scale, influencing both the actions and self-understanding of citizens, the goals of politics and the routines of social institutions (Beck, Bonß and Lau, 2003: 4). The six premises of first modern society can be summarized thus (Beck, Bonß and Lau, 2003: 4–6):

1 *Society as nation-state society.* First modern society is 'defined by territorial boundaries'. The nation-state is perceived to be a 'container', holding and containing a certain society, a certain people within a certain territory. Therefore, most social institutions of first modernity are closely tied to the nation-state as institution and principle of organization (see Chapter 5).
2 *Programmatic individualization.* In first modern societies, a controlled kind of individualization takes place. Individualization, here, is limited by collective ways and patterns of life, which are 'heavily reminiscent of pre-modern structures that determined one's status by birth.' This means that the social position of the individual is largely predetermined. Individuals may be freed from traditional, feudalized structures of inequality based on heritage and family, and the individuals may be 'theoretically free and equal' but their freedom and equality is, in fact, 'molded' by social institutions, such as the nuclear family, their class and their nation. The 'sexual division of labour', too, is explicit and understood as a natural fact – man was made to provide for the woman, who, in turn, was made to take care of the children and housework. The nuclear family is perceived to be the ideal and its task is to function as a production unit, generating a – predominately male – workforce.

3 *Society as employment society* or perhaps rather *gainful employment society*. With its ideal state being one of full employment, Beck and colleagues call first modern society a *full employment society*. This means that 'status, consumption and social security all flow from participation in the economy'. *Every* (male) individual thus must be given the opportunity to obtain full-time, gainful employment. The norm is business-confined work and production. Lifelong, standardized full-time work is a given, which paves the way for standardized biographies of trade and labour (see Chapter 7).

4 *Nature is perceived as being separate from society.* As we have already mentioned in Chapter 2, industrial society perceives nature to be a neutral, accessible and perpetually available resource to society. Not only does this instrumental approach to nature serve to reduce it to a resource, 'which can and must be made available without limitation', it also turns nature into a 'prerequisite of an industrial dynamic growth', in which the normal state of society is one of endless, unlimited growth that can actively displace the 'negative effects so that they seem to originate elsewhere' (see Chapter 2).

5 *Leaning on a scientifically defined concept of rationality.* Instrumental control is given pride of place. Progress is perceived to a process of demystification which can, potentially, go on forever. The belief, then, is essentially that science will ultimately provide society with perfect control over nature. Rationality becomes a monopoly of science and is primarily used to exercise power over nature. This leads to a certain hierarchy between experts and laypeople, with the former being in control thanks to their professionally controlled monopoly on knowledge and expertise. Put differently, a restructuring of social knowledge takes place, whereby the hierarchies of knowledge are changed in such a way that experience and hands-on, work-based knowledge becomes devalued while, conversely, the status of theoretical knowledge becomes much greater (see Chapter 6).

6 'First modern societies understand and manage their development according to the principle of functional differentiation.' Over a period of time, the differentiation of social and societal subsystems (economy, politics, culture, science etc.) has led to an understanding of them as separate, unique and hierarchical systems. The consequence of this kind of fracturing of society is that social development becomes synonymous with rising complexity. Furthermore, it is assumed that the continued differentiation of societal functions, through increasingly narrow specialization of fields, subsystems and 'patterns of social action' will ultimately lead to 'a better and better calibration of ends with means' (see Chapter 6).

These six premises of modern society, which gradually came to be institutionally and individually internalized matters of course, can be divided into two groups (Figure 3.2). The first group, consisting of the first three premises, addresses the structural and systemic preconditions for first modern societies, that is the institutions and systems on which society rests. The second group of

Modern societies are:
- nation-state societies
- characterized by a programmatic individualization (institutionalized individualism)
- gainful employment societies with full employment

They are founded on:
- an instrumental view of nature
- a scientifically defined concept of rationality
- the principle of functional differentiation

Figure 3.2 The premises of first modernity.

premises, 4–6, addresses the self-description of social action, that is the way in which human action is thought of and understood in first modernity (Beck, Bonß and Lau, 2003).[4]

The five challenges of second modernity

The securities, wisdoms and core institutions of first modernity are, little by little, being dissolved. This goes for the nation-state, predetermined communities (such as class and the nuclear family), the traditional gender divisions of labour, the notion of full employment (work for everybody), work and production in a factory or business setting, science's monopoly on truth and rationality, the view of nature as external and separate from society and so on. It is these observations that have made Ulrich Beck claim that modernity is undergoing a transformation; that we are transitioning from first to second modernity.

Why, exactly, is this happening? Why are all these well-established social structures being undermined? How did all these premises of first modern society lose their status as self-evident truths? To Beck and colleagues the answer is clear. They point out five specific phenomena, processes of change which have influenced the agenda of recent decades and undermined first modernity, leading us into second modernity. These five processes are a multidimensional globalization, a radicalized/intensified individualization, a global environmental crisis, an all-out gender revolution and a so-called 'third industrial revolution' (Beck, Bonß and Lau, 2003: 6–7; Figure 3.3).

Since these five processes of change will be handled in depth throughout the book, we will here simply summarize them briefly.

Multidimensional globalization
Radicalized/intensified individualization
Global environmental crisis
Gender revolution
The third industrial revolution

Figure 3.3 Second modernity's five processes of change.

1 *Globalization* must be understood as a multidimensional process with an influence that reaches beyond its effects on the economy. The cultural and political dimensions of globalization should be taken into consideration as well, as they are currently causing significant changes in the relationship between local and global affairs as well as between domestic and foreign affairs, effectively undermining national borders and boundaries (see Chapter 5).

2 *Intensified/radicalized individualization*, springing from the first modernity's agenda of freedom and equality, has – fuelled by the modernization of the welfare state and a politically engineered boom in education – led to the distribution of several social and political rights to every individual in society. The idea of living 'a life of one's own', free from traditional ties and bonds, has become very prevalent because of this. The result, according to Beck, has been the dissolution of traditional, collective patterns of life and the occurrence of new and hitherto unknown social forms meant to replace or supplement many of first modernity's key institutions (see Chapter 4).

3 *The global environmental crisis*, which we covered in Chapter 2, is the third challenge. It is a dynamic process which, according to Beck, is already undermining the validity and relevance of many of the assumptions on which first modernity was founded. With the public's 'discovery' or acknowledgement of the global ecological crisis – which entails a subsequent acknowledgement of the fact that we have only a very limited supply of natural resources available to us – the elimination of the causes of the global environmental crisis is turned into a political matter. The industrial process in itself did not occur as a political issue in first modernity, but, as a result of the new dynamics of politicalization at play in second modernity, it becomes one. In addition to this, the global environmental crisis makes it impossible to maintain a view of nature in which nature retains its status as a neutral resource, wholly available to man. Nature and society must instead be approached as two interconnected entities. Nature is put in an immediate relationship with society.

4 A fourth, central aspect of the transition from first to second modernity, is the sweeping *gender revolution*, which has led to the denaturalization and deconstruction of traditional male/female roles in society. As a result of this the internal, traditional relations and dynamics of the (nuclear) family are changed and weakened, and the gender-divided distribution of labour is wholly dissolved. Consequently *love* is now the sole adhesive that can hold the family unit together (see Chapter 4).

5 Full-time gainful employment as the primary means of securing one's existence and self-realization has become increasingly scarce. There is simply not enough paid work to go around. This sets the stage for the emergence of the flexible, plural kinds of underemployment, which have become increasingly popular because of the process of change which Beck calls '*the third industrial revolution*'. The term refers to the rationalization processes brought on and made possible by advances in information technology, which has created new and flexible kinds of underemployment. Because of this, Beck remains

sceptical of the notion of a full-employment society, which he considers to be an illusion in this day and age (see Chapter 7).

It is because of the combined effects of these five processes that we have been led from first to second modernity (Figure 3.4). Over the course of this transition, the semi-feudal traits and properties on which first modernity rested have all been called into question. They are traits and properties which, according to Beck, effectively made first modernity into a democratically *halved* modernity. First modernity, for example, denied women and children certain fundamental rights, and women were excluded almost entirely from the labour market. However, while the five processes above have effectively led us beyond all this, they have also led us into a second modernity which is characterized by a new, generalized kind of insecurity, having to do with the new, global environmental risks, the release of individuals from the communities of industrial modernity, the lack of full-time gainful employment and the multidimensional process of globalization which has undermined the authority of the nation-states. Thus it would be wrong to simply claim that second modernity is simply and automatically 'better' than first modernity or to believe second modernity to be somehow plainly an 'improved' version of first modernity. It does, however, come with certain possibilities for positive development and growth (we will return to this in depth in Chapter 5).

Basic institutions and basic principles

The main premise, then, in Beck, Bonß and Lau's account of second modernity, is that the premises of first modern society are being actively undermined by a multidimensional globalization, a radicalized individualization, a global environmental crisis, a gender revolution and a third industrial revolution, which is causing a transition into second modernity (Beck, Bonß and Lau, 2003). This theory is refined and explained in more depth by Beck and Lau in a theoretical article from 2005 (Beck and Lau, 2005). This article forgoes discussing the broad notion of 'premises of first modern society' and makes a clear distinction between what are called 'basic institutions' and 'basic principles'. Rather than discuss how the 'premises of first modern society' are being generally undermined by the processes of change outlined above, the 2005 article further refines the theory by arguing that the 'basic principles' of first modernity live on in second modernity, while 'basic institutions' of first modernity, such as the nation-state and the nuclear family, are forced to change. Thus a transformation of first modernity's institutions takes place *while* its ideas and ideals live on:

> The transition from first to second modernity by no means signifies a complete break in the process of modernization. Unlike postmodernity, second modernity maintains that there is an overlapping of continuity and discontinuity that needs to be defined both theoretically and empirically. In order to do this, it is helpful to interpret and refine the distinction between first and second modernity by using the distinction between basic principles and basic institutions.

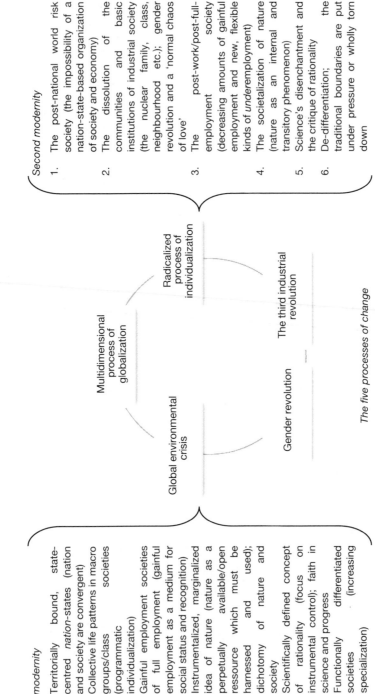

First modernity

1. Territorially bound, state-centred *nation*-states (nation and society are convergent)

2. Collective life patterns in macro groups/class societies (programmatic individualization)

3. Gainful employment societies of full employment (gainful employment as a medium for social status and recognition)

4. Instrumentalized, marginalized idea of nature (nature as a perpetually available/open ressource which must be harnessed and used); dichotomy of nature and society

5. Scientifically defined concept of rationality (focus on instrumental control); faith in science and progress

6. Functionally differentiated societies (increasing specialization)

Multidimensional process of globalization

Radicalized process of individualization

Global environmental crisis

Gender revolution

The third industrial revolution

The five processes of change

Second modernity

1. The post-national world risk society (the impossibility of a nation-state-based organization of society and economy)

2. The dissolution of the communities and basic institutions of industrial society (the nuclear family, class, neighbourhood etc.); gender revolution and a 'normal chaos of love'

3. The post-work/post-full-employment society (decreasing amounts of gainful employment and new, flexible kinds of *under*employment)

4. The societalization of nature (nature as an internal and transitory phenomenon)

5. Science's disenchantment and the critique of rationality

6. De-differentiation; the traditional boundaries are put under pressure or wholly torn down

Figure 3.4 From first to second modernity. Illustration of how the five processes of change come together to transform the premises of first modernity.

Second modernity shares certain basic principles or lasting imperatives with first modernity (such as the principle according to which decisions can and must be backed up by rational reasons), which, when fulfilled to the optimum extent, constitute the dynamic element of modernization. By basic institutions we mean the institutional responses to the fundamental imperatives of these basic principles in particular historical contexts, each response being associated with a particular phase of modernity. Thus, for example, a distinction needs to be made between the basic principle of statehood and the basic institution of the nation-state, which is subject to change. While institutional responses, once found, possess a considerable degree of inertia, they are none the less rendered null and void by the ongoing imperatives of modernization, which remove the foundations of their rationales and decision-making. It can therefore be expected that the continuity of modernity will be guaranteed by the basic principles, while the transition to reflexive modernity [second modernity] will be brought about by the discontinuous transformation of basic institutions.

(Beck and Lau, 2005: 532)

From simple-linear to reflexive modernization

Who is responsible for these new phenomena? Whom can we reasonably hope to accuse of having caused the utter collapse of a whole historical era and an entire societal system? Beck's answer, in short, is: no one. Or perhaps rather: *no one and everyone.* The subversion of the industrial social order of first modernity have exactly *not been* engineered or set in place by anybody in particular. It is not appearing, now, as a result of any specific political decisions, of revolution or of social uprising. Rather, it occurs as a series of *unintended side effects* of the industrial or simple-linear modernization process of first modernity:

> radicalized modernization consumes the foundations of first modernity and transforms its institutions and its frame of reference, often in a way that is neither desired nor anticipated. Or, in terms of systems theory: the unforeseen consequences of functional differentiation can no longer be controlled by further functional differentiation. In fact, the very idea of controllability, certainty or security – so fundamental to first modernity – collapses.

(Beck and Lau, 2005: 526)

First industrial modernity's transition into second modernity, then, must be viewed in the light of the logic of consequences and side effects which we have described in Chapter 2. The changes that occur are the unseen and unintended side effects which have followed in the wake of first modernity's attempt to make its societies more free, equal and wealthy. The result of these efforts, however, has been not merely a general rise in wealth and prosperity, but also the emergence of certain phenomena that have caused modernity itself to become a problem; in other words, phenomena that have forced modernity to *modernize* itself.

When these processes are considered more carefully, the thing they all have in common emerges more clearly: they are all unforeseen consequences, not of the crisis but of the victory of the first, simple, linear, industrial moderniza- tion based on the nation-state (the focus of classical sociology). This is what we mean when we speak of 'reflexive modernization'.

(Beck and Lau, 2005: 526)

Whereas Beck characterized first modernity as *linear* or simple *modernity* – since the process of modernization occurred in a relatively straightforward manner – he characterizes second modernity as *reflexive*. The reason for this change is that the process of modernization is starting to relate actively to itself. Beck's use of the word *reflexive* is meant to evoke the notion of the classic traffic safety reflectors. Much like how safety reflectors on our clothes may reflect the light from the headlights of a car, modernity is now being reflected back on itself. Second modernity pits modernity against itself in the shape of all the *new risks* and *man-made jeopardies* which were covered in the previous chapter: the holes in the ozone layer, greenhouse gases, chemical fertilizer residue in our drinking water and so on.

We would be wrong to think that reflexive modernization will lead to increased reflection overall, however. In fact, because of second modernity we are currently experiencing what can be called a planned or even well-considered moderniza- tion. Whereas the process of modernization during first modernity was largely programmatic, the process of modernization of second modernity is, by and large, wholly powered by the unintended side effects of industrial modernity. It is an unseen, unwanted and unintended modernization that is taking place. In other words, it is the side effect revolution.[5] Beck, Bonß and Lau summarize the conse- quences of the reflexive modernization process thus:

> Modernity has not vanished, but it is becoming increasingly problematic. While crises, transformation and radical social change have always been part of modernity, the transition to a reflexive second modernity not only changes social structures but revolutionizes the very coordinates, categories and con- ceptions of change itself.

They go on to say that:

> In the transformation from a *first modernity* that was largely synonymous with the nation-state to a *second modernity,* the shape of which is still being negotiated, modernization ends up stripping away the nation- and welfare state, which at one time supported it but later restrained it. In so doing, mod- ernization is calling into question its own basic premises.
>
> (Beck, Bonß and Lau, 2003: 2)

This means that reflexive modernization ends up giving rise to 'a new kind of capitalism, a new kind of labour, a new kind of global order, a new kind of society, a new kind of nature, a new kind of subjectivity, a new kind of everyday life and a new kind of state' (Beck, Bonß and Lau, 2003: 2–3). Beck sees this reflexive process of modernization as an open process which – as will be covered in more depth later in the book – has the *potential* to lead us to a better society, without making any specific promises whether or not that will, in fact, happen.

Liquid modernity, late modernity and second modernity

Ulrich Beck is far from alone in emphasizing the *development* of modernity rather than the unwinding of modernity itself. Zygmunt Bauman, for example, makes an attempt towards the same goal, with his concept of *the liquid modern,* in order to open our eyes to a new and, according to him, even more problematic phase of modernity. According to Bauman, the traditional, modern securities and wisdoms all disappear in the intensified, liquid modernity that has been caused by the new social complexities and opaqueness brought on by market-driven globalization (e.g. Bauman, 1998a, 2000). Because of this, Bauman wishes for a post-modernity with the courage to face the impossibilities of modernity: its cravings for order and unambiguity. He dreams, in other words, of a self-reflecting (post)modernity which is willing to embrace the ambivalences, contingencies and ambiguities of modernity. Giddens, too, emphasizes the development of modernity itself by working from a concept of late or high modernity. He agrees with Beck that we have not moved beyond modernity but 'merely' witnessed a radicalization of the modern (Giddens, 1990; Beck, 1994a). According to Giddens, the development of the modern is due in part to a rising amount of reflexivity.[6] The term is used here in the sense of *reflection*, and Giddens's incarnation of late modernity is to be seen as self-*reflexive* modernity – a kind of modernity which reflects on itself, using *knowledge* as its prime catalyst for development and growth. Although Beck, Giddens and Bauman are aware of many of the same phenomena – primarily globalization and the effect of individualization on society – there are several important differences between their respective diagnoses of modernity. As outlined, the transition into a second, radicalized modernity is, to Beck, not a product of reflection and knowledge. It is anything *but* that. Rather, this modernity is a direct consequence of *non-knowledge*. It is a kind of self-reflection, or in Beck's words a side effect revolution (e.g. Beck, 1994a). This fundamental difference in how to understand reflexivity is what causes Beck's concept of second modernity to be tied into the notion of the risk society, whereas the late modernity of Giddens is tied into the notion of the *post-traditional* society, wherein social reflexivity is undermining tradition.[7]

Early sketches of the theory of second modernity

In our treatment of the theory of second modernity, we have primarily leant on a series of Ulrich Beck's more recent texts as well as on his main work *Risk Society*. However, thematically speaking, Beck's work with modernity and modernization goes much further back, starting with a series of articles in the early 1980s. The notions were treated in such early articles as 'Folgeprobleme der Modernisierung und die Stellung der Soziologie in der Praxis' (Beck, 1982a) and 'Das Krisenbewusstsein in der Arbeitsgesellschaft' (Beck, 1982b) from 1982, and the article 'Soziologie und Modernisierung: Zur Ortsbestimmung der Verwendungsforschung' (Beck and Bonß, 1984) co-authored with Wolfgang Bonß in 1984. In these articles, Beck outlines an initial, early sketch of the theory which he later went on to elaborate as his theory of the risk society and second modernity.

It is interesting to see how Beck, this early on, seems fairly confident about the nature of the cornerstones of what would become his theory. Among other things, he puts forth an argument to the effect that scientific-technological progress, which carries the 'scientific civilization' (Beck, 1982a: 10), has not *just* brought us benefits in the shape of overwhelming wealth and man's liberation from the oppressive bonds of nature. It has also produced new problems, in the shape of human error and self-produced risks. According to the article, the rising awareness of the problematic aspects of scientific-technological progress leads to an increasingly critical attitude towards the sciences, resulting in a much more critical stance towards technology and a rejection of earlier times' blind faith in science's ability to keep fuelling a steady, social progress (Beck, 1982a: 3). As a way of elaborating on this new critical stance of society towards science, Beck then for the first time presents his argument that our discovery of the side effects of modernization – and thus our 'discomfort with modernity' (Beck, 1982b: 40) – is leading us into a new, reflexive 'developmental phase of the civilization of science' (Beck, 1982a: 10). When science is confronted with its own creations and side effects, it ends up losing its monopoly of truth and rationally and is, thus, utterly demystified. Although the reflexive phase of the scientific-technological development at this point in time is perceived to coexist alongside a more traditional one, says Beck, the 'other, reflexive constellation' (Beck, 1982a: 9) will eventually end up dominating entirely. All things considered, this means that we should not consider Beck's 1986 book on the risk society to be the point of origin or the 'ur-work' of his writings on second modernity. Rather, it is the first collected presentation of a theory of second modernity which Beck is still, to this day, actively developing and refining.

Core terms

Basic institutions: Institutions built to handle the imperatives given from the basic principles. Basic institutions change throughout history. For example, first modernity's basic institutions would include the nation state and the nuclear family.

Basic principles: Defined by Beck as the 'cognitive–normative problems and minimum requirements of the "project of modernity", which represent its "driving force" and thereby keep its developmental dynamic going' (Beck and Lau, 2005: 532). One might say that they are ideas and ideals which date back to the enlightenment and which provide the foundation for the dynamics and successes of first modernity. They are ideals about science, rationality, the principle of citizenship, human rights (e.g. property rights, freedom of science and research, freedom of movement, freedom of speech), wealth and growth.

First modernity: The era or phase of modernity which began in the 1700s but came to full fruition only after the Second World War. This era, according to Beck, is characterized by its clear attitude towards the concept of *society* as being a matter of a nation-state with full, gainful employment, a programmatic individualization, an instrumental view of nature, faith in science and progress and the principle of functional differentiation.

Premises of first modern society (basic premises): The premises of first modern society are 'the foundations of its self-description: the explicit or implicit assumptions expressed in the actions and self-understanding of citizens, the goals of politics and the routines of social institutions' (Beck, Bonß and Lau, 2003: 4).

Reflexive modernization: A reflex-like, uncontrolled kind of modernization which is both undesired and unforeseen. Reflexive modernization occurs in the wake of a successful initial, industrial modernization. It is the modernization of modernity itself. Reflexive modernity is what occurs when modernity encounters itself, in the shape of the side effects and the unintended consequences of the first, simple-linear modernization.

Second modernity: The era or phase of modernity into which, according to Beck, we have been slowly transitioning; the transition began in the 1960s and continues to this day. Beck understands this, the transition into second modernity, to be an unintended side effect of the success of first modernity. The era is characterized by five dynamics of change which converge to dictate the social agenda and transform the basic premises of first modernity: a multidimensional process of globalization, a radicalized individualization, a third industrial revolution, a gender revolution and the global environmental crisis.

Simple-linear modernization: The modernization that occurs in the first modernity. It is a kind of modernization which finds its foundation in science and belief in progress. Technological progress, here, is equated with the progress of society. Historical advance is considered a linear and progressive phenomenon.

Further reading

Beck, U. (1992) *Risk Society: Towards a New Modernity.* London: SAGE Publications.

Beck, U. (1994a) 'The Reinvention of Politics: Towards a Theory of Reflexive Modernization', in Beck, U., Giddens, A. and Lash, S., *Reflexive Modernization.* Cambridge: Polity Press.

Beck, U. (2003) *Conversations with Ulrich Beck.* Cambridge: Polity Press.

Beck, U., Bonß, W. and Lau, C. (2003) 'The Theory of Reflexive Modernization: Problematic, Hypotheses and Research Programme', *Theory, Culture & Society*, vol. 20, no. 2, pp. 1–33.

Beck, U. and Lau, C. (2005) 'Second Modernity as a Research Agenda: Theoretical and Empirical Explorations in the "Meta-change" of Modern Society', *British Journal of Sociology*, vol. 56, no. 4, pp. 525–557.

4 Individualization

Doomed to live a life of one's own

How should one live one's life? In the old days it all used to be so simple. Tradition or nature issued the guidelines and told us how we ought to act and behave. This, however, is no longer the case. Today it seems everything is up for discussion. Nothing really seems to be determined or fixed in advance. Most of the conditions and affairs that come together to form the life of an individual today demand of each individual that he or she be involved in an active and ongoing process of decision-making. This is the case for every life decision, from the most trivial everyday thing to the large, existential questions of life. In earlier days, people would often have a fairly limited number of options when it came to making choices concerning partners, marriage and parenthood. Their options with regard to education and career, too, were largely determined in advance, as were religious and national affiliations. Today, an individual cannot even be said to be bound by his or her gender or appearance. Almost everything is open to reconsideration, negotiation, alteration. Generally speaking, the individual's overall trajectory of life is becoming less and less determined by his or her family, class relation and religious background. What has happened? The short answer is: *individualization*.

The subject of individualization takes up a lot of theoretical space in the works of Ulrich Beck. He is, in Germany as well as internationally, one of the most prevalent thinkers of individualization today. In a lengthy series of books and articles from 1983 on, he has described the contemporary process of individualization (Beck, 1983, 1995b, 1996b, 1992, 1998a, 2000b, 2003, 2007a,b, 2009a). Beck has also developed his thought of individualization in close cooperation with his wife, Elisabeth Beck-Gernsheim, who is a professor of sociology at the University of Nuremberg. Together, they have published an extensive range of articles and books on individualization (Beck and Beck-Gernsheim, 1993, 1994, [1990] 1995, 2002b, 2003, 2007a,b, 2010).

A new, radicalized kind of individualization

Over the course of the last 20 years Ulrich Beck has played a large role in turning individualization into as much of a central theme in the social sciences as it now is. Individualization is perceived as one of the most influential and socially transformative contemporary social phenomena. It is often perceived to be as influential as – and work in a dualistic manner with – globalization. When the talk turns to individualization today, however, it often does so in a way that might lead us to believe that individualization in itself is a *new* phenomenon. Nothing could be further from the truth. Individualization, which has always been a stable part of modernity, has been studied by sociologists since the 1800s and the dawn of sociology as a field. It occurs as a kind of theme in Émile Durkheim's main works *The Division of Labour in Society* (Durkheim, [1893] 1997) and *Suicide: A Study in Sociology* (Durkheim, [1897] 1970). Georg Simmel, too, engages the phenomenon in his works *On Social Differentiation* (Simmel, [1890] 1989), *The Philosophy of Money* (Simmel, [1900] 1978), *Fundamental Questions of Sociology* (Simmel, 1917) and *The Metropolis and Mental Life* (Simmel, [1903] 1950). Beck, too, has commented on the fact that individualization, more or less explicitly, has been a part of sociology since its conception. In *Risk Society* (Beck, 1992), he attempts to illustrate how the theories of Marx and Weber are part of the corpus of the debate surrounding individualization and argues that the work of Durkheim and Simmel, too, can be approached from this kind of angle, thematically (Beck, 1992: 95–99, 127).

Most classically trained sociologists share a basic notion of individualization as being a kind of process which frees the individual from having choices made on his or her behalf by any kind of collective and community, essentially allowing the individual to choose a life with a unique trajectory that is much more his or her *own*. This is also Ulrich Beck's notion of individualization but we must, he stresses, stay aware of the distinction between two particular 'waves' or 'phases' of individualization which take place in industrial society and risk society, respectively. The first wave, the one studied and charted by classically trained sociologists, really does free the individual from feudal social structures and religious dogma; it catapults the individual into industrial society, where he or she can then be 'picked up' by *new kind*s of collective ways of life and community.

Beck himself points out that individualization, in Marx's work, ends up being attenuated by the notion of a collectively experienced impoverishment in capitalist society, which ultimately leads to a process of class formation. To Weber, on the other hand, individualization ends up being cushioned by certain 'status group founded' traditions and subcultures which, to ensure their viability and relevance, merge with ownership of competencies and market chances in capitalist society, thus ultimately ending up as real, differentiable social classes (*sozialen Klasselagen*) (Beck, 2009b: 229–234).

The second wave or 'individualization push' (Beck, 2009b: 225), on the other hand – the phase we are currently experiencing – goes a step further, freeing the individual from the surrogate communities of industrial society, forcing him or her to undertake hitherto unmatched – and unheard-of – solitary strides towards inventing and living a life of his or her own: 'The protective in-between which (as it is called in sociology) "intermediates institutions" – social classes, small families, the ethnic group, male and female role models, the welfare state – has, while it still exists, slipped from our grasp' (Beck, 2007a: 582–83). The first modern basic institutions are no longer able to relieve the individual by providing it with certainty or direction.

Because of this, Ulrich Beck speaks of contemporary individualization as a new and *radicalized* kind of individualization and his basic thesis is that individualization has never before been as profoundly significant – so influential to so many aspects of the lives of so many people – as is the case today. Thus the subject of individualization, its possibilities and, to Beck, its fundamental tragedy, comes to be a central pivot point in his work. (Beck, 2007a: 578).

Institutionalized individualization

With the rise in general wealth, the gradual expansion of the welfare state and political and civil rights, the development of social safety nets based on social rights, rising labour market regulation, labour market participation and the massive, explosive growth in education, it is obvious that the collective ways of life that were predominant in industrial society have by now come under intense pressure. This development, which has been gathering momentum more or less non-stop since the 1950s and 1960s is, according to Beck, the source of the new, radicalized individualization that is taking place today (Beck and Beck-Gernsheim, 2003; Beck, 2009b: 233). Beck sees the current trends in individualization as a result of the new demands that the labour market and educational system are making of the individual, and as a side effect of the success with which welfare states have secured the freedoms and social rights of each citizen (Beck and Beck-Gernsheim, 2002a: 205; Beck, 2000a: 163). What we are witnessing, then, is a welfare state-driven labour market which forces a significant degree of individualization on life situations and ways of life by making ever-increasing demands for mobility (both geographic and social), education and education/labour market-based competition between individuals (Beck, 2009b: 229).

The contemporary individualization process then, says Beck, should be seen as a case of *institutionalized individualization*: the institutions take their starting point in the individual, rather than in the family or any other collective entity or community, and thus end up acting like vehicles for the individualization process (Beck and Beck-Gernsheim, 2002b: 22). In this way, individualization 'really is imposed on the individual by modern institutions' (Beck, 2007b: 681). The labour market provides an excellent example of this: apart from certain, very specific kinds of work – e.g. foster families – the labour market is directed towards, and geared for, individuals. One seeks *an individual* with certain qualifications and skills necessary to perform a certain kind of job – one does not seek a couple or a family.

This fact, combined with the rising mobility and dynamics of the labour market – the demand for constant reinvention, adaptation and flexibility – has by now made it so that the ideal labour market subject is the *single* person, the kind of person who is not in any way 'held back' or 'restrained' by relationships, marriage or family. The *single* maintains full mobility (Beck, 1992: 116).

'For now'

Combining a working life and career with a family thus becomes increasingly difficult; the contemporary family is turning more and more into a kind of 'temporary agreement family' which provides nothing more than the formal framework and boundaries for the life and self-realization projects of its individual members.

In the words of Zygmunt Bauman, the notion of '*for now*' prevails (Beck and Beck-Gernsheim, 2002b: 15–16). We stay together as a family 'for now' – until something better comes along. The same thing goes for our work, education and living arrangements. Radicalized individualization puts the individual in a state of restlessness, continually searching for something better. The value of our relationships, says Beck, is constantly weighed against our knowledge of the fact that things could be *different*, that there is no need or requirement that we stay together; that we do not have to keep living where we live, working where we work or being who we are. This kind of knowledge is the source of great uncertainties, as it requires that we always ask ourselves whether or not we have made the right choices.

Having us act as the authors of our own life stories will have large ramifications for our relations and for the connections we form with other human beings – especially those who are supposed to be closest to us. Marriage and family are put under great duress. In a relationship, the individualization of one person becomes the delineation and restriction of the other – which is a constant source of uneasiness, quarrel and conflict. In fact, says Beck, radicalized individualization actively undermines one of the core institutions of industrial society: *the nuclear family.*

During first modernity, the nuclear family provided the natural boundaries and framework for the emotional and social life of its individuals. Radicalized individualization, however, has completely changed the internal relations and dynamics of the family unit; it undermines and dissolves the gender-determined distribution of work and it is the main force behind the transformation of gender roles that has taken place since the 1950s and 1960s (Beck, Bonß and Lau, 2003: 6; Beck, 2009b).

According to Beck, individualization leads to a conflict of interests between love, family and personal freedom, thwarting our attempts at the notion of 'the family' as we have known it. But how and with what, ask Beck and Beck-Gernheim in their book *The Normal Chaos of Love* – should we replace the family? They answer their own question with:

> the family, of course! Only different, more, better: the negotiated family, the alternating family, the multiple family, new arrangements after divorce, remarriage, divorce again, new assortments from your, my, our children, our past and present families. It will be the expansion of the nuclear family and its extension in time; it will be an alliance between individuals as it always has been, and it will be glorified largely because it represents a sort of refuge in the chilly environment of our affluent, impersonal, uncertain society, stripped

of its traditions and scarred by all kinds of risk. Love will become more important than ever and equally impossible.

(Beck and Beck-Gernsheim, [1990] 1995: 2)

To put it bluntly: we are beyond the normal family and normal class, experiencing 'the *normalization* of diversity, both with regard to family law and to the self-image of family members' (Beck, 2007b: 684). Individualization simply places us in a situation in which we cannot maintain the core principles and role distributions of first modernity's nuclear family. Some of these core principles were the exclusion of women from the labour market, the lack of basic women's rights and the unquestioned assignment of home- and family-related chores to women in general. When women are granted the same rights as men, when they are given new freedoms and liberties, when they start to educate themselves and – to the benefit of the (welfare) state – start gaining a foothold in the labour market, it all swiftly leads to the institution of marriage losing its function as a means for social and material security. As a direct consequence, the prime reason for entering into marriage is changed. Rather than material and financial security, it is now *love* which is the decisive factor of the relationship. Should the love disappear, so will the relationship. In this sense, individualization entails 'two faces: individuals are not merely reproducing, they are also destabilizing the social order of things. Individualization becomes a cross point of the unintended side effects, putting into question the foundations of the key institutions of industrial society' (Beck, 2007a: 581). This is also the case for the institution of the family.

If we wish to study the status of marital relationships and the situation of the family today, we will need a new kind of framework of thought to do so, given the consequences and effects of individualization and globalization on human relations. Beck points out, in the spirit of his rejection of methodological nationalism, that there is a need for a new cosmopolitan turn in the science and research of the family; a turn which will enable us to understand the situation of families in an interconnected world which is characterized by transnational relations, marital migration and transnational modes of cohabitation (Beck and Beck-Gernsheim, 2007a,b, 2010).

Beyond class and nation

Radicalized individualization, however, did not just do away with the nuclear family. The consequence of the intensified individualization, according to Beck, is a much more general dissolution of the traditional social structures of first modernity, i.e. of the industrial, collective ways of life. In *Risk Society*, Beck argues that the individual has been freed from the traditional bonds of class:

subcultural class identities have dissipated, class distinctions based on status have lost their traditional support, and processes for the 'diversification' and individualization of lifestyles and ways of life have been set in motion. As a result, the hierarchical model of social classes and stratification has increasingly been subverted.

(Beck, 1992: 91–92)

Bluntly put, we are currently witnessing the general dissolution of social status and class and thus the end of traditional macrosociety. Individualization – occurring as a result of the general labour market strategies of the welfare state – has weakened the ties between individuals and their families, class, neighbourhoods, workplace colleagues and so on. Because of this, it is the welfare state itself which is responsible for the de-traditionalization and undermining of the social structures of industrial society. Beck, in *Risk Society*, says:

> The expansion of the welfare state has, by preserving and maintaining inequality, caused a cultural erosion and evolution of our life circumstances and thereby put the inequalities between men and women in plain view. This is exactly the dynamic of individualization which, along with the other factors I have mentioned – less time spent performing paid work, more money, mobility and education etc. – is now exercising its ability to cause structural changes by gradually transforming the life-relations and conditions for the social classes *and* the family.
>
> (Beck, 1986: 130)[1]

In recent years, Beck has been focusing intently on delineating the relationship between radicalized individualization, class and inequality. His article 'Beyond Class and Nation: Reframing Social Inequalities in a Globalizing World' (Beck, 2007b) is a clear indication that Beck takes the distinction between 'class' and 'social inequality' quite seriously indeed. Although the kind of radicalized individualization taking place today may well mean, according to Beck, that we have by now moved far beyond the industrial class society, it does not mean that social inequality has been abolished. Quite to the contrary: 'Individualization implies no (final) state, but a process, more precisely: a process of the transformation of the *grammar* of social inequalities' (Beck, 2007b: 680).

Social inequality and the many potential conflicts tied to it are simply *individualized* away in second modernity, leading to a radicalization of social inequality itself – which goes on to exist in the shadow of individualization and the success of the welfare state.

> Evident here is the *irony and paradox of the welfare state.* The class struggles of class society achieve the welfare state and with it the principle of individual assignment of claims and contributions with the consequence that individualization becomes permanent, and the internal structuring principle of modern societies (classes) become less important. It is the *collective success* with class struggle which institutionalizes individualization and dissolves the culture of classes, even under the conditions of radicalizing inequalities.
>
> (Beck, 2007b: 682)

The question of whether or not there can exist such a thing as a collective class identity under the pressure of institutionalized individualization and the demand for reflexive life styles and individualized life biographies – which require of each individual that they themselves manufacture all meaning and every identity aspect of their own lives – is, to Beck, an easy one to answer. The notion of a collective class identity is done away with once and for all by:

> capitalism without classes, more precisely: without classes *for themselves*. Individualization uncouples class culture from class position; as a result, there are numerous individualized class conflicts without classes, that is, a process in which the loss of significance of classes coincides with the categorical transformation and radicalization of social inequalities.
>
> (Beck, 2007b: 686)

Put bluntly, the radicalization of social inequality may end up taking place as a consequence of class conflicts becoming individualized, paving the road for the utter dissolution of social classes. Another driving force behind the new patterns and categories of inequality is the transnationalization of social inequalities, which can be traced back to the (varying) capacities and resources of individuals working to move beyond national boundaries, that is to the varying degrees of mobility in individuals. This leads to a socially uneven distribution of global risks – and, in this sense of the word, risks and social inequality are two sides of the same coin. However, owing to the methodological nationalism of the social sciences, says Beck, this development has so far gone unnoticed. We will return to this in Chapter 6 below.

Choosing everything

In general, contemporary radicalized individualization has caused a larger degree of mobility in the lives of individuals. This is evident from the rising prevalence of serial monogamy and, in labour, from the rising frequency with which people change between jobs. Zygmunt Bauman asks us to consider the notion of *the tourist* as an illustration for the terms and conditions under which one is an individual today (Bauman, 1997).

Always on the move, the tourist jets happily from place to place. We are not all part of this 'globetrotting elite', however; far from it (Bauman, 2001b: 107). Some of us are much more related to *the vagabond*, the antithesis of the tourist. The vagabond is simply *forced* to move from place to place out of sheer necessity, since he is unwanted everywhere and lacks the resources to fight or oppose the prevailing logics and systems where he is. He must keep moving. The vagabond is the ultimate loser in the current processes of individualization, since he is not able to meet the demands for flexibility and life-long competency development which is demanded by the labour market and by second modernity in general. However, the tourist, too, ends up losing in the end. The tourist and the vagabond both share a new kind of existential anxiety and uncertainty, stemming from the processes of individualization (Bauman, 2001a: 89–96). Both their situations seem to share a certain element of random *tossedness*. Both the tourist and the vagabond have been more or less tossed into their current way of life; a way of life which neither of them has asked for and which is characterized by uncertainty and anxiety. It is a life in which everything must always be actively chosen and nothing is determined in advance (Bauman, 2000: 34; 2002: 68).

Even though Beck is not nearly as pessimistically black and white as Bauman in his appraisal of the consequences of the current process of individualization, both still largely agree on their analyses of the process itself. Like Bauman's, Beck's analysis hinges on the observation that, today, everything must be actively *chosen*. Everyone is constantly being forced to consider how to live his or her life. There are no more predetermined answers to that question:

> Today's individual feels steamrolled, smothered by options which, although they are not actual choices, none the less demand that decisions be made as fast as possible, in an almost reflex-like manner, so to say . . . the individual . . . in this way is no longer able to construct linear, narrative biographies.
>
> (Beck, 2007a: 583; our translation)

In this way, the individual is 'forced' into a fragmented mode of existence. At the core of this fragmented new existence is a fundamental sense of uncertainty and incalculability, which has come to govern every aspect of the individual's life.

The question 'What do you want to be?' used to have to do merely with education and trade; today, it covers every aspect of our human existence: religion, identity, marriage, parenthood. Not even gender is determined. Today, it is possible to have one's gender changed, if one feels trapped in the wrong body.

Nobody forces us to make the most unusual of choices, however, and nobody expects of us that we answer each and every existential question of life in the most novel or revolutionary manner. We can still choose to do what our parents did and opt for doing as our friends do. The point, however, is that we must now actively *decide* that we want to live this way or that. This kind of choice always happens at the expense of knowing that things *could* have been done differently. The radicalization of life choices often ends up weighing the individual down. We are *condemned* to individualization, says Beck (taking a cue from the French philosopher Jean-Paul Sartre[2]). We cannot choose to *not* be individualized.

Because of this, we should not confuse individualization with egoism and we should not think that individualization has anything to do with *individualism* as an ideology. Individualization is not *individualizing* in the psychological sense of the word: the process whereby a child separates and detaches mentally from the mother in order to become an independent individual. Nor should we take terms such as Thatcherite or Bushish *market-individualism, freedom of choice, autonomy, emancipation* (Habermas), *atomization, value decay* and others to be proper synonyms for individualization (Beck and Beck-Gernsheim, 1993: 179; 2002a; Beck, 1994a: 13; 1997a: 94; 1998a: 33; 2002a: 61; 2009b).

On the contrary, Beck sees the current processes of individualization as institutionalized individualization and thus as a *societal* matter (Beck, 2003a: 76). He says of the current individualization processes that it is an 'unavoidable product of the societal evolution' (Beck, 1998a: 7, 132) and also to be understood as a historically specific, self-contradicting societalization of the individual. (Beck, 2009b: 226). We are individualized, without regard for our gender, age, race, religion, wealth and general demographics. The current, radicalized individualization thus represents a kind of democratization and generalization of individualization: everyone is individualized in the same way and to the same extent, regardless of whether they *want* to be or not (Beck, 2009b: 234).

An ambivalent process

The current, radicalized process of individualization is, according to Beck, an ambivalent one (Beck and Beck-Gernsheim, 1994, 2002a). On one hand, the individual is increasingly put in a position in which he or she can live a life of his or her own and author his or her own biography in a way that he or she feels corresponds well with his or her choice of social networks and connections (Beck, 1994a: 7, 14; Beck and Beck-Gernsheim, 2002a: 22–29). On the other hand, this new freedom of choice is entirely dictated by the premises of the educational system, the labour market and the welfare state (Beck, 1994a: 14). Beck therefore emphasizes that it is 'important to distinguish between institutionally individualized *opportunities* to make decisions and institutionally individualized *obligations* to make decisions', as:

> many features, functions and activities which were previously assigned to the nation state, the welfare state, hierarchical organization, the nuclear family, the class, the centralized trade union, are now transferred outwards and inwards: outwards to global or international organizations; inwards to the individual.
>
> (Beck, 2007b: 682)

Thus, while the individual is set free from the micro- and macro-structural connections of industrial society, he or she is also 'delivered' more or less automatically to such modern institutions as the labour market, the social security system and the educational system. Contemporary radicalized individualization, then – much like earlier processes of individualization that have taken place – is closely connected to new *standardizations and institutionalizations* of the life trajectories of individuals (Beck, 1992: 89–90; Beck and Beck-Gernsheim, 2002a). When Beck makes a point out of emphasizing that the setting free of the individual from the communities of industrial society also entails an *institutionalization and standardization* of the life trajectory of that individual, he does so because he sees it as point which is tightly connected with his argument that an increase in individualization does not necessarily lead to more freedom for individuals (Beck, 2009b). We are individualized within certain frameworks, boundaries and institutions which – as a direct consequence of individualization itself – we come to grow more and dependent on. This is especially the case for the labour market. The welfare state defines the boundaries and limits to how the individual organizes his or her own life, but the market itself plays an active part in the process as well:

> Individualization means market dependency in all dimensions of living. The forms of existence that arise are the isolated *mass market*, not conscious of itself, and *mass consumption* of generically designed housing, furnishing, articles of daily use, as well as opinions, habits, attitudes and lifestyles launched and adopted through the mass media. In other words, individualization delivers people over to an *external control and standardization* that was unknown in the enclaves of familial and feudal subcultures.
>
> (Beck, 1992: 132)

A similar line of thought can be found in the work of Bauman. According to him, we are set free mainly as consumers, that is as atomized market agents in a new kind of consumer society which has replaced political society (Bauman, 2002).

'All-risk' individualization

The 'self-culture' of second modernity, then, should not be taken to entail total freedom of the individual.

In the wake of the new ethics of self-development – and all its interesting possibilities for self-individualization and development – follows a massive demand for *individual* reliability and responsibility. It is an 'all-risk' individualization (Beck, 1994a: 20) which forces each individual to bear the weight of the global and collective risks and uncertainties on his or her own shoulders. Life becomes quite a risky affair indeed, filled with 'risky freedoms' (Beck and Beck-Gernsheim, 1994). Because of this, the biography of the run-of-the-mill individual ends up being not only a kind of 'biography of choices' or a 'self-assembly' biography, but even a 'hazard biography' or the biography of a tightrope walker working without a safety net (Beck, 2001: 119; Beck and Beck-Gernsheim, 2002a: 48). To Beck individualization is:

> in the middle of its gestation period, undetermined, chaotic not as an exception but as the rule, utterly normally chaotic, so to say; what matters here is the grand question: how do I expect the unexpectable? How do I plan the unplannable? Everything is full of risk and risky liberties.
>
> (Beck, 2007a: 581; our translation)

The large degree of freedom and chance for self-expression and realization is also accompanied by a 'privatization' of collectively produced risks. The individual is constantly forced to think up his or her own, biographical solutions to the *systemic* challenges he or she encounters (Beck and Beck-Gernsheim, 2002a: 22); or, as Beck puts it in *Risk Society*, 'how one lives becomes the *biographical solution of systemic contradictions* (as for instance between education and employment, or the legally presumed and the actual standard biography)' (Beck, 1992: 137).

It is, in other words, simply up to the individual to learn how to life his or her life under conditions and terms which are utterly beyond the individual's control.

> One feels forces to live in a world of risks, in which knowledge and life opportunities have become principally uncertain. It is this new immediacy – '. . . the condition of immediacy' (John Tomlinson) – which enforces the non-linearity.
>
> (Beck, 2007a: 583; our translation)

Currently, one of the largest systemic contradictions is the one we find between work life and family life. On one hand, modern work life requires an almost inhuman amount of efficiency, willingness to adapt and mobility. Our children and partners, on the other hand, are just not all that easy to simply exchange, uproot or move about. It is not easy to take your daughter out of a school that she's happy to attend, to move out of a city after living in it for many years, leaving one's social networks behind, or to follow one's spouse to the other end of the country for his or her career, forgoing one's own in the process. In their attempts to solve such systemic contradictions, individuals take to experimenting; they begin searching out *biographical* solutions to the systemic contradictions. A married couple, for example, may agree to let one person focus on his or her career for a period of time, while the other stays at home on child care leave, spending his or her free time on personal development projects such as further educating him- or herself part-time, learning a new language and so on. Alternatively, people may 'choose' to 'live together separately' – living in two different homes during the week and spending weekends together – allowing both members of the relationship to focus wholly on their careers while remaining a 'family' during weekends (Beck and Beck-Gernsheim, [1990] 1995: 11–44).

The danger of atomization

When Beck speaks of individualization as being the social structure of modern society (e.g. Beck, 2003: 63), he does so in a very ambivalent way. Being radically individualized might well mean to be set free from the (suffocating) bonds of the surrogate communities of industrial modernity and from the confines of a standardized family unit which is wholly based on gender roles, but also means that we end up individualizing the risks and social inequalities of today's society. The structural inequalities and crises of society, such as poverty, social peril, structuralized unemployment, divorce and illness are all 'individualized away' (Beck and Beck-Gernsheim, 2002a: 50). They are turned into *personal* failures and fiascos, and attributed to the weakness and lack of resources of the individual, and his or her lack of ability to see through and utilize the institutional possibilities that are at all times available (Beck and Beck-Gernsheim, 2002a: 44). When the highly educated, after five or six years of education, are unable to find proper employment, they are told perhaps little else than that they ought to have thought ahead and picked another field than the humanities or social sciences. The unemployed person is forced to accept the blame for his or her own unemployment. The individual is held responsible for social circumstances that are entirely beyond his or her own control and influence. This can, according to Beck, manifest itself in very specific, concrete ways: 'Thus social problems turn into immediate psychological dispositions, into personal inadequacy, guilt, anxiety, psychological conflicts and neuroses' (Beck, 2009b: 236; our translation).

Attempting to avoid the forced choices and uncertainties, a growing number of people are trying to return to the safe and trusted framework of first modernity. They do so by seeking enrolment in closed, exclusive subcultural movements and milieus or radicalized political groups (Beck, 2003a). Certain people may join new religious movements that offer 'package deals' which promise to answer all the questions and doubts of second modernity, so that the individual will not have to do so (Beck and Beck-Gernsheim, 2002b).

To Beck, this is an unfortunate – albeit entirely understandable – strategy for handling uncertainty. If we wish to stop this tendency from gaining further ground in society, we must assign new possibilities and options to the politics of individualized society; we must imbue the culture of political freedom with a new kind of organizational structure, for example by allowing civil society to wield a greater amount of authority by itself (Beck, 2003a). Doing so will open a new institutional space between state and market – a space for individual creativity and self-responsibility, which may help us to once again re-invent sociality and community. The aim, in other words, is to reshape the creative and collective impulses – which are *also* a part of socially experimental individualism – into new political-public issues and shapes (Beck, 2003a).

One possible development which Beck finds especially worrisome is that radicalized individualization might, at some point, turn into full-fledged atomization. However, even though Beck believes that he already sees the early signs of atomization taking place, he does not see the need to resort to any doomsday prophecies just yet (Beck, 2003: 80). Rather, he emphasizes the fact that the process of radicalized individualization is still an entirely open one, which is taking place in the space between the entirely positive scenario of respectful, mutual individualization and the entirely negative scenario of counter-individualization (Beck and Beck-Gernsheim, 2002a: xxiv), which has led to a transformation of the social structures of western society, resulting in a greater amount of individual uncertainty. However, says Beck, there is a certain positive potential to this transformative process of our social architecture as well, since it might well imbue new, individualistic, self-determined sociocultural forms of community with life and thus supply us with new ways of thinking about politics and social action that can go toe to toe with second modernity, meeting its challenges.

Second modernity, says Beck, is characterized by exactly this kind of cooperative or altruistic individualism (Beck and Beck-Gernsheim, 2002a: 28), which creates opportunities for re-embedding the individual into the new kinds of community and sociality: new family constellations, social movements, different transnational fractions of a new 'global generation', experimental youth subcultures and so on (Beck and Beck-Gernsheim, 2007a; Beck, 2009b; see Table 4.1). In these new 'individualization movements' and the rising willingness to partake and participate in social work, transnational citizen projects and other, similar activities, Beck even sees the contours of a kind of 'cosmopolitical individualism' being drawn (Beck, 2000a: 89, 139; 2009b: 226). The largest and most vital questions of the future, says Beck, will be how to combine individualization with our duties and commitments to others, both locally and globally (Beck and Beck-Gernsheim, 2002a: 212).

Table 4.1 Simple individualization versus reflexive, radicalized individualization

First wave of individualization		Second wave of individualization
Industrial society/first modernity	→	Risk society/second modernity
Individualization in relation to the social structures and communities of feudal society	→	Individualization in relation to the social structures and communities of industrial society. Institutionalized individualization (the labour market, educational system and rights of the welfare state are all directed towards the individual)
Replacement communities: class status family nation	→	Replacement communities are subjected to fundamental changes and loss of significance
Born into a certain status and class	→	Born into the framework of second modernity: institutionalized individualism
The life trajectory of the individual is (largely) predetermined	→	The life trajectory of the individual must be created/chosen. Autobiographies of choice. DIY biographies. Reflexive autobiographies. Tightrope walkers' biographies. Risk biographies. Hazard biographies. We are condemned to individualization (Sartre: condemned to freedom)
Fixed connections, forced connections, predetermined connections (work, education, love, family etc.)	→	The 'for now' prevails (Zygmunt Bauman)
Nature and tradition will decide: religion gender identity marriage parenthood	→	Must be chosen/created/invented by the individual: 'Who and what would you like to be?'

Individualization theory prior to Ulrich Beck

Although Beck makes a distinction between a first and second wave of individualization which correspond to first and second modernity, he does not draw a particularly clear picture of the first wave of individualization or of the theory of individualization which has gone before him. Reading Beck and other contemporary thinkers of individualization, it is often hard to determine to what extent the relations and phenomena being discussed have already been touched upon by earlier sociologists. In order to shed a bit of light on what kind of work has been done on individualization before Ulrich Beck, we are going to finish off this chapter with a closer look at how classic sociologists such as Georg Simmel and Émile Durkheim – along with sociologists from the generation immediately before Beck's own, such as Norbert Elias and Talcott Parsons – have approached the issue of individualization.

The German sociologist Markus Schroer has pointed out that we have to make a historical distinction among three separate, theoretical strands in the theory of individualization (Schroer, 2000, 2001). He identifies the first strand as leading from Weber through Adorno and Horkheimer to the work of Foucault, and identifies this as the strand of *negative individualization.* The second strand, from Durkheim through Parsons to Luhmann, he calls *positive individualization.* The third strand is the one that ends with Beck. Schroer calls this third strand *ambivalent individualization,* since individualization, here, is understood as both a negative and positive phenomenon, from Simmel through Elias to Beck.[3] The question, however, is whether one can make quite such sharp distinctions as Schroer does. As we will illustrate below, beginning with Schroer's own account, it is obvious how Beck's notion of individualization follows the line of reasoning in the work of Simmel and Elias and their sociological thought. None the less, we should remember that certain elements of Beck's theory of individualization seem to be discernible in, and preconceived by, the sociology of Durkheim and Parsons.

Simmel and Durkheim

As early as the year 1900, the rising tendency to free individuals from their traditional communities inspired Georg Simmel to characterize modern society as a 'strongly individualized society' (Simmel, [1900] 1989b: 520). According to Simmel, this kind of society robbed individuals of their traditional instances for orientation and points of reference and, essentially, suspended them in a sort of 'agony of choice' (Simmel, [1890] 1989a: 132). To Simmel, the 'fool in fashion' might well be seen as a reaction to exactly the kind of loss of stability and process of disillusionment that followed in the wake of individualization (Simmel, 1998). No longer was the individual part of any predefined, collective identity; likewise, one could no longer hope to obtain a secure place in the world through family ties, lineage, class or the like. In this regard, that is the abolishment of the traditional certainties and the disenchanting of traditional social structures, Beck's thoughts on individualization follow closely in the line of those of Simmel.

To Simmel, individualization is intricately tied with the spread and growth of monetized economy and the largely anonymous social space that is characteristic of the major metropolitan area (Simmel, [1903] 1998a). Urbanization and market economy are, he believes, the engines of individualization since it is the money and the large cities – allowing complete freedom for individuals in a modern society – that end up making it possible for individuals to engage one another in new kinds of fleeting, unemotional connection. The social circle of the individual, then, is widened at the same pace at which the individual is freed from his or her local communities and responsibilities. Furthermore, the growing social differentiation that is brought on by urbanization and money ends up encouraging each individual to cultivate and emphasize his or her own particular uniqueness and the ways each may differ from others. As the individual becomes more and more independent and society grows more and more complex, social reality as a whole ends up becoming much more *impersonal,* as its people become more and more individualized. As Simmel puts it: 'What is of importance is no longer to be a free, particular being; what is of importance now is to be a specific individual who cannot be confused with any other individual' (Simmel, [1917] 1990: p. 9; our translation).

Unlike Beck, then, Simmel does not believe that it is the (welfare) state and educational system that are responsible for fuelling the process of individualization and creating the expectations for *one's own life.*[4] To Simmel, rather, it is the money economy and major metropolitan areas that together – by creating a special kind of social space – end up having that same effect.

On the other hand Simmel emphasizes – as did Beck a century later – that individualization does not equal anomie, moral decline and *the fall of society*, but rather that it equals a characteristic sort of change of social contracts and responsibilities. According to Simmel, society consists of reciprocal actions and configurations between individuals that have *always already* been weaved into networks of social relations. This entity of specific reciprocal action Simmel dubs 'societalization' (*Vergesellschaftung*). It is the kind of shape into which the 'contents' of individuals grow – their desires, goals, wishes, interests and so forth – in order to be unified and made real (Simmel, [1908] 1998). Simmel's foundational thesis, in other words, is that the individual is *never* simply in a state of *non-reciprocity.* This is also the case for individuals in modern, highly individualized societies; these are merely characterized by new and other kinds of reciprocity than in premodern societies. Individualization, to Simmel, does not equal complete social independence since each affected individual will remain within his or her boundaries and framework of new, *non-optional* commitments, even while his or her social connections and positions may grow enormously in number. Simmel believes that it is money and major metropolises that create a sort of *standardization* of individual ways of life, whereas Beck argues that it is the welfare state, the educational system and the labour market that perform the controlled integration.

Like Beck, Simmel was not only concerned with the negative aspects of individualization, such as individual insecurity and the new kinds of forcedness that followed in the wake of the liberation of the individual from the bonds of traditional social structures. Simmel also believed that individuals, as they found themselves increasingly condemned to making their own choices and constructing their very own (social) lives, might well end up inventing new social forms and networks. He is reminiscent of the humanists of the Renaissance, who saw themselves as members of a cosmopolitical, abstract brotherhood (Hansen, 1990).

In other words, individualization and universalization – and, in today's terms, globalization – were already joined at the theoretical hip in the works of Simmel. However, this also makes it clear that Simmel – like Beck – approached individualization as an ambivalent, three-dimensional process and as a question of (1) liberation/disembedding, (2) destabilization/disenchantment and (3) re-embedding/reintegration (Simmel, 1989a: 245; Beck, 1992: 128).

If we turn our attention to the French sociologist Émile Durkheim, we find a notion of individualization as a natural side effect of the rising social differentiation of modern societies; a *functional necessity* for highly developed, labour-organized societies (Durkheim, [1893] 1997). Durkheim's main point is that individuality and community, seen from a historical perspective, are both developed in a mutual relationship of rise and decline. This means that individualization grows in a way which is proportional with the 'socialization' of the individual. The explanation for this puzzling phenomenon is, says Durkheim, that modern, functionally differentiated society is capable of both socialization and individualization.

As a consequence of the growing division of labour, each individual gets tied closer and closer to society as a whole, becoming increasingly dependent on his or her fellow citizens, while also becoming more and more *individualized*, simply because, in order to survive in a labour-divided society, one needs to be highly specialized in one's field. This kind of process forces the individual to focus narrowly, to self-develop and spend all available time honing his or her own individual skills and abilities. As a result, labour division ends up acting as the main force behind the rising individualism, by encouraging greater respect for the rights and needs of the individual and granting the individual certain inalienable rights.

To Durkheim this kind of development is essentially a positive one, which poses no immediate threat to society or social communities in general; rising individualization is a result of a rising division of labour, which is taken to be a moral phenomenon, since it encourages a sort of organic solidarity which acts as an adhesive agent, binding together the parts of modern society (Durkheim, [1893] 2000).

What are the consequences of individualization, according to Durkheim? As mentioned, Durkheim does not at all take individualization to entail the dissolution or weakening of social structures or society in general – quite the opposite. Individualization – which is necessitated by the division of labour in modern societies – actually means the dissolution of exactly the highly collectivistic kinds of community which, says Durkheim, are characteristic of those traditional, segmented societies. Such community always completely eradicates the notion of individuals by enrolling everyone into groups that are so strongly saturated by shared norms and religious beliefs that the consciousness of the collective always ends up absorbing the consciousness of the individual. So, in this case, Beck is right in his claim that classic sociologists have always sought to describe

the liberation of the individual from previous religiously organized social con-
structs. But Durkheim does more than this. Having pointed out that the concept
of solidarity occurs, in modern society, as a result of social differentiation (and
that social divides thus act as adhesive agents which strengthen unity and sense
of community), he emphasizes that the kind of organic solidarity which is created
by division of labour stems from a principle of social heterogeneity which, ultimately, also ends up affecting basic institutions such as the family. The division
of labour and the organic solidarity which allows the appearance and appreciation
of the personality of individuals, the attribution of inalienable rights to individuals
and the rising possibility for expression and development within the institutions
of differentiated society, thus end up loosening not only the ties that bind the
individual to religion and religious communities, but also the ties that bind the
individual to his or her family, class, birthplace and traditions. To Durkheim,
modern society is 'a mobile and plastic society' (Durkheim, [1893] 1997) which
undermines all static and predetermined hierarchical systems.

It is not much of a theoretical leap, then, from the thoughts of Durkheim to
those of Beck. Durkheim's work obviously precedes Beck's point about second
modernity's meltdown of the (nuclear) family and of class. At the same time,
Durkheim emphasizes that the development in labour division and individualization is reflected in the conditions of the legal and judiciary system, with a growing
number of laws and rights being added that focus primarily on the status of the
individual in the system. According to Beck, it is exactly these rights that have
caused the radicalization of individualization in second modernity.

Elias and Parsons

The concept of individualization was widely discussed by the generation of
sociologists immediately prior to Beck's own, as well, with several influential
contributions to the field made by Norbert Elias and Talcott Parsons in particular.
To Elias, twentieth-century modern, functionally divided society is a 'highly individualized society' (Elias, 1978: 126) which is characterized by an unprecedented
degree of individualization (Elias, 1991: 22). In both his *Was ist Soziologie?* (Elias,
1970 [English: *What Is Sociology?*, 1978]) and the posthumously published *Die
Gesellschaft der Individuen* (Elias, 1991a [English: *The Society of Individuals*,
1991b]), however, Elias – like Beck – categorically rejects the notion of a completely free individual, because individualization, according to Elias, can be
understood only as a decidedly *social* process. Like Simmel, Elias does not enter-
tain any ideas of the complete dissolution of *all* social relations, but sticks simply
with discussing their characteristic changes and transformation. The process of
individualization, to both Simmel and Elias, is a continuous, ongoing, complex
and synchronous one of embedding and disembedding. This means that Elias,
prior to Beck, is able to determine that the 'highly individualized' society is both
an *individualizing* and a *typologizing* or *standardizing* one (Elias, 1991b: 22–23).
Elias's main point is that the modern individual is increasingly freed from *non-
optional* communities, leading to more freedom of acting and more possibilities

and choices, in the shape of *self-chosen* social networks, more possibilities for living a life of one's own: putting oneself first, developing one's own abilities and skills and so on. However, says Elias, there is also a kind of standardization taking place, as individuals are forced to rewrite their autobiographies within the conforming structures of modern, capitalist society (Elias, 1991b).

The notion of individualization as an ambivalent process which Beck puts forth, then, can also be found in the works of Elias, to whom individualization and standardization are highly intertwined entities. Elias points out that it is impossible to live a life of one's own *completely*. On the one hand, modern and functionally divided society encourages each individual to cultivate and accentuate his or her own uniqueness and irreplaceability – to *individualize* – which leads to the individual expecting to be able to live a life which is wholly his or her 'own'. On the other hand, everyone is constantly faced with specific external, social demands. Elias then, like Beck, does not see individualization to be tantamount to freeing the individual from all bonds, since the process of individualization will unavoidably end up producing new, latent 'structural bonds' as it unfolds (Elias, 1991b: 160).

Also, like Beck, Elias too saw what once used to be certain *non-optional* relations being transformed into *voluntary, chosen* social connections. A series of basic 'us' constellations or *we-groups*, as Elias calls the basic communities such as the family, become suddenly matters of individual choice, which can be abolished or rejected should the need arise. Thus, even family becomes a voluntary connection that can be revoked (Elias, 1991b: 204). The same goes for occupation and – says Elias – even national citizenship. Everything must be *chosen* and, with regard to this one simple circumstance, the individual has *no choice* (Elias, 1991b: 121). However, as the number of available choices and possibilities increases, so does the risk of the individual becoming paralysed by uncertainty and losing his or her sense of direction in the labyrinth of modern life (Elias, 1991b: 109). Yet Elias feels confident – like Beck – that this kind of individualistic culture also opens up new ways of reintegration, as individuals become increasingly proficient at self-control and self-regulation.

In this way, Elias's work on individualization resembles Beck's in a number of ways, especially when it comes to his argument that individualization goes hand in hand with standardization and the dissolution of 'natural' communities such as the family, and that individualization always entails some kind of re-embedding. With regard to this point, we should probably mention Parsons, who was the first to use the term *institutionalized individualism*, which Elias hints might be affecting modern society. To Parsons, rising individualization is not at all a symptom of crisis but rather – as it was to Durkheim – a consequence of a functional process of differentiation which heightens both the freedom and autonomy of individuals and, simultaneously, the mutual dependency of individuals in general.

The rise in freedom means that the individual is no longer simply assigned a place and position in society and life, but is now asked to find one on his or her own. Parsons calls this 'self-localization' (Parsons, 1980: 81). Interestingly, however, he also speaks of 'institutionalized individualism' (Parsons, 1964: 13,

101, 116–17, 198–201), which he believes is influencing the functional systems of modern, differentiated society, increasingly shifting its focus towards the individual, and thus ultimately ends up benefiting individualization. Institutionalized individualization, to Parsons, is a functional, goal-oriented kind of individualization which springs from functional systems and provides the foundation for community and social order. Wholly in line with Durkheim, Parson's counter-scenario to this 'institutionalized individualism' is 'utilitarian individualism' (Parsons, 1964; Durkheim, [1898] 1969), which allows egotism and hedonism to flourish.

Institutionalized individualism – which presupposes that the individual is included in an array of learning and socialization processes – forms the foundation of the (linear) reproduction of social systems, since it is institutionalized individualism which ensures that individuals adapt to the structures and expectations of differentiated society. Institutionalized individualism then, according to Parsons, ensures a process of individualization that allows for the individual to both live a life of his or her own and simultaneously fulfil his or her social obligations. However, this also makes it clear that Parsons – unlike Beck – does not view institutionalized individualism as any kind of paradoxically 'individualizing structure' (e.g. a non-linear, ambivalent and continuous process which undermines the basic systems and institutions of modern society). So Beck, although he can be said to have inherited the notion of institutionalized individualism from Parsons, adds a socially transformative potential to it – whereas Parson's merely remains socially *stabilizing* – by making it the prime engine of the radicalized individualization of second modernity.

Core terms

First and second wave of individualization: Ulrich Beck makes a distinction between two waves of individualization in modern society. The first wave is tied to first modernity, in which the individual is set free from the feudal structures of society and led into the new communities of industrial society. The second wave is tied to the risk society and second modernity. Here, individuals are set free from the surrogate communities of industrial society.

Individualization: A process which frees the individual from prior, given and collective identities and which, to a much larger extent, forces the individual to pick his or her own trajectory of life.

Institutionalized individualization: Beck's term for the kind of individualization that takes place in second modernity. The prime engine of individualization here is, according to Beck, modern institutions such as the labour market, the educational system and the welfare state. These institutions all take the individual as their starting point and thus help accelerate the process of individualization that is already taking place.

Radicalized individualization: Beck makes a distinction between the first and second wave of individualization, by arguing that the second wave represents a much more radicalized kind of individualization.

Further reading

Beck, U. (1992) *Risk Society: Towards a New Modernity*. London: Sage Publications.

Beck, U. (2007b) 'Beyond Class and Nation: Reframing Social Inequalities in a Globalizing World', *British Journal of Sociology*, vol. 58, no. 4, pp. 679–705.

Beck, U. and Beck-Gernsheim, E. (1995) *The Normal Chaos of Love*. Cambridge: Polity Press.

Beck, U. and Beck-Gernsheim, E. (2002) *Individualization: Institutionalized Individualism and Its Social and Political Consequences*. London: Sage Publications.

5 Globalization and cosmopolitanism

Living in an interconnected world

Scenario 1: 11 September 2001

Nobody who has seen the live footage of the two hijacked passenger jets crashing into the twin towers of the World Trade Center – or watched, mere hours later, as both towers collapsed into rubble and dust – will ever forget the images from that day. Most people recall vividly where they were and what they were doing when they first heard of the coordinated terrorist attack, which struck both the World Trade Center in New York and the Pentagon in Washington more or less simultaneously. The 9/11 attacks were far from the first acts of terrorism to be aimed at the USA and they were not the first to critically hit American interests but they were by far the single gravest and most extensive blow that had ever been inflicted on the world's mightiest nation. Claiming the lives of almost 3,000 people, the attacks were also heavily charged with symbolism in their choice of targets, with the hijacked commercial airliners being aimed at the nexus of world free trade and the headquarters of American military efforts, respectively. Less than one month after the attacks, on 7 October 2001, the USA launched its 'war on terror' as American air forces initiated a bombing campaign in Afghanistan, seeking to destroy the terrorist organization of al-Qaeda, which was behind the 9/11 attacks, capture its leader Osama Bin Laden and remove Afghanistan's Taliban regime, which had provided al-Qaeda with training, support and shelter.

Scenario 2: 19 December 2009

They had all been there; throughout the week they had been arriving at Copenhagen airport at a steady pace, to participate in the 15th Conference of the Parties (COP 15) climate summit. The US was represented by President Barack Obama, China had sent its Prime Minister, Wen Jiabao, and India its Prime Minister, Manmohan Singh. President Lula da Silva of Brazil, South Africa's President Jacob Zuma and every European leader, spearheaded by Angela Merkel, Nicolas Sarkozy and Gordon Brown, had all been in attendance. Even some of the more problematic figures of international political society participated. Zimbabwe's President Robert Mugabe, Iran's Mahmoud Ahmadinejad and Venezuela's Hugo Chávez had all flown in for the Copenhagen summit. But all to no avail. When the summit came to a close, it had failed to produce the large, binding agreements that most of the world's leaders claimed they had been hoping for and which the international community had been working towards, behind the scenes, for years. It was supposed to be the agreement that would come to replace the Kyoto protocol and, once and for all, make a serious effort to address the perils of global warming. However, despite the increasingly apparent problems that were starting to surface in the wake of the emerging climate changes – and despite the increasingly alarming predictions and environmental prognoses being put forth by scientists to detail exactly how badly things may turn out unless the international world manages to come to an ambitious, binding agreement that will drastically reduce the emission of CO_2 – no such ambitious agreement was put in place.

Scenario 3: 27 October 2011

In the early hours of 27 October, a tired but ultimately contented group of European leaders, headed by Germany's Angela Merkel and France's Nicolas Sarkozy were – after 10 harrowing hours of intense negotiations – finally able to release a statement proclaiming that an agreement had been reached, allowing Europe to put a new bailout package for its economically struggling member state Greece into effect. The agreement, including severe haircuts to Greece's debt repayment obligations, had been deemed necessary not just for the sake of the Greeks and their economy but indeed for the future viability of the joint European currency, the euro. The agreement was designed, first and foremost, to stabilize the euro in the wake of the financial crisis which had struck Europe in 2008 with the collapse of the American housing market. Throughout Europe, and especially for a series of southern European countries headed by Greece, the financial crisis had begun to take on the looming aspect of a threatening debt crisis – a debt crisis which might well prove to end up spreading and affecting other countries in the eurozone, whose banks and financial institutes held large amounts of southern European government bonds that would be rendered wholly valueless in the case of a Greek national bankruptcy. International stock markets reacted swiftly and positively to the released statement. The Japanese Nikkei index closed up 2 points and the Hong Kong stock exchange saw a rise of 2.2. Later, the European and American markets would – as they closed – follow suit and present even larger rises. The next week, however, indexes all over the world went on to plummet once again, as the Greek Prime Minister, George Papandreou, suddenly suggested that the bailout package might have to be subject to a national referendum before it could be accepted.

These three scenarios all occurred in (and because of) the kind of new *world risk society* which, according to Ulrich Beck, has come to replace the old national, industrial societies. The scenarios are all characteristic of our time, in that each illustrates the new dimensions of hazard and danger which Ulrich Beck believes to be trademarks of the world risk society: first, ecological crises; second, global financial crises; and third – since 11 September 2001 – terrorist dangers caused by transnational terror networks. In this chapter, we will be taking a closer look at these three dimensions but, before we dive into the hazards themselves, we will need to examine the process which is, at the heart of things, responsible for our becoming members of the world risk society, namely *globalization.*

What is globalization?

Coming up with a quick and easy definition of globalization, however, is no easy task. In his book *What is Globalization?* Beck writes that the task of defining the concept of globalization is 'like trying to nail a blancmange to the wall' (Beck, 2000b: 20). He tries, nonetheless:

> Globalization means that borders become markedly less relevant to everyday behaviour in the various dimensions of economics, information, ecology, technology, cross-cultural conflict and civil society. It points to something not understood and hard to understand yet at the same time familiar, which is changing everyday life with considerable force and compelling everyone to adapt and respond in various ways. Money, technologies, commodities, information and toxins 'cross' frontiers as if they did not exist. Even things, people and ideas that governments would like to keep out (for example, drugs, illegal immigrants or criticisms of human rights abuses) find their way

into new territories. So does globalization conjure away distance. It means that people are thrown into transnational lifestyles that they often neither want nor understand – or, following Anthony Giddens' definition, it means *acting and living (together) over distances, across the apparently separate worlds of national states, religions, regions and continents.*

(Beck, 2000b: 20)

Beck's notion of globalization is quite broad and dictates the rules for not only the transfer of money and goods across national borders, but also transboundary pollution, migration, civil activities, information technology and so on. This multidimensional process of globalization, says Beck, effectively changes our conceptions of society in general. When people 'do business internationally, work internationally, love internationally, marry internationally, research internationally, grow up and are educated internationally' (Beck, 2000c: 80) they also dismantle the claim that it is possible to separate and distinguish one specific nation-state from any other. These kinds of transboundary acts, in other words, undermine what Beck calls the container theory of society and state; the idea of a united state-entity, consisting of one people and one society, within one specific territory, all contained within the nation-state (Beck, 2000b: 23).

On the topic of globalization, Beck does not share the views of the neoliberals and the protectionists, to whom globalization is mainly a matter of economy and trade (Beck calls this approach to globalization *globalism*) as he sees the notion of globalization as being a matter of *globality*. To approach globalization as a matter of globality is, according to Beck, to acknowledge that a certain process of globalization has already taken place, that this process is by now wholly irreversible and that it has introduced profound and fundamental changes to our understanding of what constitutes a society: 'Globality means that we have been living for a long time in a world society, in the sense that the notion of closed spaces has become illusory. No country or group can shut itself off from others' (Beck, 2000b: 10).

Beck argues that this development requires of us that we engage the situation in a new way, at eye level, and that we develop new methods for discussing, researching and acting within this new kind of globalized society. Throughout the last 15 years, he has published a large number of books and articles, arguing that the social and political sciences should focus on replacing the myopic nation-state-centric perspectives of first modernity with a more contemporary, up-to-date cosmopolitan perspective on the world of today (e.g. Beck, 1996a, 2000b,c, 2003b, 2004, 2005, 2009a,b, 2010).

New risks and zombies

One might also say that Beck's work on globalization started with his analysis of the risk society and the global and globalized characteristics of the so-called new risks (e.g. Beck, 1991a, 1992, 1995b). It has always been a point of Beck's that, although we could feasibly interpret and analyse the properties of industrial society from within the framework of the nation-state, we have little choice – when it comes to the risk society – but to interpret it as a world risk society (e.g. Beck, 1996a, 1997b). In *World at Risk*, he puts it thus: 'risk society, thought through to its conclusion, means world risk society' (Beck, 2009a: 81). This is mainly because of the fundamental nature and properties of the kind of risks we are confronted with, living in the risk society. Whereas classic industrial society exposed its citizens to risks which were more or less limited in range, scope and effect – risks that affected only *certain groups* of people in *certain areas* for *certain periods* of time – risk society also, in addition to these risks, confronts us all with risks which are not at all limited to certain demographic groups, certain areas or certain periods of time. These risks – which Beck calls *man-made disasters* (Beck, 2000b) or *new risks* (Beck, 1991a) – are kinds of risks that, in principle, will affect everybody, everywhere, for a non-specific period of time (Beck, 1988: 120–122; 1991a). Beck, in *World at Risk*, says:

> its basic principle is that humanly generated, anticipated threats cannot be restricted either temporally, spatially or in social terms. This annuls the framework conditions and basic institutions of the first, industrial modernity – class conflict, national statehood and the notion of linear, technical-economic progress.
>
> (Beck, 2009a: 81)

Beck is talking about such new risks and man-made disasters as radioactive leaks from malfunctioning nuclear power plants – as we have seen happening in Chernobyl and, recently, Fukushima – and the complications and perils of global warming.

With the rise of these new risks, it is no longer the case that society and (nation-)state map onto one another. Whereas society must be understood as a world risk society and, therefore, as a global entity, the state as *nation*-state remains tied to a particular, demarcated territory. Because of this, regulation of societal activities grows to be more and more difficult, an unmanageable task for the nation-state. We still have a tendency, nonetheless, to turn expectantly towards our respective nation-states when we desire certain, political action or measures against unfortunate/undesirable social affairs and problems. Because of this, Beck has compared the condition of the nation-state to that of a *zombie*: an entity which, although effectively long dead, lives on in our minds and experience. This comparison between the nation-state and the zombie is the crux of Beck's work from the 1990s on, all the way to the present day. Beck is driven by a desire for *enlightenment*. He wishes to open our eyes to the new, cosmopolitan reality of things. He wants us to think and act differently from how we do today.

Only very few social theoreticians, however, are willing to go as far in their denouncement of the political possibilities of the nation-states as Beck does, or used to do. In fact, there exists today a rather broad, international consensus among political scientists that the nation-state as entity still has a very important, political part to play on the world stage. The English political scientist and theoretician of globalization David Held,[1] when asked in an interview to comment on Beck's comparison of the condition of the nation-state to that of a zombie, said:

States can, in their space, still make a big difference to dampen inequality, to empower citizens through education and learning, to increase the competiveness of their economy while also ameliorating the worst consequences of exposure to the world economic market. And this is true not just for advanced countries but for many developing countries as well. We live in a world where politics is now multilevel and multilayered.

(Thorup and Sørensen, 2004: 4)

Today, Beck would probably not disagree with Held's claim that today's politics is a multi-level practice which occurs in a number of different dimensions. Indeed, this is exactly how Beck himself characterizes the political game in both *Power in the Global Age* (Beck, 2005) and *Cosmopolitan Europe* (Beck and Grande, 2007). Beck does not, in either of these, completely disown the notion of the nation-states or their usefulness. However, as we shall see, Beck firmly maintains that nation-states throughout the world have indeed lost much of their power, as a direct consequence of globalization and that, consequently, they will be able to redeem themselves and re-establish a fundamental kind of influence on the world stage only in so far as they are able to *re-invent* themselves.

Real cosmopolitanization

Beck, in other words, seeks to warn us against putting our blind faith in the nation-states and hoping that they might somehow shelter us from the perils of globalization, if we only manage to keep each nation-state strongly secured and rigid enough. As early as in *Risk Society* Beck pointed out that the precautions and safety-measures which can be provided by individual nation-states will in no way suffice to protect anybody properly against the kinds of hazards we face today. Considering the radioactive emissions from Chernobyl, for example, Beck, in his foreword to the German edition of *Risk Society,* wrote:

Stunned, the world – interconnected by a network of information technology – watches. The minuscule hope in itself, our holding out for a 'fortunate' *wind direction* (the poor Swedes!) speaks louder than any number of words in expressing our helplessness, the helplessness of this, our highly civilized world, which has sought to protect its borders by use of barbed wire, walls, military force and police. Should the wind suddenly turn in an 'unfortunate' direction, or should it begin to *rain* – how very unfortunate – we would have to put a number of hopelessly inefficient measures in place, in the hope that society might somehow be able to defend itself against polluted nature and limit the nuclear hazard to the 'surrounding' environment.

(Beck, 1986; our translation)

Rather than try to hide ourselves behind the walls of our nation-states – walls which are, by now, not very protective at all – we ought, says Beck, to open our eyes to the cosmopolitan reality we are now part of. Although we have not noticed it, our world has grown increasingly cosmopolitan. Beck calls this phenomenon *banal cosmopolitanism* (Beck, 2006). The food we eat comes from places all over the world; even the simplest meal will often contain ingredients from several continents. The clothes we wear are produced on the other side of the globe. So are the music we listen to and the movies we watch. Reality, in other words, has become cosmopolitan. According to Beck, a cosmopolitanization of reality has taken place:

> Global interdependence means that reality is becoming cosmopolitan, though in a thoroughly uncosmopolitan way, one which no philosophical cosmo-politanism or cosmopolitan philosopher anticipated or even thought possible: without publicity, unintentionally, independently of political decisions and programmes, in other words, in a thoroughly deformed way. Real cosmopoli-tanization – unwanted, unseen, in varying degrees compulsory – is entering through the back door of side effects.
>
> (Beck and Grande, 2007: 119)

Beck makes a clear-cut distinction between real cosmopolitanization and philosophical cosmopolitanism (see Beck, 2006), taking the former to be a descriptive term and the latter as an umbrella term meant to cover several norma-tive theories about how the world of politics *ought* to function. The notion of the slow but steady erasure of national borders – the sneaky self-implementation of cosmopolitanization of reality, behind the backs of agents acting in economical environments – is not, however, a new theory. Witness Marx and Engels, in *The Communist Manifesto*:

> The bourgeoisie has through its exploitation of the world market given a *cos-mopolitan* character to production and consumption in every country. To the great chagrin of Reactionists, it has drawn from under the feet of industry the national ground on which it stood. All old-established national indus-tries have been destroyed or are daily being destroyed. They are dislodged by new industries, whose introduction becomes a life and death question for all civilised nations, by industries that no longer work up indigenous raw material, but raw material drawn from the remotest zones; industries whose products are consumed, not only at home, but in every quarter of the globe. In place of the old wants, satisfied by the production of the country, we find new wants, requiring for their satisfaction the products of distant lands and climes. In place of the old local and national seclusion and self-sufficiency, we have *intercourse in every direction, universal inter-dependence of nations*. And as in material, so also in intellectual production. The intel-lectual creations of individual nations become *common property*. National *one-sidedness* and narrow-mindedness become more and more *impossible*, and from the numerous national and local literatures, there arises a world literature.
>
> (Marx and Engels, 1848; emphasis ours)

Beck and his contemporary theoreticians of globalization, then, are far from the first to anticipate the cracking-open of the nation-state containers. However, whereas Marx and Engels's description was meant to provide a extrapolated prediction, a prognosis of how the future might pan out eventually, rather than a diagnosis of contemporary society as it was, it seems safe to say that, by now, the times have more or less caught up with the theory: today, we are in many ways living in exactly the kind of future predicted by Marx and Engels – at least according to Beck.

The meta-game of power

Beck's thesis, then, is that society has long escaped the boundaries and containment of the nation-state. As a direct consequence, nation-states are no longer able to make clear-cut distinctions between national and international matters and phenomena. Foreign policy has become *world domestic policy*, giving rise to a new, global kind of meta-game of power, in which nation-states have been stripped of their privileged positions on the world stage, forcing them to act as contestants alongside – and on the same terms as – other participants such as non-governmental organizations (NGOs) and globally competing economical agents (Beck, 2005: 10). Beck has another reason for calling this new competition a meta-game of power; he wishes to underline the fact that, although this new international dynamic does indeed concern itself, ultimately, with the distribution of power, it is also a game wherein the rules are constantly changing and shifting. Nothing is certain. Even the participants of the game are vague, as they enter the fray. Most of them are formed by the process of participation in the game itself (Beck, 2005: 34). This goes for the state as well, which, as we shall see, retains the option of *reshaping* or *reforming* itself in an effort to gain an advantage in the new meta-game of power.

To this day, however, it is the global economic agents – rather than the nation-states – which have had the largest influence and have, very effectively, set the agenda for the new meta-game of power. Second modernity, in other words, has more or less turned the distribution and position of influence and power of first modernity completely on its head.

No longer do nation-states get to define the boundaries and frameworks for economical activities; these days it is the other way around, with global economics dictating how politics and nation-states ought to perform and act. This is a direct consequence of the development in the global market, which has provided economic agents with an array of options for continually moving and redistributing their investments and means of production to whichever location – foreign or domestic – will net them the most profit.

The kind of power which global, economic agents is currently wielding over the nation-states, then, is largely based on the fact that they have an 'exit-option' (Hirschman, 1970: *passim*): the ever-present option of simply abandoning one country for another, should it turn out to be beneficial. They have been given this by the formation of a global market (Beck, 2005: 53); in Beck's words:

It is not the threat of *invasion* but rather the threat of *non-invasion* of investors, or the threat of their withdrawal, that constitutes the means of coercion. There is only one thing worse than being overrun by multinationals, and that is *not* being overrun by multinationals.

(Beck, 2005: 52)

Transnational corporations are all ready to uproot from their current location and resettle elsewhere, if they believe that the move will yield lower taxes, looser environmental restrictions and more flexible labour rules. They often move where labour is cheap. The dependency of the nation-states on the corporate world is not a new phenomenon – nation-states have always depended on their corporations – but today the corporate world is increasingly inclined to sever its territorial ties and affiliations for the sake of economic gain. In Beck's figurative words, investors have *wings* whereas states have *roots* (Beck, 2005: 72).

As early as in *What Is Globalization?* Beck pointed out that the globally functioning corporate world, with its constant threats of moving its production lines and investments to cheap, low-cost countries, is effectively *undermining* the agentive options of the nation-states. The corporate world, by acting this way, is forcing the nation-states to lower corporation taxes, in order to keep their investors and production facilities; but, by doing so, the nation-states end up undermining their own basic foundations for future investment and financing (Beck, 2000b: 4). More often than not, this kind of development is not due to transnational corporations exercising any sort of *deliberate* pressure on specific states. Rather, it is a matter of subpolitics (see Chapter 6); specifically, 'passive subpolitics' or 'politics as a side effect' (Holzer and Sørensen, 2002: 72–74). The economic agents act out of a desire for economical gain, but an unintended side effect of their activities is the undermining of the power of the nation-states.

The three dimensions of danger

The power of nation-states, however, is not just threatened by global economic agents. Transboundary pollution, as mentioned above, ends up undermining their power, and recently transnational terror has come into serious play as a third specific threat against nation-states. Because of this, Beck speaks of three specific dimensions of danger in the world risk society: financial crises, ecological crises (environmental crises) and terrorist dangers (Beck, 2003b: 19; 2002b, 2009a; Beck and Grande, 2007).

But what are we supposed to do, politically, to address terrorism and the other man-made hazards which the world risk society exposes us to? According to Beck, one thing is certain: if politics clings to the nation-state in an attempt to use it as a tool, then politics will end up losing the new meta-game of power (Beck, 2005: 17, 116–165). This goes for the economy, as well as for the environment and the problem of terrorism. The influence of politics will only continue to dwindle, says Beck, if politicians do not stop clinging to theories, terms and concepts which assume that the nation-state is still the most relevant political framework for handling new risks. The first precondition for *winning* the meta-game of power, then, is that we rid ourselves of the zombie-like notion of the nation state, both in political theory and in political action. The first step is to acknowledge *globality*. Only by acknowledging the fact that we are, by now, all living in a world (risk) society, by exchanging our national perspectives for a *cosmopolitan* perspective, will we be able to see the possibilities which – alongside the many new hazards and dangers – are *also* arising, out of this, our new situation (Beck, 2000c, 2005: 110–116). By replacing the national perspective with a cosmopolitan one, we open our eyes to the fact that we all have a part in a *shared destiny*; and it is exactly this new insight which must provide us with the options for handling the new dangers and risks. Beck made us aware of this as early as in *Risk Society*:

> In this sense, the risk society produces new antagonisms of interest *and* a new type of community of the endangered whose political carrying capacity remains, however, an open question . . . Risk societies are not class societies – that is not saying enough. They contain within themselves a grass-roots *developmental dynamics that destroys boundaries,* through which the people are forced together in the uniform position of civilization's self-endangering.
>
> (Beck, 1992: 47)

In his most recent works, Beck refers to these opportunities, the historical openings and possibilities for new communities, as 'the cosmopolitan moment' of world risk society (Beck, 2009a: ch. 3). Suddenly – still shell-shocked by the new risks and hazards we find ourselves exposed to – it turns out that there are new options, hitherto unseen possibilities for establishing new communities. Beck, in the book on 11 September 2001, writes:

> In all three of these dimensions of danger, and beyond all differences, a common model of political chances and contradictions can be seen in the global risk society. In an age in which belief in God, class, nation and government disappears, the known and recognized globality of danger is transformed into a source of associations, opening up new global political prospects for action. The terror attacks have brought states closer together and have sharpened the understanding of what globalization actually is: a worldwide community of destiny confronted with violent, destructive obsession. How then is politics possible in the age of globalization? My answer is: through the perceived globality of danger, which renders the apparently recalcitrant system of international and national politics fluid and malleable. In this sense, fear cultivates a quasi-revolutionary situation, which admittedly can be used in quite different ways. Again and again, one asks and discusses: what can unify the world? The experimental answer is an attack from Mars. This terrorism is an attack from 'inner Mars'.
>
> (Beck, 2003b: 4–5)

There is, however, no guarantee that the new risks of the world risk society will necessarily lead to a cosmopolitan turn of political thought. The possibility of renationalization movements is ever present: 'We are all trapped in a shared global space of threats – without exit. This may inspire highly conflicting responses, to which renationalization, xenophobia, etc., also belong' (Beck, 2009a: 56–57).

Transnationalization

One requirement for acting on and responding to the hazards of the world risk society, then, says Beck, is to acknowledge and fathom the *globality* of the hazards. We have to acknowledge that terror, pollution and financial crises are no longer at all simply matters that pertain only to certain isolated, specific and independent nation-states; they do indeed influence the *entire* world society. Only in so far as we are able to assume this kind of cosmopolitan perspective, says Beck, can we hope to open the way for politics and society to grasp the new, positive possibilities and options which are also part of globalization. Whereas the perspective of the nation-state allows us to see only the negative aspects, the disastrous potentials of our new situation, the cosmopolitan perspective opens up to an array of new possibilities and methods for transboundary collaboration, while allowing us to address the hazards.

But what would this kind of political project – one that is capable of staying with the times and social changes – really look like? According to Beck, the challenges posed to us by such phenomena as transnational economies can be handled only by a correspondingly *transnational political project.* The aim of this project should be to establish a *second* globalization and thus a *second* modernity, and the project must be fuelled by *cosmopolitan reason* which acts out of equal concern for the entire globe (Beck, 2005: 212). Content-wise, this new project should focus on regaining democratic control over the way society is developing.

For this to succeed, nation-states will need to be reformed and reshaped into cooperative *transnational states.* This kind of transnationalization of the nation-states must be founded on a reconfiguration of what we understand by the concept of *sovereignty.* Rather than consider sovereignty to be a traditional matter or – along with Jean Bodin and Thomas Hobbes – an indivisible concept which has to do solely with autonomous states, Beck wants us to make a distinction between *sovereignty* and *autonomy* (Beck, 2003b: 54–55; 2005: 91). Phasing out national autonomy does not automatically lead to national loss of sovereignty. In fact, quite the opposite happens. It is exactly Beck's argument that a decrease in national autonomy might very well lead to a growth or increase in national *sovereignty.* What is important today, after all, is how to distinguish between *formal* and *actual* sovereignty. Transnationalization means the surrender of *formal* sovereignty – of autonomy, Beck would say – but the payoff is a growth in *actual* sovereignty. For example, by surrendering its right to determine corporation taxes nationally, opting instead for a common minimum tax level in the European Union (EU) as a whole, France would end up losing an amount of *formal* sovereignty. The nation-state of France would no longer be able to determine its corporation tax levels and would be forced to adjust to the levels and numbers decided by the EU in general. As a reward, however, for this surrendering of sovereignty, France would end up gaining *actual* sovereignty, as it would escape the spiralling, negative process of continually adjusting its corporation taxes downwards to avoid losing investments and corporations to other, cheaper countries. One would, in other words, escape a malign, spiralling process which would otherwise effectively end up undermining the tax foundation, complicating the finances and activities of the state in general.

The cosmopolitan state

In Beck's eyes, the ultimate goal of the transnationalization of the nation-states is a reconfiguration into *cosmopolitan states.* A cosmopolitan state

> extends its influence in the domestic and the foreign domains through action and governance in transnational networks to which other states – but also NGO's, supranational institutions and transnational corporations – belong. Thus the cosmopolitan state, freed from scruples concerning sovereignty, uses the unrecompensed cooperation of other governments, non-governmental organizations and globally operating corporations to solve 'national' problems.
>
> (Beck, 2009a: 103)

The cosmopolitan state is, in many ways, in opposition to our contemporary nation-states as well as to two other, potential responses to globalization as such, namely the world state and the neoliberal minimal state. Whereas neoliberals cling to the idea of the nation-state and voice their thesis on the impossibility of political conduct, that politics have been replaced by a world market and that national welfare states must now all be reduced to national minimal states, Beck argues that we – especially considering the events of 11 September 2001 – have now reached a situation in which the thesis of the impossibility of political conduct has *itself* become an impossible thesis (Beck, 2005: 249–279). Once again, we *do* need the state. 11 September 2001 put it in painfully clear terms for us, that the present shape and condition of the state does not enable it to protect its citizens wholly. The states, in other words, cannot provide their citizens with the necessary sense of protection and security which – according to Thomas Hobbes – is the main reason motivating people to establish political communities in the first place.[2] Beck, by pointing our attention to 11 September, and the privatized, radically elaborate air security measures of American airports, concludes that it is in fact possible for states and countries to neoliberalize themselves to death (Beck, 2003b, 2005).

On the other hand, neither does Beck exactly care for the idea of a world state that would function more or less as an inflated, novelty-sized version of the nation-state (Beck, 2005: 217). To Beck, there is only one proper, political response to the current process of globalization: we must transnationalize our current nation-states and move them towards the *cosmopolitan state.* Such a cosmopolitan project needs

> a transnational, political architecture, that must be founded on a global version of *the New Deal.* Such an architecture would consist of transnational courts of law with the power to impose sanctions, as well as new transnational parties, world citizen parties, that address cosmopolitan issues *within* nation-state public spheres and political arenas as well as beyond nation-state borders (i.e. transnationally), while attending to them in national contexts.
>
> (Beck, 2005: 217)

The specific *kind* of cosmopolitanism which every cosmopolitan state must be founded on is also one that lies in direct opposition to the kind of universalism required by a world state. Whereas universalism as a concept will always end up emphasizing *similarity* at the cost of respect for *diversity*, Beck's brand of cosmopolitanism seeks to accept the *otherness* of others, as well as their likeness to us (Beck, 2005: 227). This is the case, not least, with regard to national differences. It is a fundamental requirement for the cosmopolitan state, then, that we reconsider not only our idea of what sovereignty ought to be, but also our very *concept of the state.* Beck, in support of this argument, presents us with an elegant analogy:

> Cosmopolitan states are based on the principle of the indifference of nation-states. In a manner similar to the way in which the Westphalian peace ended the confessionally charged civil wars of the 16th century through the separation of state and religion, the global (civil) war of the 20th century and the beginning of the 21st century – this is the thesis – is answered by a separation of state and nation.
>
> (Beck, 2003b: 266)

Much like how today's British citizens, for example, do not need to be of the same religion, Beck imagines that the future citizens of the cosmopolitan states will not need to be of the same nationality. These citizens will, as true cosmopolitans, effortlessly be able to live with dual affiliations: to both a nation and a state. In this sense, Beck's understanding of cosmopolitanism is very much akin to that of the Greek and Roman stoics, to whom a cosmopolitan was a person who was as a citizen in both the entirety of the universe (*cosmos*) as well as in one, particular city state (*polis*) (Beck, 2005: 35).

Beck has often – not least in his responses to the attacks of 11 September 2001 – expressed a certain amount of cautious hope for this particular project. After 11 September he saw, in the immediate political reactions to the attack, a certain *willingness* to act in a transnational manner. However, he nonetheless warned us that, rather than establishing the *open-to-the-world,* accessible, cosmopolitan world states, we might well end up establishing *closed-to-the-world* transnational *surveillance states* or *citadel states,* in our attempts to politically delimit and contain the threat of terror and the other perils which we are facing today (Beck,

2005: 258–270). A transnationalization of our current nation-states, then, does not necessarily and automatically lead to cosmopolitan states – but transnationalization is a fundamental *requirement* for moving in that direction.

The cosmopolitan Europe

To Ulrich Beck, it remains an important point that transnationalization does not specifically need to occur as the result of any kind of idealistic or altruistic aspirations of particular nation-states. Rather, transnationalization should be understood from the kind of raw logic of causes and effects, which we covered in Chapter 2. Transnationalization will often assert itself behind the backs of the agents bringing it about, as an *unintended side effect* of the egoistically driven actions of the nation-states. This is, according to Beck, exactly what happened in the case of the EU. Beck and Grande describe the EU as an ever-expanding construct, in terms of both geographical spread and policy areas. It is, they say, a construction which follows 'the *logic of side effects*, the logic of the unintended consequences of political decisions' (Beck and Grande, 2007: 6). Beck and Grande refer to their idea of Europe, both inside and outside the EU, as 'realistic cosmopolitanism': the European nation-states are forced, by their own national interests, to commit themselves to a tightly knit venture of cooperation within Europe. In order to achieve their own goals, they must accept and respect those of the others. According to Beck and Grande, national interests go hand in hand with a quite intensified 'Europeanization'. Although technically, of course, each country may choose to withdraw from the cooperation and agreements that are in place, it is no longer a real option for anybody:

> However, there is no way back to the nation-state in Europe because all of the actors are caught up in a system of dependencies from which they could withdraw only at very high cost. After fifty years of Europeanization, the individual states and societies are capable of acting only *within* the European synthesis.
>
> (Beck and Grande, 2007: 22)

For several years, Beck has been interested in Europe and the EU. Whenever he has been asked to point to a second modern alternative to the paralysed, ineffectual nation-states, he has always made reference to Europe. In his earlier books, Beck has often included several chapters and paragraphs on Europe, although exactly how he imagined the EU would develop and progress over time has always remained somewhat unclear. For a long time, it looked like as if the EU would come to be the kind of cosmopolitan state which we have outlined above. However, in their 2004 book on Europe (English: Beck and Grande, 2007) Beck and Grande more or less abandoned this idea. They now began to describe Europe as an *empire* (Beck and Grande, 2007: 50–93). The main difference between a state and an empire is that a state – even a cosmopolitan state – is tied to a specific territory and founded on formal rule, whereas an empire is not tied to any specific territory and is founded on both formal and informal rule. By understanding Europe as an empire, we escape having to partake in doomed, fruitless discussions about where to draw the proverbial line for Europe – is Turkey a part of it or not? To Beck and Grande, the main aspect of European identity is that it is an identity of movement. Beck and Grande, with Günter Verheugen, speak of it as the *Baustelle Europa* (the European construction ground) and the 'Doing Europe'. European identity, to them, has to do with what is to come: the expectations for the future, rather than any kind of certain religion or territory.

This concept of empire is both a refinement of and in opposition to Michael Hardt and Antonio Negri's bestseller *Empire* (Hardt and Negri, 2000). Whereas Hardt and Negri start their analysis in postmodern territory – a vantage point which leaves no room for nation-states at all – Beck and Grande claim that their concept of the empire should be approached as a modern (second modern) one; modern because nation-states do still, in fact, exist and have a part to play in the empire of Europe. Compared with Beck's previous work, *Cosmopolitan Europe* does in fact seem to emphasize the significance of nation-states quite a bit more strongly. The nation-states fuel Europeanization, simply by their own egoistically driven actions, but at the same time these actions end up pushing the nation-states along, furthering their transition towards becoming cosmopolitan states.

A main driving force in the cosmopolitanization of the European process is the EU courts: the voluntary acknowledgement and utilization of the courts as a means for solving international conflict. Violence as a means of conflict resolution has been abolished within Europe. The European empire 'secures its internal domination not through force, but through a *taboo* on force' (Beck and Grande, 2007: 66). As a means of making its countries adhere to its rules and conventions, Europe threatens not violence or bullets, but exclusion.

However, Beck and Grande are not awestruck by the EU of today, which they call a *deformed* cosmopolitan EU. They describe the EU of today as a 'decentralized, territorially differentiated, transnational negotiation system dominated by elites' (Beck and Grande, 2007: 53). The task at hand, then, is to free the EU from this deformity; to somehow turn it into a truly cosmopolitan entity. The EU of today is only *inwardly* cosmopolitan, in so far as the internal differences of the other participants are being respected; outwardly, this is not the case. Quite the opposite. The global financial crisis has proven to be an especially grand challenge for the shared European currency, the euro, as well as for the entire EU project in general. In summer 2011, this caused Beck, Habermas and 17 other prominent sociologists, political scientists and politicians to publish a proclamation in several European newspapers in which they urged the EU to address the challenges that are looming over Europe today (Habermas *et al.*, 2011). In the proclamation, the 19 authors warned against the dissolution of the eurozone – which would have unfathomable political and economical consequences – unless immediate action were taken and measures put into place to establish a closer, more focused cooperation within the Union.

Beck used to be more certain that cosmopolitan reason and sense would eventually prevail. The egoistically motivated European nation-states would eventually, he thought, come to realize the benefits and gains in sovereignty that would follow if they committed themselves to the cosmopolitan, European project. In 2002, when he wrote *Macht und Gegenmacht im Globalen Zeitalter* (Beck, 2005), Beck held high hopes for the EU convention which was to begin in March 2002 and, in June 2003, resulted in the 'Draft for a treaty for the implementation of a constitution for Europe'. Beck compared the effort to that of founding the United States of America in 1778:

> The objections to such a cosmopolitan draft constitution for Europe that are raised today are quite similar to those with which the American convention had to struggle in Philadelphia in the year 1778 [sic]. At the time, the issue that was the subject of heated debate up until the very last was whether the loose union of thirteen American states needed a powerful central legislature, executive and judiciary. Even the subsequent ratification of the draft constitution was achieved only by a narrow margin. Those who wanted more centralized authority were accused of being 'oblivious to the wishes of the people', the South distrusted the North, the small states distrusted the big ones. Everyone was busy defending their own sovereignty. But ultimately all the parties were winners by dint of realizing that federalism brought about an *increase* in sovereignty, an insight that may – or perhaps even will – eventually put a cosmopolitan Europe on the road to success. It is the increase in practical sovereignty and in political capacity in the global age that more than makes up for the loss of formal autonomy.
>
> Imagine Europe as a cosmopolitan confederation of states which work together to curb the excesses of economic globalization and which demonstrate respect for difference – especially the difference of their fellow European nations – rather than denying it or bureaucratically negating it: this could be, or become, a thoroughly realistic utopia.
>
> (Beck, 2005: 95)

It is statements like these that have led some of Beck's colleagues to claim that he and his theories express a much too optimistic stance and point of view; and in many ways these notions seem to have more to do with hope and expectancy than with any kind of raw, sociological insight. Statements such as those above have also helped Beck distinguish himself from most other contemporary sociologists; not least from the internationally renowned Polish-English sociologist Zygmunt Bauman. As we have seen, Beck and Bauman share and agree on quite an extensive number of observations and considerations of our contemporary society. This is also the case with regard to the matter of globalization (e.g. Bauman [1998] 2003). Bauman, too, perceives globality to be now a basic condition. Bauman, however, is much more pessimistically charged than Beck, in his assessment of globalization and its consequences.

Bauman sees current globalization as a process which will inevitably lead to irreversible inequality and a new kind of divide between those he calls the 'locals' and those he calls the 'globals'; between those who are bound to a specific place and geography and those who keep the entire world as their own, personal playground. The amount of common ground between these two distinct groups is dwindling, disappearing from right beneath their feet, as globalization presses on. Where Bauman ends up in pessimism – entangled in an array of new inequalities, introduced by globalization – Beck has always and adamantly insisted on accentuating the positive possibilities that are also, alongside the negative potential for disaster, an inherent part of the tumultuous process of globalization which we are currently experiencing. This is another modern element in Beck's thought, as well. Unlike Bauman, Beck still holds a basic belief in reason and enlightenment. To Beck, the current process of globalization draws both good and bad elements in its wake. Staying faithful to his own theory of second modernity – a period in which multitudes and ambivalences prevail – he opts for accentuating a specific kind of *both/and* development.

The new social inequality

This is also the case for risks and their effects on our day-to-day lives. Whereas Beck used to highlight primarily the 'democratic' aspects of the new risks – that the new risks affect us all, that the distinctions between rich and poor end up being stripped of significance, that 'smog is democratic' and that we now, for the first time in history, really and truly do find that we are 'all in the same boat', so that distinctions of class and social status end up losing their meaning – he has, in later years, become more alert to what he calls *new social inequalities* (e.g. Beck, 2007b, 2010). These are inequalities that follow in the wake of the new risks and often end up acting as amplifiers for the social inequalities that already exists. The already underprivileged and poor of the low-lying areas of Bangladesh, or drought-stricken countries and areas such as south of the Horn of Africa, also end up being struck the worst by climate changes. The new risks, then, must in a sense be seen as both *hierarchical* – since the poor and exposed cannot protect themselves against them as efficiently or expansively as the well-to-do – and *democratic* – since we are all, regardless of status and class, to some extent delivered to them and influenced by them. Beck reminds us, however, of the following: the larger the risk, the harder it is to escape it. This is true for everybody, no matter how rich and powerful they may be (Beck, 2010: 175).

The transition to second modernity, then, entails the rise of new kinds of inequality. According to Beck, however, we may well have a difficult time seeing or acknowledging these new inequalities, as we are still clinging to our principle of the nation-state, trying to maintain a conceptual notion of the world as divided into separate, particular and independent nation-states. This kind of division of the world – wherein inequality is seen to be an internal matter and a problem to be dealt with by each nation-state by its own means – functions very badly in a cosmopolitan reality and, it turns out, serves very poorly as a reflection of how human beings interpret their own living conditions:

> Confronted by climate change, the spread of AIDS, the incalculability of transnational terrorism and the unilateralism of the world's greatest military

power more and more people find themselves exposed to the experience, that their conditions of life and survival are at least as much dependent on processes which penetrate the borders of nation states as on ones which appear within nation state control.

(Beck, 2007b: 691)

Because of this, Beck suggests that politics and the social sciences make an effort to replace the nation-state principle with the side effect principle as a means of understanding social inequality. Whereas first modernity exhibited a clear convergence between the two, it is no longer at all the case that side effects are restricted to affecting the people who live in the particular nation-state that has made the risk-triggering decision, such as launching a new kind of industrial production, starting new research projects or passing new laws and legislature. Rather, the negative side effects are now in a sense 'exported' both spatially and temporally, across national borders and into the future and the realms of future generations. This leads to a radically asymmetric relationship between

those who take, define the risks and profit from them and those who are assigned to them, who have to suffer the 'unforeseen side effects' of decisions of others, perhaps even pay for them with their lives, without having had the chance to be involved in the decision-making process.

(Beck, 2007b: 692)

As long as we cling to the nation state principle, says Beck, we will stay enmeshed in our current, counterproductive notion of social challenges and inequality. This keeps us from fully *perceiving* and thus understanding the new social inequality. Worse yet, the nation-state principle amplifies and exacerbates global social inequality. The production of risks and sociality inequality is strengthened and, in a sense, nourished by our way of dividing the world into particular, sovereign nation-states. This is because the nation-state principle makes it possible to speculate in social inequalities by playing off the fact that different nation-states have different standards of wage levels, working conditions, environment, tax regulation and so on. As we have discussed, it is easy for any corporation to – with very little notice – move its production lines from one country to any other if it feels it is being regulated too tightly. In this way, dangers end up being 'deported' to other areas of the world where low safety, low wages and low rights are much more prevalent – thus ultimately amplifying social poverty and need at the site of deportation. As Beck puts it, there is 'a fatal attraction between poverty, social vulnerability, corruption and the accumulation of dangers. The poorest of the poor live in the blind spots which are the most dangerous death zones of world risk society' (Beck, 2007b: 693).

In every sense of the word, then, Beck is by all accounts a *realist* – and many of his assessments share the disenchantment and mercilessness of, for example, Zygmunt Bauman or Naomi Klein. Beck, however, does not give up hope for a better world. Rather, the state of the world has caused him to strongly advocate the abandonment of the principle of the nation-state by both politicians and social scientists. We have already covered how he imagines this kind of escape from the nation-state principle might be orchestrated. Beck's goal, as we shall see in the next chapter, is also to create a *new social science* which corresponds adequately to the kind of cosmopolitan reality we live in: a science which acknowledges and addresses the new social inequalities that have been drawn onto the world stage in the wake of the transformation of nation-state-based industrial societies into one, united society of world risk.

Core terms

Banal cosmopolitanism: The fact that an increasing amount of our everyday space is filled by the results a global division of labour. Our food and our clothes are core examples of this.

The container theory: The idea that the nation-state is an entity which both contains and encases a specific national society, people and territory; for example that the German state contains and encases German society, the German people and German territory.

Cosmopolitan realism: A counter-term to philosophical cosmopolitism. Cosmopolitan realism is the research field of the social sciences, wherein the extent and degree of real cosmopolitanism is examined.

Cosmopolitanization: Beck's theory of cosmopolitanization serves as an extension of that of the stoics, who believed that the home of humanity was both the cosmos and a specific *polis* or city. To Beck, the cosmopolitan is a person of double belonging: to a state and to a nation which is different from the state; for example the Turk who lives in France and feels a connection to both the nation of Turkey and the state of France. Central to Beck's understanding is the *acknowledgement of the otherness of others*. As opposed to *universalism*, which emphasizes the sameness of human beings, Beck's cosmopolitanism wishes to acknowledge the sameness in others, as well as their differences.

Globalism: The view that globalization is solely a matter of the economy.

Globality: To interpret globalization as globality is to recognize that we are now living in a world society and that the different national societies are no longer clearly distinguishable from one another but, rather, are tightly interconnected.

Globalization: A multidimensional phenomenon which encompasses the economy, information technology, pollution, migration, the activities of civil society and so on. Globalization is promoted and enabled by transnational operators and runs as an undercurrent beneath the powers of the national states, serving as a sort of subtle interconnection between each state.

Real cosmopolitanization: Another term for globality; the increasing amount of interconnectivity between every country in the world.

Transnationalization: The shift away from the national state, characterized by an opening up towards – and an increasingly active cooperation with – other national states.

Further reading

Beck, U. (1992) *Risk Society: Towards a New Modernity.* London: Sage Publications.

Beck, U. (2000b) *What Is Globalization?* Cambridge: Polity Press.

Beck, U. (2000) 'The Cosmopolitan Perspective: Sociology of the Second Age of Modernity', *British Journal of Sociology*, vol. 51, no. 1, pp. 79–105.

Beck, U. (2003b) 'The Silence of Words: On Terror and War', *Security Dialogue*, vol. 34, no. 3, pp. 255–267.

Beck, U. (2005a) *Power in the Global Age.* Cambridge: Polity Press.

Beck, U. (2006) *The Cosmopolitan Vision.* Cambridge: Polity Press.

Beck, U. and Grande, E. (2007) *Cosmopolitan Europe*. Cambridge: Polity Press.

6 Sociology, science and politics in second modernity

Towards a cosmopolitan turn in sociology

Sociology, according to Ulrich Beck, bears the mark of methodological nationalism: it is an approach to the study of social phenomena which, often without reflection, assumes that societies can be nationally demarked and delineated and that it makes sense to study social phenomena – legislation, economic development, inequality, unemployment, institutions and so on – in a manner that is wholly *separated* from the developments and occurrences taking place in other societies. This kind of approach is, by now, defunct. It does not work. Beck, lapidary, puts it thus: 'What remains national? Thought. What is no longer national? Reality!' (Beck, 2006: 102). If today's sociology wants to be able to truly take itself to be a *science of reality*, it must first come to terms with real cosmopolitanization and the new, interconnected world (Beck, 2000c, 2005: 10–50; 2006: 24–44). If we wish to understand the new social inequalities covered in the previous chapter, we will need to do away with the nation-state-oriented framing of social inequality which has been the predominant approach to the field. So far, research into the matter of social inequality has, writes Beck, questioned almost everything: 'classes, strata, lifestyles, milieu and individualization – but not the territorial reference, the ties to the soil, the nation-state framing of social inequality' (Beck, 2010: 168). The cosmopolitanization of reality, however, requires that this particular area of research – as well as sociology and the social sciences in general – be able to demonstrate a new and more reflective approach to the coupling between national state and society.

Thus, to Beck, it seems to be high time for the social sciences to wake up and realize that globalization has caused radical change in the world. Since the 1990s, Beck has been hard at work, trying to open the eyes of his colleagues and fellow sociologists to the new cosmopolitan reality in which they – according to Beck – now find themselves living and working. One of Beck's efforts is the expansive trilogy on 'cosmopolitan realism', consisting of the books *Power in the Global Age* (Beck, 2005), *The Cosmopolitan Vision* (Beck, 2006) and *Cosmopolitan Europe* (Beck and Grande, 2007). Throughout these books, Beck conducts a thorough analysis of globalization and the significance of real cosmopolitanization drawn in its wake, with regard to the notion of politics, the state, Europe and the social sciences. Since the turn of the millennium, the challenge which the cosmopolitanization of reality presents to the social sciences and sociology has also been the topic of a large number of Beck's research articles (e.g. Beck, 2000c, 2007b, 2010; Beck and Grande, 2010). Generally speaking, the books and articles indicate a certain desire for a *cosmopolitan turn* in social and political theory, which would entail parting with methodological nationalism in order to work from a new *methodological cosmopolitanism.*

Provincialism and varieties of second modernity

This cosmopolitan turn in social and political theory, for which Beck argues, is, not least, meant to do away with the kind of *Eurocentrism* – or *provincialism* – which he claims has dominated social theory so far. Because of this centrism, social theory is characterized by false and erroneous conclusions, wherein research conducted in a specific society is extrapolated and revalued into studies of society *as such* (Beck and Grande, 2010: 412).

There is, according to Beck, not one specific course of development for society but rather many different paths of development and many kinds of modernity. Social theory, however, says Beck, has exhibited a clear tendency to base its conclusions on the kind of development that has taken place in the western world – the 'Western path' (Beck and Grande, 2010: 416) – and apply them to the rest of the world. Inspired from insights in postcolonial theory, global history and Atlantic history, however, Beck argues that there exists not simply one single modernity – with one corresponding path for transition from first to second modernity – but in fact a *plurality* of modernities and corresponding variations of developmental paths and second modernities in the world.

However, although it is possible to identify several modernities, Beck insists on the notion of a second modernity which is asserting itself across the globe; he nonetheless stresses the point that it does so in various ways, with variations that are dependent on the particular national societies and global regions. Expanding on this notion, Beck and Grande (2010: 416) have identified four (main) paths of modernization. First is the *Western path*, which is an unintended, temporally stretched and (more or less) successful modernization of modern societies. Alongside this, there is a particularly eastern brand of modernization taking place, a so-called active, *compressed* modernization driven by developmental states such as South Korea and China. Third, it is possible to identify a reactive, enforced modernization – a *postcolonial* modernization. Finally, we have seen examples of *failed* modernization in which the institutions of first modernity are never quite properly built or put into place, or where the transformation into second modernity somehow goes wrong.

Self-criticism

Beck's reproof of the provincialism of the social sciences also ends up ringing true for his own theory about reflexive modernization and second modernity. He admits that his theory, too, has so far been primarily concerned with the 'Western path' and that, as a consequence, it needs like the others to be *de-provincialized* and *cosmopolitanized* (Beck and Grande, 2010: 420). The theory of second modernity has been making the exact claim that the entire world would, eventually, come to experience exactly the same kind of social development. However, Beck is now ready to refine his theory and add more nuance to it, by pointing out that, although there is a universal and shared exposure to the side effects of the industrial, nation-state-founded modernization, the reflexive process of modernization itself may well take on very different actual aspects across different societies and occur in them in different ways.

Methodological cosmopolitanism

As mentioned, Beck would like to see sociology and the social sciences make an effort towards replacing the dictum of methodological nationalism with a *new methodological cosmopolitanism*. Such a methodological cosmopolitanism is defined as an approach which takes theoretical reflections and research as starting points in the varieties of modernities and their global interdependencies (Beck and Grande, 2010: 412). The question, then, is how one would in fact go about replacing methodological nationalism with methodological cosmopolitanism. How are we supposed to come up with analyses that can properly grasp the interplay and variations between different modernities? And which kind of entities should we be striving to focus on in our analyses, once we have been told that we need to do away with the container theory about the nation-state?

Beck and Grande's suggestion is that, rather than take our starting point in the nation-state or national societies, we begin using thematic entities such as 'individualization', 'cosmopolitanization' or 'risk society' as new starting points for our analyses (Beck and Grande, 2010: 427). They refer to a number of theoreticians and books as good examples of what it is they desire of the new sociology and social sciences:

> Paul Gilroy's conceptualization of the '*Black Atlantic*' (1993), Saskia Sassen's identification of the '*Global City*' (1991), Arjun Appadurai's notion of 'scapes' (1991), Martin Albrow's concept of the 'Global Age' (1996) and our own analysis of 'Cosmopolitan Europe' (Beck and Grande 2007).
>
> (Beck and Grande, 2010: 427)

Thus, if we want to conduct analyses that operate in a methodologically cosmopolitan manner, there are at least four possible approaches we may take, according to Beck and Grande (2010). First, we can choose to conduct *historical analyses*: for example analyses of 'transnational spaces of remembrance' (Beck and Grande, 2010: 431), such as Daniel Levy and Natan Sznaider have worked with, also partly in collaboration with Beck (Beck, Levy and Sznaider, 2004). Second, we can conduct functional analyses of, for example, 'transnational policy regimes' (Beck and Grande, 2010: 431). Third, we can choose to look at *social practices*, in particular social conflicts and conflict structures. Here, Beck and

Grande mention 'transnational political campaigns' and 'debates' as examples (Beck and Grande, 2010: 431). Finally, we can opt for taking a closer look at the new kinds of transnational institutions which are appearing. Beck and Grande's book about Europe (Beck and Grande, 2004, 2007) provides an excellent example of this fourth kind of study.

The nation-state's return to grace

Although Beck wants to get rid of methodological nationalism, his attitude towards the nation-state today is not as entirely intransigent as it used to be. In a manner of speaking Beck has, through the years, come to hold a more nuanced view of the nation-state – both with regard to its political options and as a framework for sociological analyses. Gone, it would seem, is the claim that the only way to relate to the nation-state is to consider it a *zombie* – a thoroughly dead entity which remains somewhat alive only as a result of our own thinking. In fact, Beck (with Grande) now writes that:

> The cosmopolitization of modern societies does not, however, inevitably mean the end of the national. All predictions of the end of the nation-state in the age of globalization have so far proved premature. The nation-state does not dissolve in the process of reflexive modernization; it is transformed in the most diverse ways . . . This implies that the national, i.e. national borders, national monopolies of the legitimate use of physical force, national norms, institutions and cultures can still be powerful factors shaping societies. Consequently, a *methodological cosmopolitanism cannot entirely neglect the national. It must not, however, accept it as an unquestioned premise; it must treat it as a conceptual variable, whose significance must be empirically investigated.*
>
> (Beck and Grande, 2010: 429–430; emphasis ours)

Among other things, the research conducted by his colleagues Daniel Levy and Saskia Sassen has helped convince Beck that using the nation-state as an entity of analysis can still be a quite fruitful endeavour. According to Beck and Grande, Levy and Sassen have – in each their own way – illustrated how the processes of globalization are tightly interconnected with transformations in – and by – particular and specific nation-states. Thus the nation-state receives a (partial) pardon from Beck and is reinstated as an entity of analysis which can be utilized in exploring the cosmopolitan, as the nation-state is increasingly turning into a 'showcase of the global' (Beck and Grande, 2010: 430).

The transformation and new status of science

Turning to the status of science in general, we see that a lot of interesting things are happening here as well, which have to do with the transition from first to second modernity (Table 6.1). One of the most characteristic differences between the old hazards and risks and the new is that the new risks can be fathomed

Table 6.1 Science in the risk society

Industrial society	Risk society
The dangers/risks can be detected by the individual using his or her senses (unemployment, industrial injuries etc.)	The new dangers and risks can be detected only by means of the senses of science: theories, experiments, measuring instruments etc. (e.g. CFC gases, global warming)
Experience of risk and danger is immediate, direct	Risk awareness is second-hand non-experience
Science demystifies the world (Weber)	Science is demystified
Belief in science	Belief in science crumbles, while we simultaneously grow increasingly dependent on it
Science as problem solver	Non-knowledge as an existential precondition

– become visible – only through certain scientific theories, processes and knowledge (Beck, 1992: 26–36, 51–80, 155–183). Unemployment, workplace accidents and hunger are *immediate* and directly visible risks and dangers, whereas crop fertilizer residue in our foods, holes in the ozone layer and radioactive leaks and emissions appear to us only *indirectly*: mediated through scientific knowledge and information. We cannot, for example, use our own senses and faculties to discern *immediately* whether there is a hole in the ozone layer or harmful chemicals in our drinking water. In order for us to be able to learn about these new risks, we are utterly dependent on science. It is only through scientific theory, experiments and measuring equipment that we may be able to even *see* the new hazards. Because of this, Beck calls of our experience of these new risks a 'second-hand non-experience' (Beck, 1992: 71–72).

This development means that we are now dependent on science to an extent hitherto unheard of; we simply need it to warn us about current and future dangers. As a direct consequence, the relationship between the layperson and science turns into a quite ambivalent one in the risk society. On the one hand, there is growing awareness that science plays a fairly big part in the production of new risks – and this awareness leads to a heightened criticism and scepticism towards science. On the other hand we are utterly and undeniably dependent on science and its ability to inform us about the new and lurking hazards we are unable to see. It is no longer possible to count on our own senses to reveal hazards and dangers for us. Every time a new toxin is detected in our drinking water, every time new information about the holes in the ozone layer is broadcasted through the usual channels, the information entails a sense of a loss of in our belief in general authority. First we are shocked by the news itself. Then we are annoyed that our senses no longer suffice to keep us safe and that we are utterly delivered to a science which is often in conflict with itself. As Beck puts it, our senses have lost all use and function, with regard to the man-made hazards (Beck, [1986] 1991b: 68).

This new dependence on science is often the source of daily frustration in the risk society, since science is often prone to deliver several different interpretations of the same phenomena. One week we may be told that coffee is detrimental to our health and well being, only to be told the completely opposite thing by another source the next week. It turns out, we may in fact find out, later and from a third source, that a couple of cups of coffee a day might well have a beneficial effect on the human body. Once people start doubting and criticizing the sciences in this manner – once disgruntlement spreads to the general population and media – it leads to a devaluing of scientific knowledge. Scientific knowledge is reduced to one form of knowledge among others; it ends up losing its monopoly on truth in the risk society – exactly as Lyotard ([1979] 1984) put it in his diagnosis of the conditions of science in highly developed societies (see Chapter 3). The problem for the individual, then, is how to determine what is and is not true. What is one to believe? What is one to do? It is increasingly up to the individual to create his or her own rules and strategies for life, based on *belief* in certain scientific experts or alternative explanations and *rejection* of others (see Chapter 3).

The climate debate

This is also the case at the level of society in general; but here great consequences and importance may attach to whether one should choose to place one's faith in one specific scientific theory or another. A prime example of this would be the debate that has surrounded the greenhouse effect and its subsequent environmental problems. Although all scientific experts in the field have agreed, for quite a number of years, that the world's average temperature is on the rise, there has not been as much of a concord with regard to what might be *causing* the rise. For a while now, a majority of experts have argued that the main cause of the rising temperature levels is human activities. The theory is that a rising use of fossil fuels has led to an increased emission of CO_2 into the Earth's atmosphere. This CO_2 has, in time, come to act as a filter or screen around the globe, allowing the sun's rays to pass through the atmosphere and then subsequently blocking the ensuing heat from leaving it. The CO_2 filter, in other words, functions much like the glass panels of a common greenhouse. According to this greenhouse theory, man-made CO_2 emissions – unless halted – will lead to a level of global warming which will have dire and immense consequences for life on Earth as we know it (DMI, 2009).

It is this greenhouse theory which is behind many attempts in recent years at reducing man-made CO_2 emissions – such as the highly ambitions but, as discussed, somewhat failed attempts of the COP 15 summit – 'the Copenhagen summit' – of December 2009. This and other COP summits have operated and taken their agendas from the assessments and reports of the UN climate panel. Since 1990, the UN climate panel has been pointing to man-made CO_2 emissions as the cause of the Earth's rising temperatures. According to the UN climate panel, then, we need to change our behaviour if we want to avoid future climate disasters. Massive investment will need to be made into alternative energy sources, new and more environmentally conscious car engines and so on. In short, we need to change our way of life drastically, if we wish to stem the climate changes.

However, curiously little has been done in the field. This may have to do with the fact that, alongside the assessments and reports of the UN climate panel, other and alternative theories about the causes of the rising temperature levels have been presented. One of the most discussed alternative theories – which for a good many years presented a serious challenge to the theory of the greenhouse effect – is the theory of increased solar activity levels. This made an international breakthrough when in 1990 the Danish climate experts E. Friis-Christensen and K. Lassen published the results of their research in the renowned scientific journal *Science* (DMI, 2003). The two researchers, after comparing the sun's activity with the average temperature of the Earth from 1880 to 1980, were able to point out a remarkable accordance between the two: the higher the degree of solar activity, the higher the average temperature on Earth. Because of this relationship, they proposed a theory that the average temperature of Earth was mainly dictated and regulated by solar activity and thus only to a minor extent influenced by the activities of human beings.

This kind of situation is utterly typical of the risk society, which will often produce two or more scientific theories and try to test them rigorously, only to end up, ultimately, with wildly different theories that entail wildly different consequences to politics, society and the lives of ordinary people. One would be able to argue then, science in hand, that we need to make profound and drastic changes to our way of life if we do not wish the Earth's climate to change in a decisive and uncontrolled manner. But at the same time, one would be equally able to argue in favour of the complete opposite, on an equally scientific basis. And deciding which scientific theory is 'right' is as far from a trivial matter as it could be.

With regard to global warming, for example, it would be much easier if it were to turn out that global warming is mainly due to an increase in solar activity; in that case, temperatures will eventually end up resettling at a lower level, once solar activity once again calms down and returns to previous levels. Armed with this theory and others, a fair amount of the so-called 'climate sceptics' argued for years that we need not – and indeed would be insane to – use so many resources in our attempts to combat man-made CO_2 emission, when scientific theory had been able to illustrate that it was primarily owing to the actions of the sun, rather than the actions of people, that average temperature levels were on the rise. We ought instead to use our money and energy on combating hunger, AIDS or some other matter of real consequence for the globe.

With regard to the theory of solar activity, it should be mentioned that Peter Thejll and Knud Larsen published, in 2000, an updated analysis of data on Earth's temperature levels in relation to solar activity levels, up until the year 1999. Their analysis illustrated that solar activity levels do not suffice to explain recent years' rise in temperature on Earth. Temperatures have risen along a much steeper curve – from 1980 on – than would have been possible if they were influenced by solar activity alone. The conclusion is that there must be other things causing the current rising temperatures, or – in the words of the Danish Meteorological Institute: 'We interpret this discrepancy as a sign that contributions exceeding those of the sun are now being made to temperature variations – possibly by the greenhouse effect caused by humans' (DMI, 2003; our translation). This kind of response, in its vague dithering, serves as an exemplary instance of the kind of fundamental *uncertainty* which risk society imposes on us. The greenhouse effect may *possibly* be causing global warming – but we do not yet, apparently, know for sure.

Non-knowledge as a fundamental condition

Although scientific efforts in the field of climate research are converging, today, towards the conclusion that it is indeed human activity – primarily the burning of fossil fuels – which is the root cause of the rising temperature levels we are experiencing, this does not change the general fact that we, in the risk society, must learn to live with *non-knowledge* as a fundamental condition. Or as Beck puts it in *World at Risk*:

> Living in the world risk society means living with ineradicable non-knowing [*Nichtwissen*] or, to be more precise, with the simultaneity of threats and non-knowing and the resulting political, social and moral paradoxes and dilemmas. Because of the global character of the threat, the need and burden of having to make life-and-death decisions increase with non-knowing.
>
> (Beck, 2009a: 115)

We also need to learn to accept that we shall never – no matter how much research we may conduct – be able to wholly reveal the truth about everything. With every new scientific breakthrough comes the production of new non-knowledge. First modernity's tendency to place unlimited amounts of faith in science and the unwavering ability of science to, eventually, do away with even our most difficult problems ends up being replaced, in the society of risk, by a more nuanced view of science. This new and more nuanced, second modern view both acknowledges that we need science and research now more than ever – we depend on it to inform us about the new kinds of hazard and danger as they emerge – but on the other hand also keeps an eye on the fact that we will not be able to gain any completely certain knowledge about all the new risks. As Beck puts it: 'Non-knowledge rules in the world risk society. Hence, living in the milieu of manufactured non-knowing means seeking unknown answers to questions that nobody can clearly formulate' (Beck, 2009a: 115).

Consequently, of course, this makes the lives of politicians and authorities much harder as they try to make the right decisions about the risks we are confronted with. And the problem, says Beck, is only made worse by the relationship between risk size and knowledge; the larger the risk, the bigger our non-knowledge – and, all the while, the demand for swift decision and action grows more and more acute in proportion to the size of the risk in question. This is also the case for climate change; the question of how much CO_2 we can reasonably allow ourselves to emit in the years to come – if we wish to avoid drastic climate changes and environmental problems – is not at all possible to answer in *absolute* terms or even considered in the light of any kind of *absolute* knowledge. Even in a field like this, in which there is by now a consensus about the causes of the problem, we still often – faced with a wide array of specific questions with no immediate answer in sight – end up admitting that we just do not *know* for certain how to answer them. We may have firm ideas and we may have found strong indications that this or that may be the case, but we cannot be *certain*. Nor do we know with any kind of certainty exactly how much Earth's temperature levels can even in fact rise before the truly catastrophic, irreversible climate changes occur. Certain suggestions are being made, but so are others. In spite of all this uncertainty, however, governments, parliaments and other authorities are required to make daily decisions about these affairs. We still expect of our authorities and governments that they provide us with certain, unwavering answers to the challenges of society. Beck describes this new mode, this new situation of decision, thus:

> Since governments and authorities must continually reaffirm and reestablish their control over uncontrollable risks, people are exposed to a barrage of shifting forms of more or less (acknowledged) non-knowledge of scientific standards, biochemical categories and welfare state compensation claims.
>
> (Beck, 2009a:117)

All this means that it becomes increasingly difficult to decide whether any given response to any given risk is an expression of genuine concern, of unproductive, paralysing fear or of straight-faced blatant hysteria.

Uncertain non-knowledge

Should we find that we desire an example or case-study of exactly how difficult making the right choices and reaching the right decisions can be, in the world risk society, we need only look at the history of CFC gases. As we have seen in Chapter 2 above, it was not until the 1970s that the world began to become aware of the negative side effects of CFCs. It took, in other words, more than 40 years from when people began using CFC gases as refrigerants in refrigerators and as propellants in aerosol spray cans, before it was discovered – and scientifically proven – that CFC gasses were harmful to the ozone layer. For more than 40 years, in other words, people were unable to contain or limit this new, man-made risk – simply because nobody knew it existed. Using CFCs as an example, Beck writes:

> The boundary between knowledge and the lack of knowledge is becoming blurred. This is becoming paradigmatic because, for more than forty years, science did not even know what it did not know. Thus the issue is not the traditional problem of what is not yet known but unconscious or unacknowledged non-knowledge; and it is the inability-to-know in this form that must be regarded as the 'cause' of the threat to the human race. It is a case of unintended inability-to-know, at any rate at the moment of decision.
>
> (Beck, 2009a: 118)

Our awareness of this situation, of these terms for decision-making – that we may not know, at the time of our decision-making, what we do not know – has led to an increased adherence to the so-called precautionary principle. Wikipedia defines the precautionary principle thus:

> The precautionary principle or precautionary approach states that if an action or policy has a suspected risk of causing harm to the public or to the environment, in the absence of scientific consensus that the action or policy is harmful, the burden of proof that it is not harmful falls on those taking the action.
>
> (Wikipedia, 2011)

This principle has, for example, become a central principle in European Union law.

The precautionary principle ends up exercising direct influence on decisions about whether or not to allow the use of genetically modified organisms in nature, to grant the building permissions necessary for the construction of a new nuclear power plant, or to release a new medical product to the general public. However, it may also be applied in attempts at combating terrorism or the global financial crisis. Beck warns us, however, that there may be certain undesirable consequences to our leaning too much on the precautionary principle when we make our decisions. When one takes a certain amount of precaution in one's decision, one does so exactly because one is not entirely aware of the risks (hazards) that may be entailed by a given decision, but when one does not know anything one is prone to end up basing decisions on estimates, intuitions, guesswork, gut feelings and prejudice. This may mean that one ends up neglecting or rejecting new, useful and wholly reasonable technology or inadvertently ends up doing harm to particular demographic groups or individuals by placing them under unfair and unwarranted supervision and suspicion. Additionally, one's effort towards preventing a danger may end up triggering an even greater danger than the one one sought to prevent in the first place. This is the case, says Beck, with the war in Iraq:

> The preventive measures against catastrophic risks themselves trigger catastrophic risks, which may in the end be even greater than the catastrophes to be prevented. The Iraq War is a textbook example of this. This was presented, among other things, as a war against terrorism but has had the effect of transforming Iraq into a playground for terrorists.
>
> (Beck, 2009a: 119)

Although Beck's interpretation of the war in Iraq is definitely open to discussion, there is little doubt that the new legislative measures put into place everywhere throughout western countries, in an attempt to do away with terrorism, have had direct and negative consequences for a large number of people – consequences which may not be entirely proportionate to the actual reduction of the terrorist threat one sought to remove (increased surveillance, sealed-off piers and docks, wire-tapping, unwarranted and unexplained detention of individuals, deportation without court appearance etc.).

When these states of affairs are taken into consideration, it should be remembered that a terrorist organization such as al-Qaeda is intentionally operating in a manner that takes advantage of our non-knowledge. As Beck points out in *World at Risk*, al-Qaeda's terrorism is founded on organized non-knowledge (Beck, 2009a: 118). The organization is a flexible one, consisting of small, independent cells that possess no information about the activities or whereabouts of any other cell. This means that only a very small number of people know where the next attack will happen and that al-Qaeda, as a consequence, is a difficult organization to do away with entirely.

Subpolitics

Functional differentiation is, as discussed in Chapter 3, one of the characteristic trademarks of modern societies, according to Ulrich Beck. Much like system theoreticians such as Talcott Parsons and Niklas Luhmann, Beck sees the development of (first) modernity as a transition towards more and more complex societies consisting of undifferentiated subsystems in charge of highly specific functions. Although Beck's understanding of the development of modern societies is, in this regard, an extension of the views of Parsons and Luhmann and their system theories, it should be noted that this is only the case for the development of *first* modernity. With regard to second modernity, however, it is exactly Beck's point that a *de-differentiation* takes place which is immediately followed by a *re-differentiation* with regard to the differentiated subsystems of first modernity (see, for example, Beck, Bonß and Lau, 2001, 2003)

The most significant functional differentiation in first modern societies, according to Beck, is the one which exists between the techno-economic sphere and the political sphere. In first modernity, it is the task of the techno-economic sphere, on the one hand, to bring about a general increase in wealth through industrial production and the active use of science, whereas the political sphere on the other hand is tasked with taking care of issuing the guidelines of society's development, the distribution of wealth and the handling of the side effects of industrial production. The distribution of power and decision, too, is a fixed matter with regard to these two spheres: it is *politics* which is at the end of the table, calling the shots.

In second modernity, however, this model of distribution for work and responsibility comes under significant pressure, since it is founded on the precondition that the development of productive powers and the scientific development in the techno-economic sphere do not surpass the regulatory abilities, capacities and powers of the political sphere (Beck, 1992: 183–185).

This precondition crumbles under the pressure of globalization and the production of the new risks and man-made hazards. One very visible consequence is the deconstruction of the nation-state containers which used to provide the framework for the distribution of risk and wealth in first modernity (see Chapter 5 above). The advantages as well as the disadvantages of industrial production, however, can no longer be contained and held within the boundaries and borders of the nation-state: pollution and all the other new risks and man-made hazards from industrial production end up crossing all political and military borders as if they were not there at all. So does the economy. The techno-economic sphere, in other words, has burst from its nation-state wrapping paper. On the other hand, however, the political sphere is still to a great extent stuck helplessly in the national. This means that the political system is experiencing more and more difficulty in its attempts at balancing and handling the advantages and disadvantages of industrial production. With the rise of new inequality, there is – as we covered in the previous chapter – no longer any kind of specific guarantee that the population that ends up dealing with the costs and consequences of a given line of industrial production is the *same* population as ends up reaping its benefits.

At the same time, a common notion is spreading, a realization that societal change will come not from the political sphere but from the techno-economic one – that the political sphere's position at society's rudder is, basically, an illusion. Beck puts it thus:

> In contemporary discussions, the 'alternative society' is no longer expected to come from parliamentary debates on new laws, but rather from the application of microelectronics, genetic technology and information media.
>
> (Beck, 1992: 223)

These new phenomena convene to change the positions of power between the spheres, turning the relationship between the two on its proverbial head; in second modernity, the political sphere is forced to follow the rules of the techno-economic sphere to an ever-increasing degree.

The new premise for politics

The political sphere has also lost its right to initiative in second modernity. Time and time again it finds itself struggling to keep up the pace of the techno-economic sphere, unable to produce legislature and regulations to govern new conditions and productions until long after they have been put into place. Ironically, this is caused by the utter success of the political sphere in instating a *program of freedom*, which can be traced back to the ideals of the age of enlightenment. The development that began with the introduction of the catalogues of human rights in the constitutions of the emerging liberal state of the eighteenth and nineteenth centuries, and culminated in the modern welfare states of the twentieth century – a development which has bestowed upon the agents in the techno-economic spheres the freedom to conduct research, trade how they want and invest in what they want – has ended up making it extremely difficult for the political sphere to exercise any kind of control over the direction and development of society.

However, *globalization*, too, is causing problems for the political sphere and its options for regulation and control. Because of the expanded world economy, and with a starting point in the sanctity of private property, corporations may play off nation-states against each other in order to reap the benefits. If a corporation feels itself taxed too excessively or hampered by too many rules and regulations for its tastes, it can easily move its lines of production to another country. In this way, corporations are in a position to play off countries or individual locations against one another, in a process of 'global horse-trading' to find the cheapest fiscal conditions and the most favourable infrastructure. They can also 'punish' particular countries if they seem too 'expensive' or 'investment-unfriendly'.

(Beck, 2000b: 4)

All things considered, nation-state politics is by now severely hampered in its ability to exercise any kind of real control over the techno-economic sphere – as a direct side effect of its previous successfulness. Not only has nation-state-based politics been forced to concede power to a more and more globalized economical system, its politicians are also time and time again put into plain embarrassing positions by technology and its advances. Take for example the medical sciences, which – in a veritable stampede of innovation – are progressing wildly and continuously presenting the world with new methods of treatment and new medical products, leaving the politicians to deal with the difficult ethical questions and putting real, growing pressure on public budgets.

Politicians often end up as glorified approval machinery, wielding a rubber stamp with the word *approved* and stamping everything that comes their way, as a consequence of the development in the techno-economic sphere. The actual political decisions are made in that sphere, long before they even come to reach the desks of the politicians. After all, how can one possibly oppose the saving of lives or the treatment of hitherto untreatable serious illnesses? One cannot. Although the political system loses influence to the techno-economic sphere, it is still needed to legitimize its actions: 'The political institutions become the administrators of a development they neither have planned for nor are able to structure, but must nevertheless somehow justify' (Beck, 1992: 186–187).

As we can see, Beck's analysis of the subpolitical power of the techno-economic sphere in many ways seems to echo Marx's (and Engels's) point that the real foundation of a society is its system of production, and that changes to this foundation leads to changes in the political, legal and so on 'superstructure'. There are marked differences between Beck's thinking and that of Marx, however. For example, Marx and Engels consider the system of production to be the dominant sphere a priori whereas Beck argues that it only comes to be dominant in time. Although they agree on the necessity of gaining political control of the economy, their approaches to how one would go about doing so – revolutionary and reformist, respectively – are widely different.

The politicization of the techno-economic sphere

The transition from first to second modernity calls into question the non-political nature of the techno-economic sphere. Somewhat unorthodoxly, Beck defines politics as *the structuring and changing of living conditions* (Beck, 1992: 190, footnote 2) and he takes the techno-economic sphere to be a political one, because of its direct influence on our living conditions.[1] It is not, however, political in the same sense of the word as the political sphere is, as the techno-economic sphere does not have to legitimize itself in relation to the general public through common democratic procedures. In order to separate it from the formal, political system on the one hand and sheer non-politics on the other hand, Beck opts for calling it *subpolitical.*

Beck believes that there will be rising pressure on the techno-economic sphere to legitimize itself in the eyes of the general public:

> But that means that operational activity comes under pressure for legitimation to a degree previously unknown. It acquires a new political and moral dimension, which had seemed alien to economic action. This moralization of industrial production, which reflects the dependence of operations on the political culture in which they produce, ought to become one of the most interesting developments of the coming years.
>
> (Beck, 1992: 222).

When the technological innovation or economic dispositions of corporations leads to a demand for change in laws and legislature on the one hand, and while an increasing number of corporations are reconfigured and turn into socially responsible corporations working actively towards better conditions for the workers and environment on the other, it leads to a softening of the boundaries between the political and the techno-economic sphere. There is, in other words, a *de-* and *re-*differentiation taking place. The habitual division of work between the two spheres, with which we have been acquainted, is transformed – although it is not yet at all clear how it will end up or what it will come to look like in the future. One thing is certain, however: in the future, it will be much harder to figure out where and how the actual, political decisions are in fact made. In other words, the clarity that characterized the functional differentiation of first modernity disappears as second modernity comes into being.

The new culture of politics

The transition from first to second modernity, then, has also drawn a new kind of *obscurity* of the political realm in its wake. Beck points out that this new kind of obscurity conceals

> a profound systemic transformation of the political in two respects. The first of these is the loss of power experienced by the centralized political system in the course of the enforcement and utilization of civil rights in the forms of a new political culture; the second lies in the changes of social structure connected with the transition from non-politics to sub-politics, a development that seems to lose its conditions of application in the hitherto prevailing 'harmonizing formula' – technical progress equals social progress. Both perspectives add up to an 'unbinding of politics'.
>
> (Beck, 1992: 190)

According to Beck, we are now experiencing a politicization of the hitherto non-political. With the realization that 'the sources of wealth are "polluted" by growing "hazardous side effects"' (Beck, 1992: 20) and 'what *was* until now *considered unpolitical becomes political – the elimination of the causes in the industrialization process itself* (Beck, 1992: 24) the political dynamics of second modernity springs largely from the new risks: 'risks become the motor of the self-politicization of modernity in industrial society; furthermore, in the risk society, the concept, place and media of politics change' (Beck, 1992: 183). In this way, the boundaries of the political come to be opened up and expanded. This goes for the subpolitical nature of the techno-economic sphere, but also for the new, extra-parliamentary centres which Beck imagines will come about. Without wholly defining what it might entail, he points out that the media public, the judicial system, the private realm, citizen initiatives and new, social movements will all come to be elements in a *new political culture* (Beck, 1992: 195).

The success of the political sphere in ensuring the rights of the individual in first modernity, then, thus ends up not only hampering the political sphere's ability to intervene in the matters and doings of the techno-economic sphere; it ends up *spurring on* extra-parliamentary *counter*-activities. The theory, then, is that the subpolitics of the techno-economic sphere will be met – either entirely or in part – by the new (counter-)subpolitics of the political culture and that this will lead to extra-parliamentary conflict and power struggles over society's future development. The obvious facts of first modernity are no longer given in advance. The unquestionable authority of scientific rationality, for example, is now pulled into doubt and technological and scientific 'progress' is more and more turned into matters of debate and conflict, within the framework of the established political system. An example of one such conflict is the conflict that has surrounded genetically modified foods and the debate between consumer interest groups and production groups and companies; another is the civil protests in Japan and other countries that occurred in response to the accident at the Fukushima nuclear power plant in 2011. Somewhat histrionically, then, Ulrich Beck proclaims this to be the coming of a new era in the history of democracy:

> Basic rights with a universalist validity claim, as established in Western societies over the past two centuries or more by fits and starts, but in a generally directed process (so far), thus form the hinges of political development. On the one hand, they have been fought for in parliaments; on the other hand, centers of sub-politics can develop and differentiate themselves parallel to the parliaments, and through these a new page in the history of democracy can be opened.
>
> (Beck, 1992: 195–196)

Beck presented his first thoughts and theories on the issue of subpolitics in the 1980s, a decade that witnessed how intellectuals – as a response to the 1970s and a tendency to overpoliticize society – were otherwise turning away from the issue of the political. Beck's political thought is a clear reaction against this tendency. It is not because Beck feels any particular desire or need to revert to the overzealous focus of the political that prevailed in the 1970s that he seeks to distance himself from the postmodernists of the 1980s – whose ideas about *the death of politics* he does not hold in any particularly high esteem. Although the authority and agentive power of the traditional political system are hampered, and although politics – in the conventional sense of the word, that is as something which takes place in national, political congregations and takes as its main issue the defence and legitimization of power and interest (Beck, 1992) – ends up losing actuality, this does not ultimately mean that the political *as such* is experiencing any kind of crisis. Rather, says Beck, the political is in the midst of re-inventing itself, and its goal should be to avoid getting caught in antiquated notions of itself which would only lead it – and us – to look for the political in all the wrong places. As Beck writes:

> the laments on the loss of the political related to the normatively valid expectation that the decisions which change society should be concentrated in the institutions of the political system, even though they are no longer concentrated there.
>
> (Beck, 1992: 188)

Politics, according to Beck, will no longer be contained or captured in the traditional coordinates of the political: left versus right, socialists versus conservatives, participation versus non-participation (Beck, 1992). What is needed, then, is a new reflection on the political, which can help us in uncovering the shift of power that has happened between the formal political sphere and the subpolitical sphere.

Passive subpolitics: subpolitics as a side effect

Beck's use of the term *subpolitics* is meant to cover two very different phenomena (Figure 6.1). First, it refers to the development in the techno-economic sphere, which – unconsciously and without our direct intentions – changes our shared living conditions. Second, it covers extra-parliamentary actions and events which are deliberate attempts at influencing the development and direction of society. In order to make a distinction between the two types of subpolitics, we might call the former *passive subpolitics* or *subpolitics as a side effect* and the latter *active subpolitics*, in order to accentuate its deliberate and intentional nature (Holzer and Sørensen, 2002, 2003).

Beck uses the medical sciences as an illustrative example of how passive subpolitics may be arranged (Beck, 1992: 204–212). It is easy to locate, in the field of medicine, examples of how scientific breakthroughs seep from their original contexts and come to influence society as a whole. In this way, medical science is constantly pushing the boundaries of what can and cannot be done, both technically and scientifically, but also with regard to ethics and politics. Cloning and gene therapy, for example, are two highly relevant examples. The medical sciences are working on developing these new kinds of technology for clinical and clearly defined purposes, but it seems plausible to suspect that we

Non-politics	⇔	Subpolitics	⇔	Politics

	⤎		⤏	
Passive subpolitics				Active subpolitics
⇩				⇩
(Sub)politics as side effects				Intended subpolitics
⇩				⇩
Medical sciences, transnational corporations etc.				NGOs, political consumers, ethical investors etc.

Figure 6.1 Sub-politics between politics and non-politics.

will, eventually, see unintended side effects of this new research as well, which will end up influencing society in general, rather than just the specific groups of patients in need of a cure. This, at least, has often been the case with earlier breakthroughs in medicine. As a direct consequence of the introduction of respirators in hospitals, and the new developments in organ transplant technology, the political system came under high pressure to develop and introduce new and updated criteria for death, resulting in most of the world having to supplement its old definition of death – the heart's having ceased to beat – with a new criterion of cerebral death.

The economical decisions of large corporations, too, have an active influence on our shared living conditions and can, in this sense, be interpreted as a kind of subpolitics as a side effect. When a corporation, in response to the perceived high expenses related to operating in a specific country, chooses to uproot its production to another country, it effectively weakens the abandoned country's tax foundation while subjecting it to new and heightened expenses, such as having to pay unemployment benefits to the workers made redundant by the outsourcing. Thus, if too many corporations decide to move their productions abroad, it could easily end up destroying the economy of a country. In many countries, governments and politicians have sought to retain (and attract) corporations by lowering corporation taxes. Seen from a subpolitical perspective, this means that taxation politics is effectively dictated no longer by elected politicians but by corporate chief executives and their economically grounded decisions about whether or not to move their production and investment elsewhere. The political sphere, in other words, is still making the formal, official decisions on how tax politics are to be conducted, but the decision is dictated by the development taking place in the techno-economic sphere.

If we wish to discuss subpolitics as a side effect, however, it is important that we remind ourselves that no doctor, corporate boss or other passive subpolitician in the techno-economic sphere intends – or, at least, has as his or her primary interest – to partake in the conduct of politics. Nonetheless, their scientific or economical decisions end up having political consequences. However, as they work on their own objectives – be it to secure the profitability of their corporation or to develop a new treatment or medication – our shared living conditions are changed, without it being anybody's real intention. The political, in this sense of this word, must be understood as an *unintended side effect* of decisions which are primarily of an economic or scientific nature.

Active subpolitics

In addition to the kind of unintended politics outlined above, Beck's notion of subpolitics also refers to another, more immediate, way of conducting subpolitics: *active* subpolitics. It is this kind of politics which is at the heart of the activities of the kind of new political culture we have discussed above. Rather than utilizing and depending on the traditional channels for political participation, such as parliamentary elections or membership of specific political parties, in its efforts to influence social development and progress, the new political culture seeks to assert itself and achieve its means through extra-parliamentary activity. This, according to Beck, happens as a response to the more traditional channels for political participation, which have come to be viewed as antiquated and inefficient (Beck, 1997a).

Beck often refers to the Brent Spar case of 1995 as an illustrative example of how this new political culture – in the shape of an environmental organization and politically inclined consumers – succeeded in conducting active subpolitics (see, for example, Beck, 1997b, 2001, 2009a: 96–97). As some may remember, the multinational oil company Shell was, in early summer 1995, allowed by the British government to dump an obsolete oil storage and tanker-loading buoy in the Atlantic Ocean. Shell, along with the British government and several scientific experts in the field, concluded that dumping the buoy in the Atlantic Ocean, several hundred kilometres off the coast of Scotland, would be a both environmentally and economically sound method for getting rid of the unit. The environmental organization Greenpeace, however, strongly disagreed, opting to launch a campaign to stop the dumping. Politicians in several North Sea countries supported Greenpeace and spoke out against the British government and Shell. Greenpeace and others – including the then chancellor of Germany, Helmut Kohl – called for boycott of Shell and its products among European consumers. The ensuing boycott was most widely effective in Germany but also, to a lesser degree, in other countries, such as Denmark (Sørensen, 2001: 127).

The cumulative pressure on Shell's economical and PR interests ultimately resulted in Shell calling off its plans for disposing of the oil storage buoy at sea. According to Beck it was exactly the consumer boycott mounted against Shell and its interests that came to be the decisive factor in the corporation's decision not to dump Brent Spar in the Atlantic after all:

What such jibes overlooked was that the oil multinational was brought to its knees not by Greenpeace but by a mass public boycott, put together through world-wide televised indictments. Greenpeace is not itself shaking the political system, but it is making visible a vacuum of power and legitimacy.

(Beck, 2001: 40)

Beck, in other words, sees the Brent Spar scenario as an example of how the new political culture – operating *around* the established, political system – has begun to demand of the techno-economic sphere that should it be able to legitimize its actions and decisions. He goes on to say:

Suddenly political elements were discovered and deployed in everyday activity – in the filling of petrol tanks, for example. Car drivers banded together against the oil industry (you only need to try it once to 'get a taste for it'). And in the end the state joined in with the illegitimate action and its organizers, thereby using its power to legitimize a deliberate, extra-parliamentary violation of the rules, while for their parts the protagonists of direct politics sought to escape – through a kind of 'self-administered ecological justice' – the narrow framework of indirect, legally sanctioned agencies and rules. The anti-Shell alliance eventually led to a scene-switch between the politics of the first and the second modernity. National governments sat on the benches and watched, while unauthorized actors of the second modernity directed the course of the action.

(Beck, 2001: 40–41)

In this way, the 'new political culture' is based, in part, on the recognition of the political in everyday life. Beck points out that today we find ourselves in a position where the welfare state-regulated, late-capitalist *a*political citizen has come to be political (Beck, 1997a: 127). The reason for this is that the close interconnections between the microcosm of private life and the macrocosm of global scale problems and challenges are becoming more and more apparent. This opens the door for a new kind of politics which 'makes its entrance through the private realm, that is, through the backdoor' (Beck, 1997a: 152). Beck's term for this phenomenon is *subpolitics*, whereas Anthony Giddens and others have sought to conceptualize the same tendency by referring to the notion of *life politics* (Giddens, 1991, 1994b).

(Active) subpolitics then, to Beck, is a politics from below, a 'shaping of society from below' (Beck, 1994a: 23; 1998a: 37). Subpolitics, to him, is an indication that politics in second modernity comes to lose its institutional bindings and ties (Beck, 1997a: 100). In *World at Risk*, Beck puts it like this:

The concept of 'sub-politics' refers to the decoupling of politics from government; it underlines that politics is also possible beyond the representative institutions of the nation-state . . . the concept of 'sub-politics' directs attention to indicators of a global self-organization of non-state politics that has the potential to mobilize all areas of society.

(Beck, 2009a: 95)

Subpolitics, then, is an indication that there has emerged a new political praxis based on everyday life and, along with it, a new kind of non-institutional politics. In subpolitics, Beck sees a potentially transnational species of politics, which may develop into a strong political control system. He envisages the rise of 'risk communities' or 'imagined cosmopolitan communities . . . which come into existence in the awareness that dangers or risks can no longer be socially delimited in space or time' (Beck and Grande, 2010: 418). The political potential in such 'communities' can then come to be realized either through new transnational, or cosmopolitan, cooperative measures as we have seen in the previous chapter, or through new kinds of active subpolitics.

Subpolitics, to Beck, also contain a large amount of democratic potential, to the extent that he has argued that the official political system ought to help further this potential through '*legal protection of certain possibilities for sub-politics to exert influence*' (Beck, 1992: 234). Traditional, parliamentary politics, roughly put, ought to support and nurture subpolitics and help establish a foundation for a 'policy of politics' which may help put politics back in charge (Beck, 1997a: 99–100).

Active subpolitics, however, is not a wholly positive phenomenon to Beck. It is not, for example, entirely unproblematic to alter 'the definition of the common good' (Beck, 1998a: 37) while avoiding the influence of the established political system. Rather, it is the narrow self-interests of individuals and interest organizations which come to thrive under these new subpolitical conditions in which they are freed from the doings and functions of the traditional, established political system, which, all things considered, tend to enforce a certain degree of consideration for the common good. In addition to this, subpolitics – just like any other politics – does not simply belong to the 'good guys'. Like other forms of politics, it may manifest itself as the struggle of social movements and individual citizens against global warming, human rights violations or the effects of the global financial crisis, but it may also come to serve the agenda of the violent, the fundamentalist or political fringe groups and their attempts to influence society as a whole. Subpolitics, in other words, is also vulnerable and accessible to anti-modern and anti-democratic forces. We see an example of this in global terrorism, which, to Beck, is also a clear case of (active, intentional) subpolitics (Beck, 2009a: 104–108):

terrorist subpolitics constitute the most illegitimate and effective means conceivable to pose a key problem in the global public arena and to direct it against economic globalization.

(Beck, 2009a: 107).

The break with self-incurred immaturity

Like his notion of methodological nationalism, Beck's notion of (passive) subpolitics is a concept that is meant to help open our eyes to the true condition of our current states of affairs. The techno-economic sphere used to have a great ability to influence the direction and pace of social development in first modernity, but, with the rise and production of the new risks and man-made hazards of second modernity, this kind of influence from a globally active, non-democratic techno-economic sphere is proving to be truly problematic. On the surface, things may still be looking fine and democratically dandy, but, leaning in to take a closer look, one finds that in many ways democracy has come to be replaced by dictates from the techno-economic sphere. Democracy, in other words, is slowly being eroded.

Although in many ways, as mentioned, Beck's analyses of the influence of the techno-economic sphere on the development of society resemble those of Marx and Engels, Beck's criticism is founded not here, but rather in Kant's theory of enlightenment. Kant defines enlightenment as 'man's emergence from his self-incurred immaturity'.[2] The way second modernity has allowed the techno-economic sphere to endanger humanity and dictate the terms for the development of society is, to Beck, an archetypal example of how certain non-elected agents – acting on purely economical, scientific or technological agendas – have been granted the power to decide the path of development for society as a whole.

However, with active subpolitics, Beck imagines that there will arise the opportunity to reclaim some of our lost autonomy. It requires, however, that we have the courage and decisiveness to step into a *new age of enlightenment* wherein 'our understanding, our eyes and institutions are opened to the self-incurred immaturity of first modernity and its self-endangerment' (Beck, 1998b: 171).

Because of this, Beck has high hopes for the new political culture. It is meant to reclaim what has been lost. It is meant to democratize the non-democratic techno-economic sphere by forcing it to *legitimize* itself in the eyes of the general public. An important aspect of such a development, says Beck, is that it will allow for the *possibility* that risk society may eventually transform into a *wholly* modern society, whereas industrial society, according to Beck, was merely a *half*-modern one (Beck, 1986)[3] since the principles of its representative democracy influenced only the political sphere and not the techno-economic sphere:

> In this sense the innovation process that is enforced by modernity against the predominance of tradition is split in two democratically through the project of industrial society. Only a part of the decision-making competencies that structure society are gathered together in the political system and subjected to the principles of parliamentary democracy. Another part is removed from the rules of public inspection and justification and delegated to the freedom of investment of enterprises and the freedom of research of science.
>
> (Beck, 1992: 184)

In active subpolitics, Beck sees an incipient break with this kind of democratic bisection. Active subpolitics' criticisms of science, technology and progress are not primarily – no matter what the postmodernists might claim – counter-modern phenomena; rather, says Beck, they are an expression of a continuous and adamant *further development* of modernity beyond the confines of industrial society (Beck, 1986).[4]

From the mid-1980s, when he began work on *Risk Society*, up to writing *Was ist Globalisierung* (Beck, 1998b), Beck held, as we have tried to describe here, quite high hopes for the active subpolitics of the new political culture, which he expected would save us from the self-incurred immaturity we had got ourselves caught in. However, from 1998 on, active subpolitics came to take a less and less predominant place in his work, coming steadily to be replaced by transnational, political forums such as the EU, the World Trade Organization and the UN Human Rights Council,[5] as we have seen in Chapter 5. However, as *World at Risk* (Beck, 2009a) proves, Beck has not completely forgotten about subpolitics. *World at Risk* once again points out the opportunities and benefits of active subpolitics (Beck, 2009a: 81–108).

Core terms

Functional differentiation: Traditionally seen as a way to describe differentiated subsystems such as the justice system, the political system, the economical system and the scientific system. It is assumed that these systems have been conceived as systems each tasked with its specific tasks and responsibilities. Beck is primarily interested in two systems, or spheres, as he often calls them: the political sphere and the techno-economic sphere.

Methodological cosmopolitanism: An approach in the social sciences wherein one – even when studying the relations and affairs of specific countries – is always working from the assumption that the world is connected and that societies cannot be separated by national means.

Methodological nationalism: When social scientists conduct research they are predisposed – and unreflectively so – to assume that a specific, single society can be defined by its national boundaries and that thus it can make sense to study individual societies while assuming them to be unconnected to others. This goes for matters of national economy, marriage, class and social inequality in second modernity.

Non-knowledge: With the production of knowledge comes the production of non-knowledge. The more we come to know, the less we will know. Because of this, Beck sees non-knowledge as a fundamental premise of living in the risk society.

Political sphere: One of the two main spheres of first modernity, tasked with providing the guidelines for societal development, distribution of wealth and political neutralization of the side effects of industrial production. It justifies its efforts and initiatives by way of democratic procedure.

Subpolitics: Subpolitics places itself squarely between politics and non-politics. It is a form of politics which avoids or circumvents the established political system: parties, parliaments and democratic elections. Subpolitics can be divided into two different kinds: active and passive subpolitics. Active subpolitics is a kind of subpolitics which is intended; passive subpolitics is side effects that occur as unintended consequences of activities in the techno-economic sphere.

Techno-economic sphere: The other of the two main spheres of first modernity, tasked with the general advancement of wealth through industrial production and through the utilization of science and technology. Originally justified by equating techno-economic progress with societal progress.

Varieties of second modernity: The notion that there exist not one but several variants of second modern society. The notion is a break with the Eurocentric attitudes of the social sciences, including Beck's own previous work.

Zombie category: Beck's term for categories that, although they are no longer connected to any reality, still remain alive in our thought systems. Social science, for example, according to Beck, is at risk of becoming a zombie science, if it bases itself on the container theory.

Further reading

Beck, U. (1992) *Risk Society: Towards a New Modernity.* London: Sage Publications.

Beck, U. (1997b) *The Reinvention of Politics: Rethinking Modernity in the Global Social Order.* Cambridge: Polity Press.

Beck, U. (2007b) 'Beyond Class and Nation: Reframing Social Inequalities in a Globalizing World', *British Journal of Sociology*, vol. 58, no. 4, pp. 679–705.

Beck, U. (2009a) *World at Risk.* Cambridge: Polity Press.

Beck, U. and Grande, E. (2010) 'Varieties of Second Modernity: The Cosmopolitan Turn in Social and Political Theory and Research', *British Journal of Sociology*, vol. 61, no. 3, pp. 409–443.

7 The third industrial revolution
The end of full-employment society

In June 2010 Hewlett Packard (HP), one of the world's largest manufacturers of information technology (IT) equipment and a leading provider of software solutions and IT services, announced that it had plans for a series of new investments in automation technology for its enterprise service division, which would make it possible to standardize and consolidate 100 HP data centres worldwide. According to HP this would, over the course of a few years, result in an estimated 9,000 jobs being eliminated; this, it was emphasized, would mark HP's transition away from the standard practice of outsourcing back-office jobs to other countries, towards a new way of leveraging technology to perform the back-office tasks much more efficiently (Ford, 2010).

In early 2009, another international corporation made headlines worldwide as JCB – a company specializing in loading, excavation, digging and construction equipment – signed an agreement with its workers to reduce the number of daily working hours, effectively cutting the number of working days in a week from five to four, for an indefinite period of time. This reduction in working hours was a direct consequence of the recession which had followed in the wake of the financial crisis, and it effectively forced workers to choose either to submit themselves to massive lay-offs, or to work according to new and flexible schedules that would entail significant wage reductions (*The Independent*, 2009).

To Ulrich Beck, there is nothing extraordinary about either of these scenarios. They are simply, from his point of view, the kind of ramifications one can expect to follow naturally in the wake of the *third industrial revolution*. As Chapter 3 has shown us, Beck takes the third industrial revolution to be a tangible phenomenon which – along with four other processes of change – is in the midst of causing our current transition from first to second modernity. One of the immediate consequences of this transition is that first modern, industrial *work societies* are undergoing changes, being transformed into post-work societies or *post-full-employment societies* of second modernity; these societies are characterized by new, flexible and uncertain labour markets (Beck, Bonß and Lau, 2003). It is characteristic of second modernity that we, by now, live in a society in which there is a *reduced amount of available employment* and, simultaneously, one that is experiencing a transformation of whatever paid work remains available and possible to obtain (Beck, 2000a: 18). This kind of break in the labour market

– which occurs to Beck as a fundamental kind of change, one that has a direct effect on the former system of employment – is already addressed quite early on in Beck's work, in *Risk Society* (Beck, 1992). It was the transition in the labour market itself, however, that went on to become the main topic of the Beck's later *The Brave New World of Work* (Beck, 2000a). The reflections on the constitution and properties of (paid) work, however, have been theoretical constants in Beck's work from quite early on, dating as far back as the early 1970s, although certain periods of his academic work have been more preoccupied with the issues than others.

Thus Beck's periods of preoccupation with the question of paid work can be divided into three main parts or 'eras', with the first period occurring in the mid to late 1970s, the second in the mid 1980s and the third around the turn of the millennium. The perspective of Beck's later studies on work sociology has, as we shall see, changed quite a bit from the perspective he put forth in his early 1970s studies of work and employment.

The third industrial revolution

As discussed in Chapter 2, Beck believes that we are currently experiencing five processes of change that are in the midst of leading us through a transition from first modernity into second modernity. One of these processes is the so-called *third industrial revolution*, which is largely responsible for both the sheer *reduction* of employment available and the *transformation* of the shape and content of the remaining paid work that is taking place today (Beck, Bonß and Lau, 2003: 6–7). The term *third industrial revolution* is a relatively new part of Beck's theoretical glossary, occurring for the first time only in the programme article of 2001 (Beck, Bonß and Lau, 2003). Thus, although Beck already examined the causes of the 'systemic transformation of wage labor' (Beck, 1992: 141) in *Risk Society*, he did not fully summarize his position and understanding of the processes involved until 2001, which was when he started referring to the phenomenon as the third industrial revolution.

Other theoreticians have used the concept of a third industrial revolution as a means for describing the kind of microelectronic modernization of production machinery which has taken place over the course of recent years.[1] Whereas the first industrial revolution owed almost all of its momentum to the budding basic industrialization (e.g. the invention and success of the steam engine) and the second industrial revolution revolved largely around the development of electric and internal combustion engines by the turn of the twentieth century, the *third* industrial revolution has turned out to be related to the use of novel microelectronics in production. When Beck speaks of the third industrial revolution, he, too, is speaking of this development. In *Risk Society*, he speaks of 'microelectronics' (Beck, 1992: 140–150), whereas in newer publications he usually uses such terms as 'the informational-technological revolution of rationalization', 'digitalization' (Beck, 2000a: 74) and 'digital capitalism' (Beck, 2003a: 171; 2005: 1). Thus, to Beck, it is the use of new microelectronically based systems of production – the new and fully automatic, intelligent industrial robots and production machinery – *along* with the use of microelectronically based technologies of information and communication, which are the hallmarks of the third industrial revolution. Thus the third industrial revolution, according to Beck, is a revolution of rationalization, of information technology and communication technology, an IT revolution and a microelectronically based revolution of precision engineering, all at once. The third industrial revolution, in other words, occurs in the wake of highly advanced, technological, computer-based systems of production. Demand for manual labour is becoming increasingly scarce, as a direct consequence of these revolutions, which are, to Beck, unintended side effects of the kind of rationalization drive which is inherent to global capitalism.

The end of full-employment society

The third industrial revolution undermines one of the basic premises of first modernity, namely the view that first modern societies

> are *work societies* or more precisely, *gainful employment societies*; in their fully developed form, they are what was once called in Europe 'full employment societies' – that is, societies in which unemployment is so low that it can justifiably be considered frictional.
>
> (Beck, Bonß and Lau, 2003: 4)

The third industrial revolution, then, abolishes the *normal work model* of first modernity, the origins of which, according to Beck, can be traced all the way back to the triumphs and advances of the Reformation, political economy and the civic revolutions of the eighteenth and nineteenth centuries, finally to come to full fruition after the Second World War (Beck, 2000a: 11, 62), when societies came to be wholly and consistently based on gainful employment, resulting in paid work, in itself, becoming the absolute core value of society and its prime mechanism of integration (Beck, 2000a: 11). This kind of work became the centre of society, in the sense that gainful employment and admittance into the labour market came to serve as access passes to social identity and status, along with material and existential security. There were rights that were tightly connected with paid work, which one could simply not obtain otherwise. However, when one makes work into a prerequisite for social and material security, one also makes it a prerequisite for a viable democracy, as it is exactly social and material security which is required to ensure the basic utility of legally established civil rights and political freedoms. Beck views the recent significance and importance of work, and the sheer matter of course wherewith this importance is accepted by the individual, as the result of a historical process which has led to a radical reevaluation of the notion of work. As means of clarifying shift of values that has happened, Beck directs our attention to Greek antiquity (Beck, 2003a: 153; 2000a: 165). During antiquity, work was the one kind of activity which would actively cause an individual to be disengaged from his polis, and it was an activity that was perceived to be in sharp contrast to artistic or political activity. Working individuals were *un-free* and, to a large extent, stripped of basic human qualities. A working man, in other words, was not recognized as a citizen. However, this kind of irreconcilability between work and free, political life was turned on its head with the arrival of modernity, in which 'industrial society in its mature form had full employment as its precondition, from the welfare state in its broadest sense to the meaningfulness of parliamentary democracy' (Beck, 2003a: 156). Modern work societies, in other words, are based on 'the working citizen', who ensures the existence of both him- or herself and the economy of society, through paid work while using his or her spare time to contribute to, and actively take part in, the democratic system. Thus the first modern democracy was a *work democracy* (Beck, 2000a: 10–12), whereas the project of Beck – as we will elaborate later – is to *detach* the concept of democracy from the concept of paid work. So when Beck is stressing the point that any given western society is founded on work (Beck, 2003a: 153), and when he is talking about a *society of normal work* that goes along with a *model of normal work*, what he is really referring to is a specific kind of work and a specific kind of society, namely lifelong *full-time paid work* in a society of *full employment* (Beck, 2000a). Lifelong, full-time paid work was, according to Beck, the main rule and key factor of first modernity; here, one saw the notion of a *career* as something one could create for oneself under the reins of one specific employer, based on a certain kind of education. Apart from a high degree of job security, the work of first modernity was *contractually founded* and *standardized* with regard to the *time and space* it took place in. Work, in other words, was something to be performed under the protection of an employment contract – which was often negotiated collectively, along with fellow workers – during a specific, daily time interval, at a specific location; for example in the assembly lines of the large factories (Beck, 2005: 37).

It is exactly this 'system of normal work' of first modernity – the system of lifelong, contractually ensured full-time employment, an unemployment rate of 2 per cent at most, of fixed location and time for work performed, social security through one's job position, and so forth – which is, according to Beck, now starting to disintegrate (Beck, 2005: 1–10; 2003a: 158).

Flexible, pluralized forms of underemployment

But what kind of new work reality, then, might be said to characterize second modernity? To Ulrich Beck, it is a kind of reality in which paid work and employment – in its traditional amount and form – is disappearing. It is a reality which is characterized by a scarcity of full-time employment *and* by radically new, uncertain kinds of work (Table 7.1). The third industrial revolution plays a key part in this new reduction and transformation of wage labour. The reason for the ever declining amount of full-time employment available, according to Beck, is to be found in recent decades' rationalization of jobs by way of new production and communication technology. In addition to this, another of Beck's key points is that microelectronic modernization of the labour market is currently changing – in

Table 7.1 Paid work in first and second modernity

First modernity	Second modernity
Full employment (maximum of 2% unemployment)	Reduced/declining paid work and wage labour (shortness of employment)
Full-time occupation	Flexible/pluralized kinds of *under*employment
Standardization of work	Flexibilization/individualization of work: pluralized work
Contractually standardized work	Contractually flexible work
Spatially bound work: work spatially standardized	Globalization/digitalization of work: spatially destandardized work (the deterritorialization of paid work)
Temporally bound work: work is temporally standardized (clear distinction between work hours and leisure time)	Globalization/digitalization of work: temporally destandardized work (no difference between off-hours and work hours)
Depoliticized work	Politicization of work
Unemployment as collective misfortune	Unemployment as individual, private misfortune
Work and career ensured by education	Work and career no longer ensured by education

deep and fundamental ways – whatever forms of employment that remain available, because of the *flexibilization* and *destandardization* which are taking place; all this has resulted in new kinds of uncertain wage labour (Beck, 1992, 2000a).

One explanation for the emergence of this new kind of work flexibilization, according to Beck, is simply that there is no longer enough work to go around, for all those who desire a full time job. Thus, more and more are instead forced to work jobs that are time-intensive, spatially decentralized and without proper contracts. The result is a new kind of employment/unemployment synthesis (Beck, 2005: 3) – which results in more and more flexible, pluralized kinds of *under*employment, in other words varying *degrees* of employment – making it difficult for the individual to maintain an acceptable standard of living (Figure 7.1). The number of people who find themselves in this kind of situation, says Beck, is steadily rising; they are the people working in different fixed-term, time-intensive

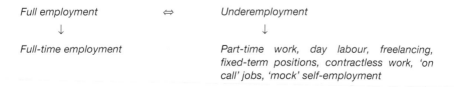

Figure 7.1 A new synthesis between full-time employment and unemployment: underemployment.

and poorly paid non-full-time jobs, without contracts, often labouring in black or grey areas which lie on the border to being informal work (Beck, 2003a: 155). The number of people who do this kind of flexible work – who are employed in jobs that are wholly flexible with regard to time, space and contractual obligations – is steadily rising, according to Beck.

Unless this development is somehow reversed, half of the European workforce will soon be employed in a way that offers no solid guidelines for when, where or how their work should be done (Beck, 2003a: 92). Beck bases this conclusion on empirical data and reports from various organizations and countries, such as reports from the International Labour Organization (ILO). One need only look as far as Spain to get an impression of exactly the kind of desperation that a flexible labour market can induce in a population. In 2011, for weeks on end, thousands of Spaniards, mainly the Spanish youth, occupied the central squares of most major Spanish cities, demonstrating and venting their frustration with the Spanish labour market – one of 20 per cent unemployment, in which having an education no longer serves as any kind of guarantee for subsequent job security at all – and to protest at the fact that it is getting harder and harder for a young person in Spain to gain any kind of foothold on the Spanish job market.[2] The uprisings in the Parisian suburbs, too, have been viewed as recent, tangible examples of the kind of rage that is felt by a whole generation of young people; a kind of rage and despair at the prospect of the steady, continual growth in the number of temporary jobs and unpaid so-called internships which most young people – even those with a high level of education – find themselves forced to work these days. Since 2005, the French grass-roots organization *Génération Précaire* has played a very active part in the public debate in France, protesting against the exploitation of young and educated French citizens who find themselves forced to work underpaid and informal jobs without any kind of job security.[3] The prevalence of these kinds of 'junk jobs' – jobs in which the wage is steadily declining, as a result of increased competition, and which are not covered by the normal guarantees and security measures of full-time employment such as pension and safety regulations – actively contributes to a kind of labour market in which more and more people find themselves in the paradoxical situation of having both *less* and *more* work to do, at the same time. They are always forced to search for enough part-time employment to secure the existence of themselves and their families (Beck, 2005: 2, 6–8). In an attempt to conceptualize the rise of a de-standardized, fragmented, plural 'underemployment system' characterized by highly flexible, time-intensive and spatially deregulated forms of paid labour (Beck, 2000a: 77), Beck speaks of the 'Brazilianization of the West' (Beck, 2000a: 1–10), pointing out that the flexibilization of wage labour is a *multidimensional* process which has meant that the notion of one's 'work' can no longer be defined by referring to contractual obligations, spatial occurrence or temporal duration. Thus Beck's thesis of Brazilianization, or perhaps more aptly *pluralization*, is *not* simply a tool for addressing the shortness of wage labour. Nor is it a matter of whether or not we are running out of available work, as others have claimed.

According to Beck, we are not faced with the end of employment (Offe and Heinze, 1992); nor are we in a situation where mass employment is disappearing (Rifkin, 1995). To claim that work and the society of work is (utterly) disappearing (Offe, 1984; Gorz, 1989) is to take things much too far. The thesis of pluralization, on the other hand, attempts to delineate the end of classical society of work as we know it, since we are, today, *beyond* full employment. We currently find ourselves in a situation in with a scarcity of wage labour and a shortness of work, the burden of which is distributed among us all, in the form of flexible amounts of *under*employment. This, all things considered, is enough to make the lives of ordinary people quite uncertain; most of the time, however, this new situation, although it affects us all, remains hidden. It is a mechanism cloaked behind a new kind of *spatial decentralization* of work. In this sense, flexibilization is also about re-arranging whatever work remains available, since new progress in the fields of information and communication technology has made work *hours* and work*place* into matters that are largely subjective, as direct, physical face-to-face interaction is no longer needed in order for individuals to work efficiently with one another.

In ch. 4 of his book *The Brave New World of Work*, Beck (2000a) offers a systematization of the discussions that have been surrounding the future of work in recent years, in order to present 11 possible scenarios for the future of wage labour. A main point of his, in the development of each scenario, is that the wave of rationalization that has followed in the wake of new information technology has left marks in every trade and industry and that it is currently reducing the number of jobs available in many different sectors. This is true of the public sector, but also the banking, trade, transport, insurance and educational sectors (Beck, 2005: 2). Thus we should not, according to Beck, expect from service society that it will be somehow able to step in and provide any sort of saving grace from our current situation or expect it to be able to create new job opportunities. The third industrial revolution has also made possible the '*deterritorialization of cooperation*' and paved the way for a new 'freedom of planning' (Beck, 2003: 171), resulting in work being robbed of the basic, commonplace practices that used to pertain to it. Instead of factory work – which was temporally and spatially founded in a specific place and time – we now see new 'delocalized' forms of production appear, which are made possible by digital networks (intranet systems and the Internet), allowing for cooperation between people – and machines – across time and space. This is especially true for certain sectors (e.g. services and knowledge production) and within certain corporate branches (administration, management, etc.), in which work can be performed at any time and in any place. The consequence of this, however, is that the occupational organization of work is eroded, leading to a decline in available work and production, while the boundaries between work and non-work (leisure time) become intangible. All of this is a direct result of the concept of work being split into separate temporal and spatial realms (Beck, 1992: 143; 2000a: 77–78).

In addition to this, the flexibilization of work also leads to a new kind of *individualization of work* (Beck, 2003a: 62; 2005: 20), thus adding further fuel to the bonfire of individualization (see Chapter 4).

The systemic changes to paid work

Although the third industrial revolution, according to Beck, is a very central part of his diagnosis of the current state of the employment system and the changes it is undergoing, it is not the only process to influence matters. In spite of the fact that it is the microelectronic revolution which has made technologically advanced capitalism possible – and it is a kind of capitalism which is currently abolishing the connection between economic growth and employment and forcing many people into various states of underemployment – Beck believes it necessary to also include other processes of change in his diagnosis.[4] The reason for the *decline* and *change* in occupational work is also, at least in part, 'the surges of moderniza-tion in information technology, as well as in social policy and law' (Beck, 1992: 141). Beck agrees with his friend and colleague Wolfgang Bonß, who argues that even developments which may appear to be remote and unassociated from the mechanics and movements of the labour market may well turn out to be highly influential and very important for its future (Bonß, 2000).

By 'social modernization processes' Beck (2000a: 67) is referring to a series of different processes such as globalization, ecological crises, the politicization of work and a radicalized individualization, which have all, in unintended ways, contributed to the rising trend of underemployment. A softening of work legisla-tion has opened up a new kind of contractual pluralization of wage labour. The deformalization of first modernity's system of full employment has, by now – as a result of the attempts at creating a more flexible labour market – become a forced political matter, propelled along by the passing of new laws. This has provided a 'legal basis for deregulation of the labour market' (Beck, 2000a: 83). Additionally, Beck points out, the flexibilization of paid work – which has opened up new, precarious kinds of occupation – is also supported by companies that have realized the benefits to production entailed by the process, that is the possibility of adjusting the number of workers and work hours needed at any given time to fit the current demand for the good being produced, thereby avoiding unnecessary expenses by paying wages to the workers only when they are needed to fulfil incoming orders. Furthermore, the new and decentralized kinds of work mean that the expenses traditionally associated with centrally organized wage labour (expenses such as building maintenance, office space, furniture, appliances and supplies) can more or less be stricken from the company expense budget (Beck, 1992: 143, 147). If we wish to see hands-on, contemporary examples of what might happen when politicians – trying to avoid the rise of unemployment and the kind of subsequent, political scandal that always follows it – end up allowing con-tractual individualization of work, we need look no farther, says Beck, than the USA or England (Hauxner, 1999). In *The Brave New World of Work*, Beck offers us an account of a USA which has been attempting to eliminate unemployment by allowing massive deregulation. Beck ultimately reaches the conclusion that US unemployment has (solely to the benefit of the corporate world) been kept under control primarily by means of a kind of rampant deregulation which has resulted in a flexibilization of employment which, although it may have resulted in more people working and being employed, has also resulted in wages now being so low, and working conditions so poor, that they often do not provide any kind of real foundation for a proper, livable life (Beck, 2000d: 27; 2000a: 110–21).

One of Beck's most central points is that the amount of paid work available is dwindling, as a direct consequence of the fact that more and more people are trying to get into the labour market (Beck, 2000a: 54–55; 2005: 3, 6), a main factor being the massive advent of women into the labour market that has taken place over the last 30–40 years. This increasingly fierce struggle over employment, he attributes to a kind of fundamentally *intensified individualization*, which has introduced a collective desire to live a 'life of one's own' (Beck, 2000a: 54–55; 2005: 3–6). As illustrated in Chapter 3, this is a kind of individualization which also affects the institution of marriage, effectively turning it into a 'for now' kind of temporary relationship. Thus women – in order to ensure their own existence – have no choice but to venture into the labour market in the search for economic independence and a life 'of their own' (Beck, 2005: 8). However, with everybody trying to gain a foothold in the labour market in order to ensure their own existence, and with new technological progress being made almost daily in order to introduce more processes of automation and rationalization, there is simply not enough work to go around. This means that the conditions for work of first modernity, lifelong full-time employment, are dissolved on both a biographical and an occupational level. Without a desire to do so, individuals inadvertently make life harder for themselves as their collective run on the labour market further boosts the transition towards underemployment and informal work, raising the demand for work even further (Beck, 2000a: 89). The simple explanation for this is that the prevalence of underemployment requires of the individual that one compensates for the loss of income by accepting other kinds of precarious work; by 'multi-jobbing'. Seen from the collective's point of view, this is an unfortunate strategy which means that the amount of *flexible* work will increase, while the position of the individual in the labour market is weakened with a resulting loss of income as a direct consequence. A rising demand for work will, bluntly put, result in lower wages, joining the traditionally incompatible concepts of *work* and *poverty* in a new kind of union. We are, in other words, witnessing processes of poverty being fuelled by the labour market, in which wage labourers are transformed into *working poor*, forced to work an ever-increasing amount of time for an ever-decreasing amount of money (Beck, 2000a: 89). This is all grist to the mill of flexibilization and thereby to the *individualization* of work, undermining the genuine liberties of the individual. Beck even goes so far as to argue that the notion of individualization as it pertains to one's way of living life and being in the world, has been 'supplemented, overlapped and thwarted by an individualization of work' (Beck, 2000a: 54). The changes to wage labour are accentuated and strengthened further, according to Beck, by the increasing globalization – primarily in the sense of an *economic globalization* (Beck, 2000a: 25).

As shown in Chapter 5, Beck – along with Giddens – understands globalization as '*acting and living (together) over distances, across the apparently separate worlds of national states, religions, regions and continents*' (Beck, 2000b: 20).

Thus, to Beck, globalization also brings with it a kind of 'social despatialization of work and production' (Beck, 2000a: 73) which means that work loses the temporal and spatial fixedness it used to have. A consequence of the contemporary globalization process is, in other words, a *globalization of work*: a new, spatially erratic way of organizing work into new and diffuse methods and places, entailing that work can and will be done everywhere (Beck, 2000a: 75). However, as a result of this 'global competition breaks out between high-priced and low-priced labour; and the fiscal conditions and controls of individual states can be played off against one another and undermined' (Beck, 2000a: 28). This is a consequence of new global or spatially de-concentrated methods of production, and leads to a *deterritorialization of the labour market*: a kind of work realm which is stretched tight across the gap between what constitutes the local and what constitutes the global. Therefore, the globalization of work is, to Beck, also tightly connected with 'the abolition of distance made possible by production based on information technology' (Beck, 2000a: 31).

To put it bluntly, digitalization has made the globalization of work possible, as it is digital technology that allows for direct cooperation without the need for physical representation and which decides the degree to which work is virtualized. Beck himself offers a curious example of this kind of development: in the Tegel airport of Berlin, the airport's own information desk closes at 6 p.m., after which all information about flight departures, delays and changes – both on monitors and through public address systems throughout the airport – is handled by staff who are physically located in California. In this way, 'no extra payment has to be made for late working because it is still daytime; and indirect labour costs for the same activity are considerably lower than in Germany' (Beck, 2002b: 18). However, this kind of practice also results in making the work uncertain in a whole new way, throwing what used to be a spatially bound, secure occupation onto the mercy of the flows of transnational capital and shifts in global work distribution (Beck, 2000a: 73).

Consequences for education, people and democracy

The systemic change of wage labour has, according to Beck, had a great impact on a number of things – not least on the future of the educational system. Or in other words: the systemic change has a large influence on the *value* of education. In a transformed work society, the post-full-employment society, the lack of paid work means that taking an education no longer provides any kind of a guarantee that one will be able to get a job – not, at any rate, a full-time, long-term and well-paid one. In spite of the fact that education provides less and less of a guarantee for employment, and in spite of the fact that changes in the labour market are swiftly turning the occupational orientation of the educational system into a kind of anachronism, it is *still* becoming increasingly important to educate oneself, in order to have a chance of obtaining one of the much sought-after jobs. If one desires to gain access to the labour market waiting room of second modernity, one's only chance is education, preferably *higher education*.

The scarcity of paid work then, plainly speaking, has put us in a situation which can be summarized by the basic headline of 'education without work' but also, simultaneously, in a situation where it is not the diplomas and credentials one obtained while going through the educational system but rather the hiring tests and processes of companies and enterprises that ultimately decide who gets to gain access to the labour market and who does not. This, according to Beck, is a refeudalization of the labour market and a relapse into 'the distribution of chance and opportunity of pre-educational society':

> It would seem that a sort of *refeudalization* is taking place – although it is admittedly veiled behind education – with concern to the distribution of chances and risks in the labour market.
> The reason for this is that employers, who have to choose between several applicants with the same formal qualifications, will make their decisions by invoking new criteria, which have nothing to do with education or diplomas and which evade justification.
> (Beck, 1986: 248; our translation)[5]

However, if one hopes to move beyond the kind of 'unstable, transitional phase where one is constantly alternating between bad jobs, unemployment, short-term work and underemployment' (Beck, 1986: 248; our translation), education is still, paradoxically, the only real opportunity to do so. Thus Beck's point is that, although education is the sole prerequisite for avoiding the looming prospect of unemployment and hopelessness, it is *not* a guarantee. So the educational system, these days, is beginning more and more to resemble a *ghost station*

> where the trains no longer run on time or according to schedule, but everything is still, none the less, conducted and managed in the same way it has always been managed. If one wishes to travel – and who would not wish to do so, since staying at home would mean staying with a dead-end future – one must get in line and wait for one's turn, in front of booths that sell tickets to trains which are mostly overcrowded and can no longer even be counted on to go in the right direction. And the public servants carry on, unaffected, still handing out tickets to nowhere with smooth, bureaucratic efficiency while they keep a watchful eye on the ever-growing queue, holding would-be passengers at bay by barking threats that '*without tickets, you're never* getting on the train!'
> (Beck, 1986: 238; our translation)

Thus, having finished his or her education, the individual is released into a work life of risk, characterized by flexible kinds of employment and underemployment, which he or she must learn to live with, since the risks that are inherent to work have turned into individualized risks, as a direct consequence of the flexibilization of work. The contractual, temporal and spatial decentralization of work result in the isolation of the individual, forcing each to carry the burden of risk, which is characteristic of the employment system, on his or her own shoulders (Beck, 2000a: 73). On an individual level, the psychological and physical risks are also privatized and made matters of personal responsibility; this is a kind of uncertainty which can turn very paralysing very swiftly, as it leaves the individual without any real possibility of predicting the future or assessing the risks that may or may not surround the individual's life. Often, it is even unclear to the individual whether he or she is currently in a situation that can actually provide the means necessary for supporting life, on a short- or long-term basis. Among other things, the flexibilization of work means that companies, with one day's notice, may make changes to daily work schedules and work hours based on the current amount of orders (Beck, 1992: 147). The transition of many workplaces towards more and more 'virtual' companies and work methods – resulting in more net-based companies and (home) employment – entails that security regulations and workplace codes are removed from public inspection and thus beyond the control of the authorities (Beck, 1992: 143–144). And, when work turns into something that one can do *wherever* and *whenever* one sees fit, it is suddenly much more difficult to draw any kind of cohesive line between work and leisure time; also, the risk of losing one's job is turned into an individual problem of one's own. When we work in a manner whereby we are physically separated from one another (e.g. in the comfort of our own homes), the lack of employment and uncertainty about our means for future existence are turned into matters for each private citizen and worker, which may have far-reaching consequences for the mental health of the individual (Beck, 1992). In Beck's critique of the new labour market, he falls in line with the American sociologist Richard Sennett, who in his book *The Corrosion of Character: The Personal Consequences of Work in the New Capitalism* sought to illuminate the human consequences of the dissolution of normalized working conditions (Sennett, 1998). Sennett emphasized that the rearrangement of work at the hands of the new, short-sighted and so-called flexible capitalism is threatening to dissolve the personalities and characteristics of the individual people on the labour market. The main reasons for this dissolution, according to Sennett, are the new and flexible kinds of work; the short-term positions that are either periodically fixed or contractually based. These new modes of 'normal' employment essentially make it impossible for the working individual to form any kind of coherent, long-lasting personal identity. This leads to a loss of self-understanding and self-worth. Simply put, these kinds of new 'normal' jobs undermine the character of the individual and 'particularly those qualities of character which bind human beings to one another and furnish each with a sense of sustainable self' (Sennett, 1998: 27).

On a broader level, from a societal point of view, the flexibilization of work is also a problem, says Beck, as it simply entails society placing itself in a sort of position of democratic peril. Unless everyone is instilled with a sense of material-existential security in their lives, through long-term employment, flexibilization will ultimately speed up the tendency towards atomization (Beck, 2003a: 164).

The rising amount of work being performed from home is thus a risk factor not only with regard to the individual but also to democracy itself, since it erodes the workplace's function as a place of socialization which helps to tie society together, by supplying the individual with a natural venue for acquainting him- or herself with the community. Furthermore, for an individual to invest his or her trust and participation in a democracy, it is a fundamental requirement that one feel sufficiently secure on a long-term basis, with regard to both one's employment situation and means of existence in general; therefore, Beck says, we *must* react to the scarcity of paid work. There is no use in clinging to the idea of full employment as if it were any kind of real and viable option any more.[6] The problem after all is that:

> Whatever is being referred to by the concept of 'economic growth' in its present phase, goes hand in hand with the replacement of jobs by 'flexible labour' and of job security by 'rolling contracts', fixed-term appointments and incidental hire of labour; with downsizing, restructuring and 'rationalizing' – all boiling down to the cutting of the volume of employment.
>
> (Bauman, 1998b: 41)

The words are Zygmunt Bauman's but Beck sees things in much the same way. In Beck's view, there is only one solution to this kind of challenge: we must move beyond the value imperialism of paid work and we must *re-invent* our notion of work itself.

Civil labour, civic money and welfare entrepreneurs

When Beck does not simply completely abandon the *work* concept but opts to stay with it and attempt to rethink it, he does so because *work* in his view is intricately tied to the maintenance and retention of any strong and functioning democracy. In the post-full-employment society, basing a democracy solely on a foundation of full time *wage* labour is no longer a secure strategy at all. Rather, Beck argues, we must learn to see the reduction in paid work as the catalyst for a new kind of *wealth of time*, instead of as a problem. Our newfound wealth gives us the opportunity to dedicate a larger amount of our time to performing meaningful work for the benefit of others (Beck, 2005: 51–115). Beck envisages a new kind of work, which he calls *paid citizen work*, which will help society's individuals secure their own material needs while also bringing people together across social divides and class, thus reinvigorating the political community.

Beck's notion of civil labour should not be understood as an alternative to paid work, nor should it be confused with, for example, communal/governmental activation programmes which have the exact purpose of bringing individuals who receive unemployment benefit, or are on welfare, into full-time jobs. On the contrary, it constitutes a *supplement* to paid work. Beck sees civil labour as a paid, independent and self-defined work effort one makes for the benefit of – and in cooperation with – one's fellow citizens: a 'project-related, cooperative, self-organized labour for others' which is meant to coexist along with traditional paid work (Beck, 2000a: 130). In this way, then, civil labour is different from housework and from *volunteer* work, in that one is paid for performing civil labour. Civil labour can basically consist of anything from working for non-profit organizations, networks and social programmes to participating in protest movements and initiatives, as long as the work one performs is performed for the *common* good (Beck, 2000a: 127–128).[7] A decisive trait of citizen work, then, is that it is an effort made specifically for the benefits of the community, one that furthers and strengthens a 'culture of creativity', bringing new life to democracy. Civil labour is, in other words, a paid kind of civic, democratic work (Beck, 2005; 2000a: 17–35). In order for paid civil labour to become a success, however, a number of criteria must be met. The most basic condition of these is that society must experience a kind of 'altruistic individualism' which effectively combines citizens' striving towards self-realization with their desire to do something for the benefit of others (Beck, 2005; 2000a: 17–35). Judging from the steadily increasing demand for volunteer work, the time seems right for the introduction of paid civil labour (Beck, 2000a: 17–35). However, for this to happen, a political effort must be made as well, in order to provide basic funding for civil labour instead of inactivity. Furthermore, labour market legislature must be reformed and employment services need to be re-invented. Beck suggests that the amount of civic money an individual would receive as compensation for their civil labour should correspond in size to what they would otherwise have received from current unemployment benefits:

> This would consist of public transfer money, social sponsoring by companies, local authority revenue (paid for things urgently needed by the community), as well as sums obtained from the civil labour itself.
>
> (Beck, 2000a: 127)

These kinds of projects come with great potential for cost cutting and economic saving, with regard to the budgets of the public sector. For civil labour to function, however, other paid work is still absolutely *essential*, as civic money must, to a certain degree, be financed by way of taxation. Beck imagines that, in addition to proper wages, citizen work should attract formal recognition, essentially by providing individuals with the opportunity to obtain degrees, certificates and diplomas as proof of their contributions to society, just as civil labour will require a kind of fictitious currency or monetary unit which can provide a solid basis for trading the goods and services made specifically through civil labour (Beck, 2000e: 430, 433–439; 2005: 22–34). To Beck, civic money is intricately tied to *civil labour*. This is a departure from the more traditional way of understanding civic money, essentially defining it as a guaranteed, fixed level of minimum income which, in a given country, is automatically bestowed on all of its citizens. This notion of civic money has been extolled by such thinkers as Claus Offe, in *Disorganized Capitalism: Contemporary Transformations of Work and Politics* (Offe, 1985), and André Gorz, who in *Paths to Paradise: On the Liberation from Work* (Gorz, 1983, 1989) speaks of a guaranteed societal income. Like Beck, these two present civic money as a measure that may provide a solution to the problems of post-full-employment society. However, Beck views civic money *not* as a guaranteed, no-questions-asked kind of base income, but rather as an earned compensation for performing 'community-building' civil labour in order to secure the material and mental state of the individual, while strengthening democracy itself by bringing citizens together to undertake social tasks and solve social problems. So civic money as a way of supplying every citizen with a guaranteed, basic income (which was one of the key demands made by the Spanish reformation movement 15M, which was formed during the waves of protests and demonstrations throughout Spain in 2011) is not what Beck has in mind.[8] Nor does Beck believe that civil labour and regular paid work should be divided between specific groups. Rather, he says, individuals should alternate between performing paid work and civil labour (Beck, 2005: 22). Beck, in other words, imagines a society of pluralized occupation, in which work is made up of a great many different *kinds* of work or work functions. Finally, for a civil labour system to function in an optimal manner, it is necessary that the public sector stay as uninvolved as possible and keep its interference at a minimum. According to Beck, it would be plain harmful if civil labour were made a regulative matter of social welfare offices, labour exchanges or even newly formed civil labour departments (Beck, 2000a: 129). Too much strictness, regulation and red tape would end up stifling all elements of spontaneity, imagination and sheer initiative, effectively smothering the democratic potential of civil labour from the get-go. Rather, we should appoint civil labour committees that 'might advise on projects and help to enlist the necessary public backing for them' and have the ability to recognize and support people that have shown a proclivity for public welfare entrepreneurship (Beck, 2000a: 128–130; see also Beck, 2000e).

Beck sees the public welfare entrepreneurs as in charge of utilizing their entrepreneurial spirit and task-oriented, problem-solving nature (that of the prosperous businessman) and combining it with their equally strong Mother Theresa-like penchant for serving the common good and utilizing their social abilities to rally the community and encourage people to work altruistically for their fellow people. In this way, their work will not only be social work; it will also have social *results*, by bringing new energy and initiative to the community (Beck, 2000e: 429–430). The welfare entrepreneur, in other words, will function as a *community* entrepreneur who – not by being an experienced community organizer but simply by his or her sheer direct knowledge of how inclusive memberships and work processes can best be brought to bear on solving a given problem – will be able to organize spontaneous efforts and initiatives. The welfare entrepreneur, thus, will play a key role in establishing exactly the kind of highly innovative networks and organizations that society will need to help to turn its social wealth into financial wealth and handle the many challenges of second modernity (Beck, 2000e: 430–447; 2000a: 127–149). Beck does not expand further on what kind of person he considers fit to undertake this kind of vital task.

Paid civil labour

Beck has high expectations for civil labour and what it may accomplish. Thus, when saying that civil labour is the very soul of democracy (Beck, 2000e), he is not simply referring to it as a sort of politico-democratic revival of the local community or the community of the nation-state; rather, he sees civil labour as an effective means of furthering the transition towards an actively engaged *post-national* society (Beck, 2005: 18, 22, 31, 37). Civil labour, in Beck's view, is a tool that can help pave the way towards a new kind of political society: the European citizen society, which is simultaneously a local and global one (Beck, 2000a: 121–149). The reason Beck equates paid civil labour with the development of a European citizen society is that he understands civil labour as a kind of work that is characterized by its political (community-building) actions and intents. Civil labour is meant to bring different social, age and income groups into contact with one another and in that way help them rediscover the notion of community. This way, everybody will experience a sense of purpose and self-worth, as part of a coherent society and community. The preoccupation with cosmopolitanism and 'project Europe' has – as we have shown – been a trademark of Beck's thinking throughout recent years. It is a preoccupation, however, that already appears in his studies of the sociology of work. Beck sees the transition from national states to a transnational or cosmopolitical democracy as an area of key importance which is very much worth our time and discussion, and he believes that civil labour is a 'decisive institutional measure that integrates helpful individualists into social and political contexts of action and work grounded upon their own tenacity and initiative' (Beck, 2000a: 152–153). Civil labour can, in this sense, help to 'de-nationalize' democracy, and thus essentially help make it *more* democratic, by creating new interconnections between new, differentiated kinds of social integration and self-made political spaces, effectively disregarding the old borders and boundaries (Beck, 2005: 24–34; 2000a: 125, 141).

There is a kind of tension or 'drive' which lies latent in the risk society, says Beck: the regime of risk harbours a kind of inherent, albeit hidden, 'community-generating' drive or force which can be pressed into service to promote the creation of new, self-organized and transnational citizen labour groups. It is because of this kind of latent drive (which is a trademark tendency of the risk regime) that it is even feasible to imagine a new kind of citizens' Europe, founded on basic European civil rights (Beck, 2000a: 163). Simply put, the formation of these new transnational civil labour groups will occur in response to 'a common problem or situation and its "translation" across cultures' (Beck, 2000a: 168). Beck sees civil labour as a potential tool for the transnational citizens' movements that already exist today. He mentions the European civil rights movement as a classic example of how civil labour can be perceived as 'a politics of new beginnings which, in opposition to the false certainty of hopelessness and failure – as Hanna Arendt put it – assumes that the capacity to start something new is an essential part of political action' (Beck, 2000a: 137). It is a direct imperative that the nation-state somehow manages to turn itself into a transnational agent. It is a necessary requirement which the state simply *must* meet; but it is struggling to do so. As a consequence of this, the nation-state ends up being more or less wholly dependent on the Civil Society International (Beck, 2000a: 131–132). This development – the impossibility of conducting traditionally 'national' politics, combined with the relative openness of the European Union – presents us with a great opportunity for furthering the development of transnational civil labour initiatives. Political openness and availability is ultimately what allows us to co-determine and define the terms of civil labour across borders. It is also an essential prerequisite which allows the member states of the European Union to rethink and revise their conception of foreigners (Beck, 2000a: 135). This kind of Europe – the Europe of citizens and civil labour – will not be wholly possible until every European man and woman is recognized as a being a citizen of all of Europe. Only after this happens, says Beck, will we be able to create for ourselves a transnational 'culture of creativity' (Beck, 2000a: 129) in which civil labour will be able to 'pull itself up out of nothing by its own efforts' (Beck, 2000a: 169).

Work as a fundamental theme in the writings of Beck

As mentioned at the beginning of this chapter, Beck has been preoccupied with the question of work since the early 1970s. In 1972, he was hired by Karl Martin Bolte to work as a researcher and coordinator for a large labour market research project, exploring the theoretical framework for labour market and workforce research in the social sciences, and he was tasked with building – from the ground up – a research programme which would bring a new perspective into the very empirically dominated work sociology of the time. Beck worked on this project until the late 1970s (see, for example, Beck, Hörning and Thomsen, 1980). The project, officially titled 'Special research area (SFB) 101', encompassed three different research programmes. Along with Beck's own programme – programme A, the 'theoretical framework for labour market and workforce research in the social sciences' – the project also contained a programme B, which concerned itself with socialization, youth and job perspectives, and a programme C, which conducted research into the corporate world and its use of labour (Bolte, 1978). If we take a closer look at the steady stream of publications from Beck – mainly in collaboration with his research colleague Michael Brater, but also with such researchers as Bernd Wegener, Eckhart Tramsen and Karl Martin Bolte – which came out during the mid to late 1970s, it is readily apparent that Beck's main interest at the time was in developing a *subject-oriented* work sociology, which was meant to answer a specific question: what kind of influence does occupation – choice and structure – have on the life of the individual (Beck and Brater, 1977a,b, 1978a; Beck, Brater and Wegener, 1979a)? Beck believed that this kind of subject-oriented analysis of work was needed, simply because all existing labour market and workforce research had consistently ignored the status of the individual, at best reducing the subject to a sort of economical–rational business-conducting entity who – striving to sell his or her work capacity to the highest bidder – did not at all care for the actual nature and content of whatever job he or she would end up working in (Beck, Brater and Wegener, 1979a). This kind of economist–functionalist approach to everything from workforce supply to workforce utilization, qualification development, production development and work distribution had led to a situation in which sociology did *not* treat work as any kind of especially central factor of an individual's life. Thus Beck tried, in his publications, to do away with this social scientific line of thought (Beck and Brater, 1978b: 907). He insisted that the subject had real significance, along with everyday experiences, and he sought to develop the conceptual framework and tools that would allow him to handle these aspects in a novel way.[9] It is a fundamental point, in the subject-oriented work theory of Beck, that it will not suffice for us to regard occupation and vocations as predetermined roles to be played, to which the individual will have to adapt if he or she wishes to work. Rather, Beck argued, the occupational structures are *not* unbreakable but indeed very open and loosely tied, which essentially allows the individual to operate freely within the confines of the developmental templates sketched by the structures of a given occupation. However, in light of this – of the fact that occupation and vocation were both loosely structured ventures on the individual level, yet at the same time also played very active roles when it came to subjects' definitions of themselves – it also became readily apparent that we need to be aware of which kinds of effects labour and labour distribution really *have* on subjects and individuals. According to Beck, we need to realize that our way of distributing labour according to a set of 'vocational' categories is not necessarily a natural and mandatory way of going about it. Rather, it is a quite specific and highly historical phenomenon, which is both a product of – and a catalyst for – the enforcement of certain social interests (Bolte, 1978: 8). Thus Beck did not at all doubt that the vocational distribution of work had far-reaching consequences for the working individual, and he believed that there was a need for a new kind of approach to the field (Beck and Brater, 1976: 178; Beck, Brater and Tramsen, 1976a,b). When labour market structures are immediately in charge of 'manufacturing' the subject structures (i.e. when they are responsible for shaping and defining which actions and thoughts it is possible for a subject to perform and to have, in a given society) they also end up serving as mediators for the distribution and legitimization of social opportunity and as deciders of life quality in general. Thus, it was Beck's conclusion that the vocational distribution of work has far-reaching social and personal consequences for the individual living in an industrial society in which social inequality is tightly interwoven with labour market inequality. The way certain vocational constructions and labour market changes 'shaped' occupations was then, to Beck, more or less the key to understanding how social inequality, identity and reality is reproduced (Beck and Brater, 1978b: 908; 1977a: 7; Beck, Brater and Wegener, 1979a: 7–14; Beck and Zeller, 1980: 80). The fact that these structures seemed to impair social mobility, said Beck, was especially because institutionally separated educational and occupational structures were, in effect, closely tied to one another, into their respective vocational structures (Beck and Brater, 1977a: 6, Beck, Hörning and Thomssen, 1980: 11). Thus the solution to ensuring a higher degree of vocational expertise and flexibility of labour – a highly prioritized venture even in the 1970s – would *not*, according to Beck, be to further strengthen the vocational profiles and orientation of specific educations (Beck, Bolte and Brater, 1978: 22).[10]

Rather, Beck believed that it would be necessary to reform the current educational and occupational system in order to get rid of the unhealthy focus on work and vocation on which the educational and occupational system was founded. It was decisive, for Beck and his colleagues, that the occupation and vocation system should *also* allow one to break with the structures of society, and thus allow one to make changes to society at large. We should, however, keep in mind the most fundamental connections between education and employment, as well as the fact that the working individual's relation to his or her job is never simply a matter of economy alone (Beck, Brater and Wegener, 1979a,b; Beck, Brater and Tramsen, 1976a: 10). By means of empirical studies, Beck sought to prove the existence of certain 'vocational ties', which meant that the individual – as a consequence of his or her choice of work and education – would inevitably end up under the influence of certain social demands, interests, commitments, traditions and the like, depending on his or her vocation (Beck, Brater and Wegener, 1979a).[11]

Thus the *social constitution* of vocations was a key factor to the young Beck (Beck and Brater, 1977a: 584). It is no wonder, then, that it would go on to become a main point of Beck's that a well-functioning labour market must always be created through reformation of the vocational system, in close synergy with a corresponding educational system, rather than through forced flexibility and appointed occupations, which fails to take into account the social boundaries of vocational flexibility. For the individual, after all, his or her vocational employment is anything *but* simply a matter of money and prestige; it is a matter of identity (Beck, Brater and Wegener, 1979a; Beck and Brater, 1982: 215). This approach, however, evaluating the world through an analytical framework focused on vocation and trade, which characterized Beck's work and publications in the mid to late 1970s, faded and lost influence throughout the 1980s. With the publication of *Risk Society* in 1986, Beck was – as we have shown – finally ready to completely do away with the notions of work as vocation and trade, which had been a large part of his early research.

Core terms

Civic money: Beck defines civic money as the compensation bestowed upon the individual for performing civil labour. This compensation is not limited to cash payment but also includes specific social welfare services (such as child care).

Civil labour: This is not, to Beck, a phenomenon to be seen as a complete replacement for paid labour, but a partial, tax-financed supplement to it, which will simultaneously make it possible for each individual to obtain financial security while strengthening democracy. Civil labour is to be understood as work performed for the common good and can, thus, consist of everything from protest activity to paid community service.

Flexibilization and pluralization of paid work: As a direct consequence of the third industrial revolution, and following a lack of traditional employment, new plural and precarious kinds of employment occur. Paid work is no longer standardized with regard to *content, time* and *space*. Instead, work turns into a contractually, temporally and spatially flexible entity.

Flexible underemployment: The shortage of paid work available has made paid work more flexible, with regard to contracts, time and space. The result of this is that more and more people must make do with flexible, pluralized kinds of underemployment; they are forced to work several small jobs and part-time jobs which do not – at least wage-wise – add up to a full-time position.

Post-full-employment society: To Beck, the risk society of second modernity is characterized by being a *post-full-employment society*, in so far as it is widely influenced by the *decline* or *reduction* in paid work and employment, as a direct consequence of the dominating processes of change that prevail in second modernity. With the scarcity of paid work, the foundation of first modernity's work society is starting to crumble.

Third industrial revolution: One of the five dynamics of change pertaining to second modernity, this has caused a change of the system of full-time occupation and employment by largely eliminating jobs within a number of fields (production, banking, science, teaching etc.). To Beck, the third revolution is synonymous with a revolution in the rationalization of industrial robotics, information technology and communication technology.

Work and full-employment society: The industrial societies of first modernity are, according to Beck, characterized by their status as work societies with full employment (with a maximum of 2 per cent unemployment). These societies were based on a tight interconnection between the labour market and the social and democratic rights of individuals.

Further reading

Beck, U. (1992) *Risk Society: Towards a New Modernity.* London: Sage Publications.
Beck, U. (2000) *The Brave New World of Work.* Malden, MA: Polity Press.
Beck, U. (2003) *Conversations with Ulrich Beck.* Cambridge: Polity Press.

8   Critique of Ulrich Beck's sociology

As we have shown in the previous chapters, Ulrich Beck has had a great deal of influence on the theoretical developments and agendas of international sociology for some years now. His theories have received an otherwise rare amount of attention, both from sociological circles as well as from the broader public. Beck, according to Gabe Mythen (2005a), has even come to be called one of the most influential and important sociologists of his time. It is obvious, says Mythen (2007), that Beck has helped introduce a new sociological agenda. Mythen points out that there have been a number of positive readings of Beck which have tended to focus on the socially progressive dimensions of his thesis of the risk society; he mentions as examples Bronner, who has called *Risk Society* a work of great analytic and epistemological potential, and McGuigan, who has called it one of the main works in the history of social theory (Mythen, 2007; Bronner, 1995; McGuigan, 1999: 125). Mythen even believes that Beck's thought has set a new agenda, as other theoreticians such as Eder, Giddens and Strydom in some of their work build on Beck's theory as a sort of starting point, and thereby have formed a kind of 'risk society school' within sociology (Mythen, 2007: 795; Giddens, 1998; Strydom, 2002). Much in the same vein, William Outhwaite says that Beck, along with Bauman, Bourdieu and Giddens, has achieved 'canonical' status in contemporary British sociology (Outhwaite, 2009) – a status which we would venture extends to many other parts of the world as well.

According to Outhwaite, Beck's sociology must be understood as a kind of 'grand theory' or a 'diagnosis of the times' (Outhwaite, 2009). Being a grand theory and diagnosis, Beck's sociology is bound to cover a broad array of specific topics and subjects, in its attempt to produce a collected description of the new socictal reality which Beck believes has arrived. Because of this, scholars from a wide number of different scientific disciplines have been able to use and adopt parts of his theory of second modernity as inspiration or starting points for their own studies – or they have been able to use his theory about the transition into risk society and second modernity as a framework for their own further studies. As Gabe Mythen has pointed out, scientific disciplines as different as sociology, political science, cultural studies, geography and environmental studies have been able to find inspiration in Beck's thought. His theory of the risk society has been used as a starting point for studies of everything from international trades of global futures to questions of the transformation of war, childhood as a social

construct and the disappearance of youth labour, and the life conditions of profes-
sional freelancer workers (Mythen, 2005a: 129–130; 2004: 6–7, 31; Heng, 2006).

A multidimensional critique of Beck

There is, then, no doubt that Beck's theories about risk society and second, reflexive modernity are highly prevalent and influential analytical perspectives which
have led to theoretical debate across the traditional boundaries between scientific
disciplines, as well as breathing life into discussions about crime, food safety,
environment and social inequality (Caplan, 2000; Adam and van Loon, 2000;
Mythen, 2004, 2007: 795). On the other hand, however, far from everyone is
excited about Beck's sociology. His theories have seen wide criticism from many
sides. Some critics have even gone so far as to claim that he is not in fact conducting any real kind of sociology and that he is much too shallow and generalizing
in his diagnostics.

He has seen especially fierce criticism from already established researchers
and scholars in fields which he has had to venture into, as part of his work on the
theory of second modernity (risk theory, insurance theory, state theory etc.). To
established scientists and researchers in these fields, Beck's theories often end up
feeling pushy, exaggerated and much too hasty in their conclusions, and a number
of established experts have pointed out that his theories tend to both general-
ize and oversimplify (see, among other, Münch, 2002; Mythen, 2004, 2005a,b;
Marshall, 1999: 267; Elliott, 2002; Ericson and Doyle, 2004: 169). In the same
vein, his theories have been accused of lacking theoretical clarity and empirical
grounding in data which could help to demonstrate that his theories are rooted in
actual existing social reality (Mythen, 2004: 71, 93, 107–117; 2005a,b; Smith,
Law, Work and Panay, 1997; Dickens, 1996; Engel and Strasser, 1998; Goldblatt,
1995; Goldthorpe, 2002; Skeggs, 2004; Scott, 2006).

As Mythen points out, these concerns, along with a number of other, similar
reservations, have led to a number of theoreticians, such as McMylor (1996) and
Scott (2000), simply rejecting Beck's sociology (Mythen, 2007: 795). In this clos-
ing chapter we will first take a closer look at the critique of Beck's sociology and
thereafter offer our own assessments of his theories.

Delving into the criticisms that have been directed towards Beck's sociology
from a wide array of different scientific fields over the recent years, one can (ana-
lytically, if not otherwise) identify four main strands or lines of critique. Each
strand is centred around one of the main dimensions of Beck's thought. These
four strands are:

1 the thesis of the world risk society, Beck's understanding of risk, and empirical documentation;
2 the theory of second modernity and the reflexive process of modernization;
3 the thesis of individualization, that is the notion of a radicalized, institutionalized individualization;
4 the theory of globalization, Beck's cosmopolitan thought (especially concerning his understanding of the political-institutional consequences of

globalization) and his cosmopolitanism and its derived critique of sociology and science.

In the following, we will expand on each of these main strands, summarize them and offer our own assessment of both Beck's sociology and of the criticisms that have been levelled against it.

Critique of the theory of the (world) risk society

As mentioned, Beck's single largest claim to sociological fame is his theory of the (world) risk society – and it is, naturally, also this part of his theory which, over the years, has received the most criticism. The criticism has always been multifaceted but it is possible, as Gabe Mythen has shown us (Mythen, 2007), to identify six particular substrands in the critique of the risk society thesis. The *first strand* has to do with Beck's making a distinction between 'natural hazards' and new, man-made/self-produced risks; the distinction has been called into question both conceptually and with regard to its actual foundation in real history. According to Mythen, much of this line of criticism comes from Anderson (1997), Dryzek (1995) and Furedi (2002). Mythen identifies a particular *second strand* in the line of critique put forth by a series of people who have commented on Beck's thesis about a new social distribution logic wherein a wealth distribution logic is replaced by a risk distribution logic in the risk society. This argument has been made, most prevalently, by people such as McMylor (1996), Marshall (1999) and Elliot (2002).

Mythen does not mention the criticisms of Beck's work that have been put forth by Bernice Bovenkerk, but these, too, tie in nicely with this particular strand. Bovenkerk likewise focuses on the new risk distribution logic, which according to Beck will come to replace the old wealth distribution logic; this shift in the logic of distribution is the pivotal point of the article 'Is Smog Democratic? Environmental Justice in the Risk Society' (Bovenkerk, 2003). In this article, Bovenkerk attacks Beck's thesis that there has come about a new kind of common, general or shared level of 'exposure' to the new risks, which affect everybody without discrimination. Beck, according to Bovenkerk, fails to take into consideration the fact that, although nobody can now be said to be able to *wholly* avoid *every* risk, it does not automatically follow – as Beck seems to claim – that *all* risks suddenly end up being fairly and evenly distributed across everybody. According to Bovenkerk, Beck fails to draw a properly clear distinction between *global* and *local* risks. The question of the inequality of the distribution of risks and 'bads' then, also leads Bovenkerk to raise the question of whether or not Beck is not, in fact, grossly oversimplifying matters in his move towards 'eliminating' differences between social groups and class distinctions in the risk society.

In this, Bovenkerk, in her criticism of Beck, falls neatly in line with Gabe Mythen, who, in the article 'From "Goods" to "Bads"? Revisiting the Political Economy of Risk' (Mythen, 2005b), takes a quite critical stance towards Beck's theory of a new, universalist risk distribution logic. According to Mythen, Beck's argument relies too heavily on too small a number of concrete examples and is much too insensitive to the continuities of social reproduction. Furthermore, Beck fails to notice a marked intensification of traditional inequalities; a claim for which Mythen's article offers empirical documentation. From a more theoretical perspective, it is pointed out that the theory of the risk society relies on a non-viable distinction between interconnected forms of distribution, that it overlooks the potential of politics to create and spawn shared interests, and that it overlooks certain obvious, unequal kinds of risk distribution (Mythen, 2005a,b).

The *third strand* of criticism levelled against Beck's thesis of the risk society has, according to Mythen (2007), focused on whether or not Beck commits a theoretical fallacy in assuming the worst accidents imaginable (nuclear accidents, global warming etc.) to be archetypical, and thus representative, kinds of risks. By doing so, he ends up grossly exaggerating the globalizing and differential significance of self-produced risks; a tendency, which according to Mythen, is picked up on by the criticisms of Scott (2000) and Hinchcliffe (2000).

The *fourth strand* of criticism, according to Mythen, targets Beck's understanding of the general public's risk perception. According to Mythen, this strand focuses on the claim that Beck illicitly fuses natural objectivism to cultural relativism and that this 'enables him to identify risks as objective hazards while keeping hold of the idea that knowledge about threats is invariably channeled through social and cultural processes' (Mythen, 2007: 800). Still, Beck remains a realist with regard to the perception of risks – and this peculiar combination of theoretical attitudes and positions has been criticized from several sides. Critics such as Alexander and Smith (1996), Wilkinson (2001) and Tulloch and Lupton (2003) are, according to Mythen, representatives of a strand of criticism that has argued that Beck, in his interpretation and understanding of risks, fails to take ordinary social and everyday contexts into proper consideration.

The *fifth strand* of criticism takes issue with Beck's unconditionally negative view of 'risk' as a harmful concept, meaning that he ends up treating risks as phenomena with nothing but losers. That view inevitably frames risks as something which the individual will seek to avoid at all costs. Beck seems to forget, however, that risks may well simply be the acceptable price one needs to pay for societal progress and development. According to Mythen, this line of criticism has been put forth most prevalently by Merryweather (2003) and Culpitt (1999).

Finally, Mythen identifies a *sixth strand* of criticism, which has focused primarily on the potential discrepancies between Beck's insistence that we understand the risk society as a *world risk society* and his somewhat narrow analytical focus on decidedly western, capitalist cultures such as Germany and the UK. This criticism has been put forth by Mackey (2000), Nugent (2000) and Elliot (2002: 41).

A broader critique of Beck's theory of the risk society

There is no doubt that the six 'strands' of criticism that have been identified by Gabe Mythen go a long way towards encompassing much of the criticism that has been directed towards Beck's theory of the risk society, throughout the years. However, these six strands are far from exhaustive. Mythen himself has acted as exponent for a more methodically oriented line of criticism, arguing that Beck's abstract theory of the risk society lacks empirical documentation and that more concrete, 'micro-oriented' research would be required for it to obtain proper validity and gain political influence (Mythen, 2007: 803). As Mythen puts it: 'The heady mix of impassioned critique, paradoxical prose and provocative irony have made *Risk Society* (1992) a sitting duck for methodological purists' (Mythen, 2007: 803). He goes on: 'Two decades from the publication of *Risk Society* (1992), there remains a need to convert the conundrums laid out by Beck into meaningful research projects that can feed into and inform policy-making' (Mythen, 2007: 804).

In his critique of Beck's theories and their lack of empirical foundation, Mythen falls wholly into line with a number of other critics (Scott, 2000; Jensen and Blok, 2008). Critics such as Dingwall (1999) and Goldblatt (1995) have accused Beck's analyses of the risk society of operating from empirically undocumented generalizations and postulates.

> It is simply not acceptable to assume that the empirical case has been made for the widespread existence of the increasing threat of risks and increasing risk perception, or that their combined impact on social behaviour and beliefs is so conclusive that we can properly herald the emergence of a new type of society.
>
> (Goldblatt, 1995: 174)

The main point here is that one cannot conclude that the new risks *generally* act as the decisive motor of our society, if all one has to support such a conclusion is a series of discrete, specific cases, happenings and events. Because of this, the question of whether or not we are in fact living in a risk society remains quite open to discussion, as a number of Beck's critics have pointed out (see, among others, Wynne, 1996; Smith, Law, Work and Panay, 1997; Mythen, 2004).

These doubts concerning the validity of Beck's theory, then, have spawned a body of criticism which has mainly taken issue with Beck's understanding of risks. In the article 'Against Beck: In Defence of Risk Analysis', Campbell and Currie (2006) launch a significant criticism of Beck's approach to risk analysis, both as theoretical discipline and as praxis. They point out that Beck's definition of risk is inconsistent as it does not make any distinction between risks and risk perception yet works from an understanding of risks – according to Campbell and Currie – as a way of handling certain conditions, as well as making certain unexplainable distinctions between 'new risks' and 'old hazards' (Campbell and Currie, 2006: 151–153).

Focusing on Beck's term *risk*, Anthony Elliot's (2002) article 'Beck's Sociology of Risk: A Critical Assessment' argues that Beck subscribes to an objectivist and instrumental approach to the social construction of risk and uncertainty in social relations, which leads to an oversimplified understanding of risks and their 'social-cultural' origins. In other words, says Elliot, Beck fails to define the relation between new risks and institutional dynamics, reflexivity and criticism in a thorough way, and he seems to fail to take existent ideologies of dominance and power into proper account in his work.

Elliot, by pointing out Beck's potentially oversimplified understanding of risk, is in complete agreement with Jensen and Blok (2008), who have argued that the social processes which surround the perception, registration and processing of risk are much more complex undertakings than Beck's theory of the risk society gives them credit for. Somewhat related to this line of criticism is that of Hanlon (2010), who warns us against Beck's understanding of risk, which he argues to be problematic as Beck does not acknowledge the sociality of knowledge and expertise, lacks an ontological and hermeneutical understanding of expert knowledge and, on account of rational objectivity, plays down the fact that expert knowledge and lay knowledge are intricately interwoven. As Hanlon puts it: 'In short, these criticisms highlight the weaknesses of a theory of risk and knowledge which is not rooted in how daily practice shapes our ability to know' (Hanlon, 2010: 217).

Campbell and Currie (2006) elaborate on their multifaceted criticism by pointing out how Beck, in a generalizing manner, claims that risk experts – through their involvement in the development of new technology – will always tend to obfuscate and deny the existence of real and actual risks. Furthermore, Campbell and Currie argue that Beck is mistaken in interpreting the use of statistical probability in risk analyses, by taking results to be static and not susceptible to change or transformation in relation to new events and new knowledge. In addition to this, they say, Beck makes use of a principle of probability, which is presumably a logical one, which he takes to function in a non-defined time frame, in a way that causes highly *un*likely events to become possible and even likely, when one calculates it in a presumably infinite time frame. As an example, Campbell and Currie mention how Beck seems to assume that nuclear power production will go on forever, an assumption which, on a long enough time frame, will ultimately lead to the probability of a catastrophic event becoming very great, and indeed almost unavoidable.

Finally, Campbell and Currie (2006) criticize Beck for lack of nuance in his critique of the entire discussion about border values. According to the authors, Beck completely misunderstands fundamental conditions and states of affairs in the scientific industry. The fact that insurance companies do not wish to insure the nuclear industry is, according to Campbell and Currie, merely indicative of the fact that the insurance companies in question would not be *economically* capable of covering the costs that would be necessary to recover the damages in the event of such nuclear accidents. It does not, however, serve as an indication that the new risks are somehow impossible to insure oneself against, in the first place (Campbell and Currie, 2006: 166).

Ericson and Doyle (2004), too, take issue with Beck's understanding of the insurance industry, in their article 'Catastrophe, Risk, Insurance and Terrorism', rebutting Beck's thesis that the terrorist attacks of 11 September 2001 have ushered in a new industry of insurance which has made it well-nigh impossible for an individual to insure oneself against this kind of 'new risks'. Quite to the contrary, however, Ericson and Doyle illustrate that it is still quite possible to insure oneself against terrorism: 'far from "dissolving", as Beck would have it, the boundaries of private insurance were reconfigured in collaboration with the state in the ongoing, neo-liberal negotiation of political economy' (Ericson and Doyle, 2004: 169).

Finally, it bears mentioning that Beck has often been accused of a lack of depth in his treatment of the main communicational factors at play in the society of risk; the influence and effects of modern mass media, in particular, seem to remain largely underexposed in his works (Cottle, 1998; Anderson, 1997).

Critique of provincialism and European perspective in the theory of second modernity

In his article 'In Search of Second Modernity: Reinterpreting Reflexive Modernization in the Context of Multiple Modernities' Raymond Lee (2008) argues that Beck's notion of a transition from first to second, reflexive modernity is an attempt to explain certain European social changes and developments from the meta-level, and that this notion is founded on the assumption that first, industrial modernity contains – or embodies – the centres of rational control and unambiguous borders. Lee criticizes Beck for 'reinventing' modernity without paying sufficient attention to the changing centres of modernity itself; according to Lee, 'second modernity' must be conceived of and analysed in close connection with the developments taking place in the non-European world, which is exactly what has given rise to the idea of 'multiple modernities'. Lee puts it thus:

> the concept of reflexivity has been directed mainly towards an interpretation of contemporary events in Europe but not specifically towards the link between these events and the advent of modernity in other societies. New regions of modernity do not receive much attention in the theory of second modernity . . . Put another way, is reflexivity exclusively European or a factor of transformation that transcends European boundaries?
>
> (Lee, 2008: 67)

In 2010, the *British Journal of Sociology* published a special issue on Beck's theory of second modernity (vol. 61, no. 3), focusing mainly on this question by Lee. The theme was 'Varieties of second modernity: extra-European and European experiences and perspectives'. Ulrich Beck served as editor, along with Edgar Grande. In Chapter 6, we have covered Beck and Grande's article (Beck and Grande, 2010) printed in this special issue; apart from Beck and Grande's contribution, the special issue is noteworthy for the fact that it contains a number of 'non-European voices' – primarily 'Asian voices' – and their takes on Beck's theory of second modernity. In the special issue, Beck's theories are discussed in relation to case studies with vantage points in Chinese relations (Yan, 2010), Japanese relations (Suzuki, Ito, Ishida, Nihei and Maruyama, 2010) and South Korean relations (Kyung-Sup and Min-Young, 2010). The authors seek, each in their own way, to investigate how Beck's theory of modernity – and his theory of individualization – applies to the actual developments in the authors' own societies.[1]

In their article 'Redefining Second Modernity for East Asia: A Critical Assessment', Han and Shim (2010) set out to investigate what kind of statement the theory of second modernity is able to make about their part of the world. They conclude that second modernity and reflexive modernization – as a tendency and as structurally determined historical transformation – have as much of an influence in East Asia as in the West. They even go so far as to argue that East Asia's highly accelerated economic and industrial growth has led to the new risks having an even larger influence in East Asia than they do in the West. On the other hand, however, Han and Shim also see certain clear limits to the usefulness of the theory of second modernity, as a means of making general statements on a global scale. They point out, for example, that the multitude of East Asian paths that would lead towards individualization would necessarily be radically different from those prevalent in the western world, simply because communities and collectives are perceived and handled in a very different manner in East Asia. The actual paths that will lead to a second modernity will vary greatly from country to country even within East Asia itself.

Another article from the same issue which bears mentioning here is '"Small Change of the Universal": Beyond Modernity?' by Sarat Maharaj (2010). In this article, Maharaj investigates two of Beck's key terms, *everyday cosmopolitanization* (*banal cosmopolitanization*; Beck, 2006) and *methodological cosmopolitanism*. Maharaj is not as optimistic as Beck in his assessment of whether or not 'really-existing cosmopolitanism' (which Beck calls real-cosmopolitanism) can even be properly understood from within the framework of one particular modernity. Maharaj writes that more research is required in order to decide whether or not different variations of second modernity will end up producing or spurring on different (competing) 'cosmopolitan visions' which would lead to friction and potentially 'clashing cosmopolitanisms'.

In his article 'Beck, Asia and Second Modernity', Craig Calhoun (2010) argues that the theory of second modernity is in dire need of more precision and stringency, and that it needs to take *history* into deeper consideration, as part of its diagnosis of contemporary matters. Furthermore, Calhoun acknowledges that the more recent works from Beck and his colleagues have sought – in their studies of second modernity – to eliminate the 'western bias', which has been criticized widely, while striving to making a clear distinction between normative perspectives and empirical analysis. Still, Calhoun sees a clear need for this particular distinction to be further elaborated on, and emphasizes that this will always be the exact challenge for any theoretical framework which subscribes to the normative idea that (empirical) change occur in a clearly delineable way.

Critique of Beck's theory of individualization

As mentioned, several of the contributions in *British Journal of Sociology*'s special issue on 'Varieties of second modernity' seek to add further nuance to Beck's theory of individualization in relation to the real historical development in a number of Asian countries. However, the strongest critique of Beck's theory of individualization in recent years has come from Will Atkinson (Atkinson, 2007a,b). In his article 'Beck, Individualization and the Death of Class: A Critique' Atkinson (2007a) levels fierce criticism at Beck's work, focusing on four general issues.

The *first issue* has to do with what Atkinson calls a very ambivalent and self-contradictory description of what Beck even supposes individualization to be and to mean, since Beck, in Atkinson's view, seems to claim that radicalized individualization is all different kinds of things: every now and then it means dis-embedding without re-embedding, then it is suddenly supposed to mean dis-embedding with new kinds of re-embedding, then it is supposed to be equivalent to atomization, then suddenly the exact *opposite* of atomization, and so forth (Atkinson, 2007a: 356). In addition to this, says Atkinson, Beck is equally unclear in his analysis of how class and class differences are influenced and dissolved by individualization as a structural phenomenon, since Beck wholly fails to provide an explanation for his claim that the distribution of wealth in the risk society will continue to be dictated by current logic of class divisions, while those same divisions will have no influence on the distribution of the new risks, which for some reason is supposed to follow another distribution logic.

The *second issue* concerns Beck's understanding and use of the concept of class, which Atkinson finds very ambiguous. A consequence of this ambiguity, according to Atkinson, is that Beck fails to properly define and conceptualize the kind of class society which he claims would disappear with the coming of the risk society.

The *third issue* is related to Beck's understanding and rejection of class analysis as a discipline based on zombie categories such as the nation state and the nuclear family. Atkinson says that far from everybody is living a cosmopolitan life which is wholly devoid of and emancipated from national processes of stratification.

The *fourth and last issue* has to do with a quite fundamental criticism of Beck's understanding of the driving forces behind radicalized individualization. Atkinson puts it thus: 'Beck fails to acknowledge the ways in which some of the key institutions he heralds as the *slayers* of class may be hindered in their allotted role by the fact that they are *riddled with class processes themselves*' (Atkinson, 2007a: 361).

Atkinson points out, as examples, how the explosion in education must be understood in relation to a series of class-defined factors such as economic, social and cultural resources available to an ever-growing middle class, meaning that individualization and class ought not be treated as mutually exclusive concepts. Atkinson elaborates on these critical reflections in his article 'Beyond False Oppositions: A Reply to Beck' (Atkinson, 2007b), which was meant as a reply to Beck's initial response (Beck, 2007b) to Atkinson's first article. In his article, Atkinson claims that Beck remains unclear and inaccurate in his analysis of radicalized individualization and its consequences; Atkinson takes special issue with the fact that Beck does not spend more energy on delineating the relationship between 'the macro, objective elements of the social cosmos (social structures) and micro or subjective elements (attitudes, behaviours, perceptions)' (Atkinson, 2007b: 709). In addition to this, Atkinson goes on to restate his claim that Beck is operating with a set of class definitions which is lacking in nuance, pointing out that one cannot simply assume that class is synonymous with collectivism and solidarity in a national context, and that Beck's notion of the 'elevator effect' (i.e. a generally rising amount of social mobility) does not in itself suffice to explain why class, as a concept and field of research, should suddenly have become utterly irrelevant. Rather, says Atkinson, Beck's 'explosion of education' is anything but 'class independent'. Finally, Atkinson presents Beck's assumption that classes are able to exist only in so far as they are homogenous – and, further, that Beck is plain wrong in assuming that other researchers in the field of class would automatically be inclined to share Beck's view of classes as homogenous entities.

Ulrich Kohler (2007) – in his contribution to the book *From Origin to Destination: Trends and Mechanisms in Social Stratification Research*, titled 'Containers, Europeanization and Individualization: Empirical Implications of General Descriptions of Society' – sets out to investigate four different models for inequality and whether or not they can be empirically shown to have any grounds in reality. Among other things, Kohler addresses what he calls the 'model of supranational inequality' and 'the individualization model' of inequality. Although Kohler attributes both of these theses largely to Beck, he ultimately concludes that he cannot verify either thesis empirically:

> As it stands, none of the four models of European social inequality can claim to be generally true. This is the general crux of theories that describe societies in broad terms. They are too general to be true in every respect, but they are broad enough that something in them is true anyway.
>
> (Kohler, 2007: 314)

Other criticisms levelled against Beck's theory of individualization have focused on Beck's tendency to overlook – or simply ignore – the contemporary relevance and influence of the so-called zombie categories, including the nation-state, the nuclear family and other primary communities (Adkins, 2002; Skeggs, 2004). Another closely related perspective is the line of criticism that has concerned itself mainly with the claim that Beck overemphasizes the concept of choice biography and thereby ends up turning every single condition of a lived life into a matter of choice – and especially a matter of the possibility of choosing freely and thereby constituting one's own self in an autonomous fashion (Brannen and Nilsen, 2005; McLeod and Yates, 2006; Dawson, 2010: 203).

Dan Woodman illustrates how this has caused a number of theoreticians to claim that 'Beck fails to account for restraints on agency and misses the extent to which inequality remains and opportunities are still profoundly structured' (Woodman, 2009: 244); or, as Dawson puts it, the problem with Beck is his that he prefers 'dis-embedded' individualization over an 'embedded' individualization (Dawson, 2010).

Globalization, cosmopolitanism and politics in second modernity

Luke Martell's main theme in his critical analysis 'Beck's Cosmopolitan Politics' (Martell, 2008) concerns Beck's understanding of politics in what Beck argues is a new real-cosmopolitical reality. In his article, Martell points out that the areas which Beck believes to hold a potential for a new, communal, *cosmopolitan* politics are all areas wherein power, inequality and conflict remain the main, structuring principle. Martell, in other words, does not believe that environmental crises and other (transnational) risks will lead to any sort of recognition of a need for a new, global politics by default. Although he acknowledges that Beck's conflict-oriented perspective may provide local answers to the challenges of globalization, Martell nonetheless scolds Beck for failing to stay sufficiently focused on this same perspective, when the time comes for Beck's analysis of the options and conditions of global politics in general. Beck, says Martell, in failing to sufficiently realize that global problem solving is still performed on a basis of conflicting interests, power and nations, ends up taking a much too optimistic stance:

> What remains is an optimistic picture of communalism in global politics. The national outlook and a role for the state is left out by Beck in a desire to establish a globalist outlook, with the consequence that state power, and interests and ideologies in state politics, are not seen as bases for global politics around which strategies need to be geared.
>
> (Martell, 2008: 142)

Martell does not claim that Beck completely overlooks the states and their inherent power struggles, interests and conflicts that come as part of that package; but Beck, says Martell, uses these factors for different purposes. 'Beck draws attention to conflict, inequality, power and the role of the state in global politics but he does so as a qualification or clarification to a picture of global cosmopolitanism rather than as structuring principles which undermine global cosmopolitanism' (Martell, 2008: 142).

Martell expands his critique of Beck's cosmopolitanism further, in his article 'Global Inequalities, Human Rights and Power: A Critique of Ulrich Beck's Cosmopolitanism' (Martell, 2009). Here, Martell criticizes Beck's promotion of a cosmopolitan approach to global inequality and human rights which, according to Martell, does not provide any kind of new or unique perspective on global inequality. Furthermore, Martell argues that if Beck's thoughts on migration were put into effect (such as a cosmopolitan sharing of jobs) it would ultimately lead to little else than a further bolstering of global inequality, leading to anti-cosmopolitan sentiments. In his article, then, Martell repeats his claim that Beck overlooks structures of inequality, conflict and power, which results in his perspective of 'both/and' in cosmopolitical thought ends up being undermined: 'However a "both/and" view runs the risk of replacing Westernization perspectives with one in which power and inequality is glossed over by an attempt to resurrect understandings of the inputs of non-Western societies' (Martell, 2009: 259). Finally, Martell argues that Beck's suggestions with regard to human rights interventionism are anything but cosmopolitan.

The issue of power and Beck's understanding of power has also been brought up by Matt Dawson, who points out that Beck operates with a lacklustre – incomplete, even – concept of power. The reason for this is that Beck connects individual agency and action with political action through a notion of 'subpolitics', which Dawson finds somewhat fuzzy. This lack of clarity causes Beck to overlook 'the ways in which the differential power of individuals is limited by the structural domination of governments and markets' (Dawson, 2010: 203).

It is this more institutional, critical perspective which Darryl S. L. Jarvis pursues in his article 'Risk, Globalization and the State: A Critical Appraisal of Ulrich Beck and the World Risk Society Thesis' (Jarvis, 2007). Jarvis, in his article, takes special issue with Beck's analyses of the consequences of globalization on both individual risks and the systematic risks of nation-states. Working from more recent, empirical data, Jarvis points out that nation-states throughout recent decades have sought to increase both their tax revenues and their welfare expenses simultaneously. Jarvis sees this as proof that Beck's idea that the states have been somehow 'weakened' (put under pressure by mobile and uprootable corporations and the entailed lowering of taxes), and that individuals have ended up shouldering a larger and larger part of the burden as a consequence, is simply not true. The nation-states, says Jarvis, are still very capable of handling risks and protecting the individual. As an example, he points out the very efficient crisis response mechanisms which, for the last decade, have been handling everything from tsunami catastrophes to mad cow disease epizootics and terrorist attacks. Furthermore, says Jarvis, there is no empirical ground for Beck's thesis about an all-risk individualization fuelled by the precarious nature of work in second modernity. Jarvis concludes that 'these assumptions seem to be less founded on empirical realities and more on a philosophy of fatalism' (Jarvis, 2007: 44).

Furthermore, recent years have seen strong criticism levelled against Beck's cosmopolitan thought, coming from a more theoretically sociological angle, for example Chernilo's article 'Social Theory's Methodological Nationalism' (Chernilo, 2006) and Inglis's article 'Cosmopolitan Sociology and the Classical Canon: Ferdinand Tönnies and the Emergence of Global *Gesellschaft*' (Inglis, 2009). The latter questions the relevancy of the classical sociological theory in relation to the effort towards initiating a new cosmopolitan turn of sociology. According to Inglis, Beck's answer is that classical sociologists are bound to nation-state-centric methods of thought and that because of this their theories can not be of much use for the cosmopolitanization of sociology. Illustrating that this assumption is incorrect, Inglis points out the classical sociologist Ferdinand Tönnies, who, according to Inglis, sketched out exactly the *how* and the *why* of a global kind of *Gesellschaft* he believed was coming. Rather than what Beck seems to believe, says Inglis, Tönnies is an example of the kind of classically sociological forerunner of the current, cosmopolitan trends in sociology which Beck claimed did not exist.

Chernilo's criticism is more specifically aimed against Beck's 'attack' on methodological nationalism, which Chernilo does not believe to be properly defined anywhere by Beck or any other sociologist. Because of this, sociology is left without an answer to the question of how we are supposed to understand the nation-state's history, main features and heritage in relation to modernity. Chernilo ends his article with the conclusion that the reservations and disputes which sociology and social theory hold towards the nation-state are simply reflections of the nation-state's own ambivalent position within modernity: its historical opacity, its sociological lack of clarity and its normative ambiguity (Chernilo, 2006).

A theory under ongoing development

It would not be feasible, here, to attempt to provide an in-depth discussion of all these points of criticism in relation to Beck's work. It bears mentioning, however, that some of the criticism is definitely quite merited – especially the claim that Beck tends to make too broad, generalized claims and that his theory about second modernity, including its subtheories, are based on a much too narrow empirical foundation. Other points of critique seem to be more irrelevant and/or outdated; this is especially the case for those points of critique that direct themselves mainly at Beck's *Risk Society* – first published in Germany in 1986 – and which tend to overlook the further refinements and improvements to the theory proposed by Beck since its publication.

Initially, the theory of second modernity was constructed around certain rigid and oversimplified assumptions, which – although they lent the theory a certain argumentative edge and allowed a good amount of impact – also left the theory empirically vulnerable. Nonetheless, for the last 25 years Beck has been continually working on strengthening and reinforcing his theory of second modernity and he has taken in much of the criticism which has been levelled against it. It is clear that he still perceives the theory of second modernity to be an ongoing work in progress. Throughout the years, Beck has repeatedly sought to reformulate his theories in response to both theoretical and empirical criticism directed against them. A good example of one such reformulation – and improvement – of the theory of second modernity occurs in Beck, Bonß and Lau's 2001 article (English: Beck, Bonß and Lau, 2003). Here, the authors specify exactly how we are supposed to understand and interpret both the *unambiguity* which Beck believes to prevail in first modernity as well as the *plurality* which, in contrast, is characteristic of second modernity. Whereas Beck's theory of second modernity used to assume that – speaking from a *real*-historical perspective – first modernity had been characterized by only one kind of family (the nuclear family), one kind of knowledge (scientific knowledge), one kind of state (the nation state) and so forth, and that a kind of pluralization of these forms was supposed to take place in second modernity, Beck, Bonß and Lau now make theoretical room for the fact that there *also* existed a multitude of forms of family, knowledge and states in first modernity. In other words, they clarify that the unambiguity of first modern institutions is an ambiguity on the level of ideas and mentality. In first modernity, only one kind of family constellation is *acknowledged*, just as there is only one kind of acknowledged state and so on. Although other forms do exist, they are understood exactly as *deviations* from the norm. What happens in second modernity, then, is that this kind of plurality – which has always existed – is simply acknowledged.

In this way Beck manages to specify how we can subject this particular area of his theory of second modernity to empirical scrutiny and testing. We would need to study the wording of laws, acts, ordinances, inheritance acts and the like in order to properly verify or dismiss the claim that we are currently experiencing a general acknowledgement of plurality. We would also need to conduct comparative, historical studies of text material in an attempt to investigate whether a transition from 'one form' of acknowledgement to 'multiple forms' of acknowledgement has indeed taken place. In *World at Risk*, Beck mentions how changes to German family laws provide an empirical example of this kind of transition (Beck, 2009a: 221–223).

Another, more recent example of Beck's ongoing efforts to reformulate his theory of second modernity in response to the criticism directed against it can be found in his reaction to the criticism of Ericson and Doyle (2004). As mentioned in Chapter 2 above, Beck has attempted to use the *insurance principle* to draw a line between the risks of first modernity and those of second modernity, the thesis being that, whereas it was possible to take out an insurance policy against the risks of first modernity, one could not take out any such policies to insure oneself against the new risks of the world risk society (the hazards of radioactive emissions, terror, financial crises, experimentally altered gene modified crops etc.). Beck, in *World at Risk*, puts it thus: 'It [the insurance principle] asserts that the absence of adequate *private* insurance protection is *the* institutional indicator of the transition to the uncontrollable risk society of the second modernity' (Beck, 2009a: 132).

One of the advantages of this thesis, then, is that we can subject it to empirical scrutiny in a manner that does not require of us that we consider specific understandings of risks that may pertain to particular cultures or geographical areas. The goal is simply to investigate *whether* it is possible to insure oneself against a given risk or not, in order to test whether or not a given area has entered the risk society. In this way, Beck provides us with an elegant, institutional borderline between industrial society and the risk society. Ericson and Doyle, however, have shown that this formula for empirical testing does not work. Based on their study of the global insurance industry and its methods for handling risks after 11 September 2001, Ericson and Doyle reach the conclusion that although 'newly discovered catastrophe risks pose unique problems of knowledge and control, insurers do not back off from this "insurance curse" but rather turn threat into opportunity' (Ericson and Doyle, 2004: 168). Rather than simply refusing to insure their clients and customers against terror, the insurance companies seek out new opportunities for cooperation and develop new patterns of reinsurance, making it possible to insure customers and clients against these new risks, which are otherwise quite incalculable.

In *World at Risk*, Beck writes that he appreciates Ericson and Doyle's criticism (Beck, 2009a: 133) and spends 10 pages of his book addressing it. Having acknowledged that his thesis does not hold, in the light of Ericson and Doyle's criticism, he goes on to utilize their argument as a means of reformulating his thesis of insurance. He puts it thus:

> There can be no doubt that the results of this study *refute* the hypothesis that there is a *sharp* line – an either/or relation – between insurable and non-insurable risks. However, the case study *confirms* my thesis insofar as it

proves that the *private* insurance industry runs up against its limits in the case of catastrophes and must rely on *public* co-insurance (i.e. subsidies).

(Beck, 2009a: 134)

He goes on to use Ericson and Doyle's study to reformulate his own work:

> My error is the (paradoxical) result of the quasi-ontological attempt to draw a sharp boundary between either being insured or not being insured, thereby ignoring a central research result in the context of reflexive modernization, namely, that a kind of both/and holds in an increasing number of fields of social action that must be carefully differentiated . . . Applied to the insurance business this means that we must distinguish between the specific forms of 'being both insured and uninsured' and reinterpret the findings of the case study accordingly.

(Beck, 2009a: 136)

This is a good example of Beck's way of using criticism as a means for further development of his theory of second modernity. The theory, in a sense, is slowly and steadily maturing as Beck makes adjustments and reformulations in response to various criticisms. This is also the case, for example, with regard to Beck's view of the nation-state. As we have covered in Chapter 5, Beck's view of the nation-state and its current political options has – empirically speaking – been a somewhat problematic one. However, with the Europe book in particular (Beck and Grande, 2004) many of his problematic assumptions, such as those about the nation state being a *zombie category*, were softened, reformulated and clarified. One last example which bears mentioning, of how the theory of second modernity is still seeing development and refinement, is Beck and Grande's 2010 article, in which Beck admits that his own theory of second modernity so far has tended to function primarily as a description of 'the Western path' and that, as a consequence, it will need to be *de-provincialized and cosmopolitanized* (Beck and Grande, 2010: 420). As we shall see below, this is also an example of how the ongoing refinement and continuous development of the theory is not always a good thing by default.

The devil in the details

All these examples come together to illustrate how the theory of second modernity is still under development. The theory is slowly being opened up to the nuances of reality. Generally speaking, this kind of care and focus on detail is exactly what Beck's theories tend to need. It is only through an increase in focus on the real-historical and theoretical details that the theory of second modernity will be able to see any further, serious development. This part of the job, however, does not seem to hold as much interest for Beck as the work of formulating and reformulating new theory drafts. If we may use a playful image akin to those Beck himself has a proclivity for using, we can compare Beck's approach to – and the developmental history of – the theory of second modernity to the process of washing an old-fashioned hardwood floor: the first step of the process is to pour soapy water across the floor; the second, then, is to carefully clean the floor by scrubbing the individual floor boards and, finally, mopping up leftover water. Ulrich Beck's interest has always seemed to be mostly centred on the first part of the process, on pouring the water out over the floor and theoretical field, and then leaving the job of nitpicking, scrubbing and actual mopping-up to others. Many of the intermediate results in his theories, then, are not provided by Beck but can be found in the works of others – primarily the work of those working on the research project SFB 536 in Munich (see Chapter 1). Wolfgang Bonß, for example, has written an excellent book on risks and the history of risk thought (Bonß, 1995) and Christoph Lau has put in work to clarify the exact kinds of risks Beck is operating with in his theory of the risk society (Lau, 1989). Of course, Beck himself has also worked on refining his theory – not least through his cooperation with Wolfgang Bonß, Christoph Lau, Elisabeth Beck-Gernsheim, Edgar Grande, Boris Holzer and others (e.g. Beck, Bonß and Lau, 2003; Beck and Lau, 2005; Beck and Beck-Gernsheim, 1994; Beck, Holzer and Kieserling, 2001; Beck and Holzer, 2004; Beck and Grande, 2007, 2010). Still, one could well wish that Beck himself had paid a little more attention to this part of the work himself. It seems as if, throughout the last 25 years, he has been in somewhat of a hurry to publish new theory drafts and has occasionally tended to do so without completely working them through and without always taking the consequences of his new adjustments into consideration.

The occasional lack of intermediate, theoretic results and calculations, for example, is exemplified in Beck's way of reactualizing his theory of the risk society after 11 September 2001, in which he puts special emphasis on terrorism as one of the three dimensions of hazard in the world risk society. However, by crediting terrorism with this kind of prevalent place in his theory, Beck ends up breaking with his theory's previous principle of risk categorization. On the one hand, there can of course be little doubt that terrorism shares many traits with other new risks: it has, as much as anything, been made the centre of political and societal action and development in the wake of 11 September 2001. Wars have been fought in Iraq and Afghanistan because of terrorism. Most countries on Earth spend enormous amounts of political, economical and safety-related resources on fighting terrorism. The risk of a terrorist attack is omnipresent and is often used, for both good and evil, as a means for suggesting and implementing political reforms. Furthermore, terrorism poses a real challenge to traditional, private insurance measures.

On the other hand, however, terrorism-as-risk seems to lack a trait which is otherwise characteristic of Beck's new risks: it is quite hard indeed to understand terrorism as something that operates within the same *side effects logic* which has otherwise been the cornerstone of his theory of second modernity (see Chapter 2). It is, in other words, difficult to see terrorism as an *unintended side effect* of industrial modernity. Whereas environmental problems can easily be seen as the unintended side effect of our industrialized way of life, and economical hazards can be interpreted as the unintended side effects of the largely successful implementation of first modernity and its agenda of freedom and liberty – especially private property rights which make it possible for individuals and corporations to transfer capital across international borders – it turns out to be much more difficult to understand terrorism as somehow being the same kind of unintended side effect of first modernity. Only very abstractly can we speak of terrorism as an unintended side effect of first modernity, as Beck does in *World at Risk*:

> The hatred of Western modernity is a product of its *triumph*. Terrorism is the response to the dilemma of those who have long since become part of the West while at the same time being unable to reconcile themselves to the fact that the West is shaping the world according to its image.
>
> (Beck, 2009a: 108)

Unlike financial and economical risks, then, terrorism can be viewed as an unintended side effect of first modernity only in a very abstract way. In his Europe book, Beck himself points out this mismatch between terror and the other two primary dimensions of hazard in the world risk society; but he does not appear to believe it to be much of a theoretical problem (Beck and Grande, 2007: 207). In our view, Beck still has some theoretical work to do to explain why certain risks are (and need to be?) unintended side effects of first modernity, whereas others are not and need not be, in order to qualify as the kind of risk that is constituent of the risk society. When new phenomena that do not exactly fit the criteria of the theory are nonetheless implemented and made part of the theory, they end up causing the theory to lose its coherence and its sense of consequence, putting it in danger of turning into a kind of elastic theory, which can too easily be stretched and manipulated in ways that allow for it to cover most empirical phenomena. We can find another example of this tendency to overstretch the theory, in the newest reformulation of the theory of second modernity, which is delivered to us by Beck and Grande (2010). As we have seen in Chapter 6, Beck seeks to combine an idea about 'multiple modernities' with his own idea about 'discontinuity' in modernity and a transition to a second modernity. This means that his theories about second modernity must now be expanded in a manner that allows for them to cover (at least) four different paths of modernization and their entailing real-historical details and empirical data. Apart from the modernization of western societies, we are now dealing with new types of modernizations, which Beck calls '*compressed*' modernizations (as seen in, for example, China), reactive, enforced modernizations or *post-colonial* modernizations and, finally, the '*failed*' modernizations which never succeeded in establishing the institutions of first modernity or otherwise went wrong during the transition to second modernity.

Future development

The question is whether or not the theory of second modernity can withstand – and is suitable for – being made to stretch ever more thinly over an increasing number of different kinds of modernization (and failed modernization). Can the theory contain such a multitude of different developments? Does it not run the risk of becoming nothing but an empty shell surrounding a series of different developmental tendencies? Should Beck not come to terms with the fact that the theory about second modernity – along with all its subtheories – is exactly a theory which is placed in a western context and that it is primarily of use in illuminating the developments that take place in the western world?

Rather than run the risk of draining the theory of second modernity of its power by spreading it too thinly across an ever-increasing number of phenomena and regions, it might perhaps be beneficial for the theory to seek to *limit* itself to making statements about a smaller number of phenomena and locations, and to focus more on environmental and financial risks and less on terrorism, while preoccupying itself mainly with the western world. Although the theory of second modernity is an interesting suggestion for a contemporary diagnosis of western societies – and although it offers an interesting perspective on the development in other parts of the world – it simply does not function at the same level of depth in its analysis of non-western development. Rather than always and impatiently turning his attention to new theory drafts in an attempt to expand its scope and describe an ever-increasing number of phenomena and geographical areas, the theory would benefit from having Beck spend more energy on thoroughly reviewing and test-ing his current theory about second modernity, including its subtheories. If one seeks to shed light on the development of the entire world, one runs the risk of emptying one's theory of actual content, leaving it to stand as a hollowed-out set piece, wherein the drama of change can be put on as performance. This would be a shame. Although the desire to rid one's theory of methodological nationalism is a very sympathetic desire indeed, there is no shame in having constructed a theory which, although it cannot cover *all* of the development taking place in *all* the world, nicely covers *much* of the development in *one part* of the world, namely the west. This is what Ulrich Beck has proven himself to be capable of, if not more.

Notes

2 Risk society

1 Earthquake Report (http://earthquake-report.com/2011/08/04/japan-tsunami-following-up-the-aftermath-part-16-june/).
2 See IAEA's website on the Fukushima Nuclear Accident (http://www.iaea.org/newscenter/focus/fukushima/) and Wikipedia: 'Fukushima Daiichi nuclear disaster' (http://en.wikipedia.org/wiki/Fukushima_Daiichi_nuclear_disaster).
3 United Nations Environment Program (UNEP) (Ozone Secretariat, http://ozone.unep.org, especially http://ozone.unep.org/new_site/en/montreal_protocol.php).
4 See Lau (1989) for a thorough discussion of these 'new risks'.
5 This corresponds with Nassehi's view that Beck 'assumes that the risks have a certain extent of *objective* reality' (Nassehi, 2000: 255). As we have just seen, there is reason to believe that Beck would not directly oppose this claim. On the other hand, however, other discussions of Beck disagree with this view, for example Rasborg's treatment of the 'ontological status' of risks in Beck's works (Rasborg, 2001).
6 http://earthquake-report.com/
7 That is a natural disaster such as the one that hit Japan in 2011.
8 This quote as it occurs here is our own translation, as it does not appear in the English edition of *Risk Society* (Beck, 1992). It is taken from the introductory chapter 'Aus gegebenem Anlaß', pp. 7–11 in the German original.

3 The theory of second modernity

1 Lyotard is not at all the first to discuss the concept of postmodernity. The history of the term is a long one. In 1917, Rudolf Pannwitz used it as a philosophically charged cultural term which drew much of its inspiration from Nietzsche (Wikipedia, 2011). It was not until Lyotard's work, however, that the term became widely used.
2 There is a distinct difference between postmodernity as an ideal to strive for – as Bauman does – and the use of *postmodern* as a diagnostic term, which is how Lyotard uses it.
3 The other institutional dimensions which Giddens refers to are (1) capitalism, (2) military force/monopoly of force and (3) surveillance.
4 Beck and colleagues take care to make us aware that the list is not meant to be an exhaustive one; it merely provides the most significant premises.
5 See for example Beck (1994a,b, 2009a: ch. 12); Beck, Bonß and Lau (2001); Beck and Holzer (2004); Beck and Lau (2005).
6 In addition to this kind of reflexivity, Giddens speaks of two other dynamics, which he calls (1) the separation of time and space and (2) understanding social practices (Giddens, 1990). For a thorough introduction to Giddens's works, see Kaspersen (2000).

7 For a discussion between Beck and Giddens on how to understand reflexive modernity, see Beck, Giddens and Lash (1994).

4 Individualization

1 Translated from Beck's *Risikogesellschaft* (1986); the corresponding passage is
   omitted in Mark Ritter's translated edition (1992).
2 Cf. Sartre's 'Existentialism Is a Humanism', wherein he argues that we are *condemned to be free* (Sartre, [1946] 1975).
3 The 'kinship of individualization theories' among Simmel, Elias and Beck has been
   commented on previously, in Nicola Ebers's *Individualisierung – Georg Simmel
   – Norbert Elias – Ulrich Beck* (Ebers, 1995). Ebers, like Schroer, points out clear
   similarities in the three theoreticians' understanding of certain aspects of individualization, and that they all share a common sense of ambivalence towards the process
   itself.
4 However, as Beck himself points out, it is important that we remember that the conditions that, according to Beck, trigger a radicalized individualization came into being
   only at a relatively late stage in the welfare state's development (Beck, 2009a: 230).

5 Globalization and cosmopolitanism

1 David Held, a professor of political science at the LSE, is one of the authors of the
   expansive *Global Transformations: Politics, Economy and Culture* (Held, McGrew,
   Goldblatt and Perraton, [1999] 2000), which was first published in 1999 and has
   since been printed in several revised, updated editions. *Global Transformations* operates with a multidimensional concept of globalization, spanning politics, organized
   violence, trade and commerce, the financial market, corporations and production
   networks, migration and culture as well as the environment and pollution, and the
   authors conduct empirical, as well as historical, research into the global effects and
   reach of each particular dimension.
2 In his political-philosophical main work *Leviathan*, from 1651, Thomas Hobbes
   warns us – speaking with a clear retrospective eye to the English civil wars – of the
   dangers of reverting our society to a natural state of peril in which it is up to every
   man to fend for himself. To Hobbes, the primary task of any society is to limit such
   conflicts and main basic *security* for its individual citizens. Society, he argues, should
   be based on a social contract in which the citizens of a society voluntarily entrust
   their liberty and freedom to the sovereign, who in turn is then obligated to secure
   the citizens against random attacks, intrusions and violence from other members of
   society (Hobbes, [1651] 1985).

6 Sociology, science and politics in second modernity

1 The most widely used definition of politics is probably the American political scientist David Easton's system-theoretical definition from his book *The Political System*.
   Here, Easton defines politics as 'the authoritative allocation of values for a society'
   (Easton, 1953: 146).
2 Kant's full definition of enlightenment is:

   Enlightenment is the human being's emergence from his self-incurred immaturity. Immaturity is the inability to use one's own understanding [= reason] without
   the guidance of another. This immaturity is self-incurred if its cause is not lack of
   understanding, but lack of resolution and courage to use it without the guidance
   of another.

   (Kant, [1784] 1991: 54)

3 This distinction is made in the foreword of the German original – as well as the Danish translation – of *Risk Society/Risikogesellschaft*, which does not occur in the 1992 English translation.

4 From the foreword of the German original of *Risk Society/Risikogesellschaft*, which does not occur in the 1992 English translation.

5 Beck also, during this period, expects much to come from political consumers (see, for example, Beck, 2005).

7 The third industrial revolution

1 Among those to have used the term *third industrial revolution* are Joseph Finkelstein (1992), Jeremy Greenwood (1997) and Harry Stine (1975), who was in all probability the first to do so.

2 CNN, 18 May 2011 (http://edition.cnn.com/2011/WORLD/europe/05/18/spain.protests/index.html).

3 http://generation-precaire.org/. This is also the main topic of the French sociologists Anne and Martine Rambach's book *Les nouveaus intellos précaires* (Rambach and Rambach, 2009).

4 Beck talks about a 'capitalism without work' (Beck, 2000a: 38) which is now showing us the paradoxical logics at play in a standard of work society. It is a paradox wherein – on the one hand – we insist on turning wage labour into the central cog in the machinery of society while, on the other hand and in the name of productivity, we constantly focus on rationalizing and abolishing the need for human labour by introducing more and more efficient means (e.g. robotics, outsourcing) into our production lines.

5 Mark Ritter's translation (Beck, 1992) does not include the chapter 'Geisterbahnhof: Ausbildung ohne Beschäftigung' (pp. 237–249) from which the passage is quoted.

6 For example, Beck called for action from German political parties during the 2005 parliamentary election in Germany (Beck, 2005).

7 Beck views civil labour as an entity which has a real, mobilizing and integrating function in society; a social phenomenon which may well help rally the public sector and political parties, essentially by supplying society with a kind of outlet for 'creative disobedience' (Beck, 2002c: 130).

8 http://p2pfoundation.net/15M_Movement_-_Spain

9 In Chapters 5 and 6, we took a closer look at Beck's current efforts towards doing away with what he has dubbed *zombie sciences* and *zombie categories*: antiquated theory and thoughts that keep us from properly understanding reality as it is. His ambitions to modernize sociology, however, are not new. They have been a recurrent part of his work since the mid 1970s. Just as, today, Beck is harshly criticized by colleagues for accusing them of conducting zombie science, he was criticized in the 1970s for approaching work sociology from the perspective of the individual. Especially harsh was the criticism from the 'programme C' researchers, who accused the individualized perspective of being both irrelevant and ideologically charged.

10 Beck's earliest work is largely preoccupied with the debate and political climate surrounding education in Germany at the time, addressing questions in relation to the reconfiguration of the educational sector and the handling of inequalities in the labour market, such as rising unemployment and lack of apprenticeships (Beck, Brater and Wegener, 1979a; Beck and Brater, 1978a).

11 Beck and colleagues did conduct a series of empirical studies in order to verify this theory. These studies were focused mainly on German youths and their acceptance or non-acceptance and decision-making process in deciding whether or not to agree to undertake certain apprenticeships, during a period when those were in short supply (Beck, Brater and Wegener, 1979b). In this sense, Beck conducted much more empirically based research during his early academic years than he does today.

8 Critique of Ulrich Beck's sociology

  1 It should also be noted that in recent years Beck's theory of second modernity has been used as a theoretical starting point and inspiration for studies of equality and democracy (Hier, 2008; Sandell and Mulinari, 2006).

Literature

Adam, B. and van Loon, J. (2000) 'Repositioning Risk: The Challenge for Social Theory', in Adam, B., Beck, U. and van Loon, J. (eds.), *The Risk Society and Beyond*. London: Sage.

Adkins, L. (2002) *Revisions: Gender and Sexuality in Late Modernity*. Buckingham: Open University Press.

Aharoni, Y. (1981) *The No-Risk Society*. Chatham, NJ: Chatham House Publishers.

Albrow, M. (1996) *The Global Age*. Stanford, CA: Stanford University Press.

Alexander, J. and Smith, P. (1996) 'Social Science and Discourse: Risk Society as Mythic Discourse', *Zeitschrift für Soziologie*, vol. 25, no. 4, pp. 251–262.

Anderson, A. (1997) *Media, Culture and the Environment*. London: UCL Press.

Appadurai, A. (1991) 'Global Ethnoscapes: Notes and Queries for a Transnational Anthropology', in Fox, R. G. (ed.), *Recapturing Anthropology: Working in the Present*. Santa Fe, NM: School of American Research Press.

Atkinson, W. (2007a) 'Beck, Individualization and the Death of Class: A Critique', *British Journal of Sociology*, vol. 58, no. 3, pp. 349–366.

Atkinson, W. (2007b) 'Beyond False Oppositions: A Reply to Beck', *British Journal of Sociology*, vol. 58, no. 4, pp. 707–715.

Bauman, Z. (1989) *Modernity and the Holocaust*. Ithaca, NY: Cornell University Press.

Bauman, Z. (1997) *Postmodernity and Its Discontents*. Cambridge: Polity Press.

Bauman, Z. (1998a) *Globalization: The Human Consequences*. New York: Columbia University.

Bauman, Z. (1998b) *Work, Consumerism and the New Poor*. Philadelphia: Open University Press.

Bauman, Z. (2000) *Liquid Modernity*. Cambridge: Polity Press.

Bauman, Z. (2001a) *The Individualized Society*. London: Polity Press.

Bauman, Z. (2001b) *Community: Seeking Safety in an Insecure World*. Cambridge: Polity.

Bauman, Z. (2002) *Society under Siege*. Cambridge: Polity Press.

Bauman, Z. ([1998] 2003) *Globalisering: De menneskelige konsekvenser*. Copenhagen: Hans Reitzels Forlag.

Beck, U. (1982a) 'Folgeprobleme der Modernisierung und die Stellung der Soziologie in der Praxis', in Beck, U. (ed.), *Soziologie und Praxis: Erfahrungen, Konflikte, Perspektiven*. Göttingen: Otto Schwartz & Co.

Beck, U. (1982b) 'Das Krisenbewusstsein in der Arbeitsgesellschaft', *Österreichische Zeitschrift für Soziologie*, vol. 7, no. 3–4, pp. 39–49.

Beck, U. (1983) 'Jenseits von Stand und Klasse?', in Kreckel, R. (ed.), *Soziale Ungleichheiten: Sozialen Welt*. Göttingen: Otto Schwartz & Co.

Beck, U. (1986) *Risikogesellschaft: Auf dem Weg in eine andere Moderne*. Frankfurt am Main: Suhrkamp.

Beck, U. (1988) *Gegengifte: Die organisierte Unverantwortlichkeit*. Frankfurt am Main: Suhrkamp.

Beck, U. (1991a) 'Überlebensfrage, Sozialstruktur und ökologische Aufklärung', in Beck, U. (ed.), *Politik in der Risikogesellschaft*. Frankfurt am Main: Suhrkamp.

Beck, U. ([1986] 1991b) 'Der anthropologische Schock: Tschernobyl und die konturen der Risikogesellschaft', in Beck, U. (ed.), *Politik in der Risikogesellschaft: Essays und Analysen*. Frankfurt am Main: Suhrkamp.

Beck, U. (1992) *Risk Society: Towards a New Modernity*. London: Sage Publications.

Beck, U. (1994a) 'The Reinvention of Politics: Towards a Theory of Reflexive Modernization', in Beck, U., Giddens, A. and Lash, S. (eds.), *Reflexive Modernization: Politics, Tradition and Aesthetics in the Modern Social Order*. Cambridge: Polity Press.

Beck, U. (1994b) 'Self-Dissolution and Self-Endangerment of Industrial Society: What Does This Mean?', in Beck, U., Giddens, A. and Lash, S. (eds.), *Reflexive Modernization: Politics, Tradition and Aesthetics in the Modern Social Order*. Cambridge: Polity Press.

Beck, U. (1995a) *Ecological Politics in an Age of Risk*. Cambridge: Polity Press.

Beck, U. (1995b) 'Die "Individualisierungsdebatte"', in Schäfers, B. (ed.), *Soziologie in Deutschland: Entwicklungen, Institutionalisierung und Berufsfelder Theoretische Kontroversen*. Opladen: Leske + Budrich.

Beck, U. (1996a) 'World Risk Society as Cosmopolitan Society? Ecological Questions in a Framework of Manufactured Uncertainties', *Theory, Culture & Society*, vol. 13, no. 4, pp. 1–32.

Beck, U. (1996b) 'Was halt hochindividualisierte Gesellschaften zusammen?', *Mittelweg 36*, vol. 5, no. 1, pp. 33–48.

Beck, U. (1997a) *The Reinvention of Politics: Rethinking Modernity in the Global Social Order*. Cambridge: Polity Press.

Beck, U. (1997b) *Weltrisikogesellschaft, Weltöffentlichkeit und globale Subpolitik*. Vienna: Picus Verlag.

Beck, U. (1998a) *Democracy without Enemies*. Cambridge: Polity Press.

Beck, U. (1998b) *Was ist Globalisierung?* Frankfurt am Main: Suhrkamp.

Beck, U. (2000a) *The Brave New World of Work*. Cambridge: Polity Press.

Beck, U. (2000b) *What Is Globalization?* Cambridge: Polity Press.

Beck, U. (2000c) 'The Cosmopolitan Perspective: Sociology of the Second Age of Modernity', *British Journal of Sociology*, vol. 51, no. 1, pp. 79–105.

Beck, U. (2000d) 'Wohin führt der Weg, der mit dem Ende der Vollbeschäftigungsgesellschaft beginnt?', in Beck, U. and Bonß, W. (eds.), *Die Zukunft von Arbeit und Demokratie*. Frankfurt am Main: Suhrkamp Verlag.

Beck, U. (2000e) 'Die Seele der Demokratie: Bezahlte Bürgerarbeit', in Beck, U. and Bonß, W. (eds.), *Die Zukunft von Arbeit und Demokratie*. Frankfurt am Main: Suhrkamp Verlag.

Beck, U. (2001) *World Risk Society*. Cambridge: Polity Press.

Beck, U. (2002a) *Samtaler med Ulrich Beck: Frihed eller kapitalisme*. Copenhagen: Hans Reitzels Forlag.

Beck, U. (2002b) 'The Terrorist Threat: World Risk Society Revisited', *Theory, Culture & Society*, vol. 19, no. 4, pp. 39–55.

Beck, U. (2002c) *Fagre nye arbejdsverden*. Copenhagen: Hans Reitzels Forlag.

Beck, U. (2003a) *Conversations with Ulrich Beck*. Cambridge: Polity Press.

Beck, U. (2003b) 'The Silence of Words: On Terror and War', *Security Dialogue*, vol. 34, no. 3, pp. 255–267.

Beck, U. (2004) *Der kosmopolitische Blick oder: Krieg ist Frieden.* Frankfurt am Main: Suhrkamp.

Beck, U. (2005) *Power in the Global Age.* Cambridge: Polity Press.

Beck, U. (2006) *The Cosmopolitan Vision.* Cambridge: Polity Press.

Beck, U. (2007a) 'Tragische Individualisierung', *Blätter für deutsche und Internationale Politik*, vol. 5, pp. 577–584.

Beck, U. (2007b) 'Beyond Class and Nation: Reframing Social Inequalities in a Globalizing World', *British Journal of Sociology*, vol. 58, no. 4, pp. 679–705.

Beck, U. (2009a) *World at Risk.* Cambridge: Polity Press.

Beck, U. (2009b) 'Jenseits von Stand und Klasse? Soziale Ungleichheiten, gesellschaftliche Individualisierungsprozesse und die Entstehung neuer sozialer Formationen und Identitäten', in Solga, H., Powell, J. and Berger, P. A. (eds.), *Soziale Ungleichheit: Klassische Texte zur Sozialstrukturanalyse.* Frankfurt: Campus Verlag.

Beck, U. (2010) 'Remapping Social Inequalities in an Age of Climate Change: For a Cosmopolitan Renewal of Sociology', *Global Networks*, vol. 10, no. 2, pp. 165–181.

Beck, U. and Beck-Gernsheim, E. (1993) 'Nicht Autonomie, sondern Bastelbiographie', *Zeitschrift für Soziologie*, vol. 22, no. 3, pp. 178–187.

Beck, U. and Beck-Gernsheim, E. (1994) *Riskante Freiheiten: Individualisierung in modernen Gesellschaften.* Frankfurt am Main: Suhrkamp.

Beck, U. and Beck-Gernsheim, E. ([1990] 1995) *The Normal Chaos of Love.* Cambridge: Polity Press.

Beck, U. and Beck-Gernsheim, E. (2002a) *Individualization: Institutionalized Individualism and Its Social and Political Consequences.* London: Sage.

Beck, U. and Beck-Gernsheim, E. (2002b) 'Individualisering i moderne samfund: En subjektorienteret sociologis perspektiver kontroverser', *Slagmark: Tidsskrift for idéhistorie*, no. 34, pp. 13–39.

Beck, U. and Beck-Gernsheim, E. (2007a) 'Generation global und die Falle des methodologischen Nationalismus: Für eine kosmopolitische Wende in der Jugend- und Generationssoziologie', in Villányi, D., Witte, M. D. and Sander, U. (eds.), *Globale Jugend und Jugendkulturen: Aufwachsen im Zeitalter der Globalisierung.* Weinheim: Juventa Verlag.

Beck, U. and Beck-Gernsheim, E. (2007b) 'Generation Global', in Beck, U. (ed.), *Generation Global: Ein Crashkurs.* Frankfurt am Main: Suhrkamp.

Beck, U. and Beck-Gernsheim, E. (2010) 'Passage to Hope: Marriage, and the Need for a Cosmopolitan Turn in Family Research', *Journal of Family Theory & Review*, vol. 2, no. 4, pp. 401–414.

Beck, U., Bolte, K. M. and Brater, M. (1978) 'Qualitative Veränderung der Berufsstruktur als Voraussetzung expansiver Bildungspolitik', *Beiträge zur Arbeitsmarkt- und Berufsforschung*, vol. 30, no. 2, pp. 21–52.

Beck, U. and Bonß, W. (1984) 'Soziologie und Modernisering: Zur Ortsbestimmung der Verwendungsforschung', *Soziale Welt*, vol. 35, no. 4, pp. 381–407.

Beck, U., Bonß, W. and Lau, C. (2001) 'Theorie reflexiver Modernisierung: Fragestellungen, Hypothesen, Forschungsprogramme', in Beck, U. and Bonß, W. (eds.), *Die Modernisierung der Moderne.* Frankfurt am Main: Suhrkamp.

Beck, U., Bonß, W. and Lau, C. (2003) 'The Theory of Reflexive Modernization: Problematic, Hypotheses and Research Programme', *Theory, Culture & Society*, vol. 20, no. 2, pp. 1–33.

Beck, U. and Brater, M. (1976) 'Grenzen abstrakter Arbeit', *Leviathan: Zeitschrift für Sozialwissenschaft*, vol. 4, no. 1, pp. 178–215.

Beck, U. and Brater, M. (1977a) 'Vorwort' and 'Berufliche Arbeitsteilung und Soziale Ungleichheit: Konzeption einer subjektbezogenen Theorie der Berufe', in Beck, U. and Brater, M. (ed.), *Die soziale Konstitution der Berufe, vol. 2*. Frankfurt: aspekte Verlag.

Beck, U. and Brater, M. (1977b) 'Vorwort' and 'Problemstellungen und Ansatzpunkte einer subjektbezogenen Theorie der Berufe', in Beck, U. and Brater, M. (ed.), *Die soziale Konstitution der Berufe, vol. 1*. Frankfurt: aspekte Verlag.

Beck, U. and Brater, M. (1978a) *Berufliche Arbeitsteilung und soziale Ungleichheit*. Frankfurt: Campus Verlag.

Beck, U. and Brater, M. (1978b) 'Berufliche Qualifikationsstrukturen als Medien der Verteilung und Legitimation sozialer Chancen', in Martin, K. (ed.), *Materialien aus der soziologischen Forschung: Verhandlungen des 18. Deutschen Soziologentages vom 28.9. bis 1.10.1976 in Bielefeld*. Darmstadt: Luchterhand.

Beck, U. and Brater, M. (1982) 'Berufe als Organisationsformen menschlichen Arbeitsvermögens', in Littek, W., Rammert, W. and Wachtler, G. (ed.), *Einführung in die Arbeits- und Industriesoziologie* (2nd edn). Frankfurt: Campus Verlag.

Beck, U., Brater, M. and Tramsen, E. (1976a) 'Beruf, Herrschaft und Identität: Ein subjektbezogener Ansatz zum Verhältnis von Bildung und Produktion. Teil I: Die Soziale Konstitution der Berufe', *Soziale Welt*, vol. 27, no. 1, pp. 8–44.

Beck, U., Brater, M. and Tramsen, E. (1976b) 'Beruf, Herrschaft und Identität: Ein subjektbezogener Ansatz zum Verhältnis von Bildung und Produktion. Teil II: Kritik des Berufs', *Soziale Welt*, vol. 27, no. 2, pp. 180–205.

Beck, U., Brater, M. and Wegener, B. (1979a) *Berufswahl und Berufszuweisung*. Frankfurt: Campus Verlag.

Beck, U., Brater, M. and Wegener, B. (1979b) 'Soziale Grenzen beruflicher Flexibilität: Ergebnisse einer empirischen Untersuchung über Probleme der Berufswahl unter Bedingungen knapper Lehrstellen', *Mitteilungen aus der Arbeitsmarkt- und Berufsforschung*, vol. 12, no. 4, pp. 584–593.

Beck, U., Giddens, A. and Lash, S. (1994) *Reflexive Modernization: Politics, Tradition, and Aesthetics in the Modern Social Order*. Cambridge: Polity Press.

Beck, U. and Grande, E. (2004) *Das kosmopolitische Europa: Gesellschaft und Politik in der Zweiten Moderne*. Frankfurt am Main: Suhrkamp.

Beck, U. and Grande, E. (2007) *Cosmopolitan Europe*. Cambridge: Polity Press.

Beck, U. and Grande, E. (2010) 'Varieties of Second Modernity: The Cosmopolitan Turn in Social and Political Theory and Research', *British Journal of Sociology*, vol. 61, no. 3, pp. 409–443.

Beck, U. and Holzer, B. (2004) 'Reflexivität und Reflexion', in Beck, U. and Lau, C. (eds.), *Entgrenzung und Entscheidung*. Frankfurt am Main: Suhrkamp.

Beck, U., Holzer, B. and Kieserling, A. (2001) 'Nebenfolgen als Problem soziologischer Theoriebildung', in Beck, U. and Bonß, W. (eds.), *Die Modernisierung der Moderne*. Frankfurt am Main: Suhrkamp.

Beck, U., Hörning, K. H. and Thomssen, W. (1980) 'Einleitung und Überblick', in Beck, U., Hörning, K. H. and Thomssen, W. (eds.), *Bildungsexpansion und betriebliche Beschäftigungspolitik*. Frankfurt: Campus Verlag.

Beck, U. and Lau, C. (2005) 'Second Modernity as a Research Agenda: Theoretical and Empirical Explorations in the "Meta-change" of Modern Society', *British Journal of Sociology*, vol. 56, no. 4, pp. 525–557.

Beck, U., Levy, D. and Sznaider, N. (2004) 'Erinnerung und Vergebung in der Zweiten Moderne', in Beck, U. and Lau, C. (eds.), *Entgrenzung und Entscheidung*. Frankfurt am Main: Suhrkamp.

Beck, U. and Zeller, E. (1980) 'Berufskonstruktionen als Medien der Vermittlung von Bildung und Beschäftigung: Untersucht am Beispiel der Entstehung und Schneidung der Medizinisch-Technischen Dienstleistungsberufe', in Beck, U., Hörning, K. H. and Thomssen, W. (eds.), *Bildungsexpansion und betriebliche Beschäftigungspolitik*. Frankfurt: Campus Verlag.

Bell, D. (1973) *The Coming of Post-Industrial Society*. New York: Basic Books.

Bell, D. (1987) 'Informationssamfundet', in Institutionen Sociologi (ed.), *Informationssamfundet*. Copenhagen: Sociologisk Institut.

Benhabib, S. and Cornell, D. (1987) *Feminism as Critique: Essays on the Politics of Gender in Late-Capitalist Societies*. London: Polity Press.

Bolte, K. M. (1978) 'Vorbemerkung', in Beck, U. and Brater, M. (eds.), *Berufliche Arbeitsteilung und soziale Ungleichheit*. Frankfurt: Campus.

Bonß, W. (1995) *Vom Risiko: Unsicherheit und Ungewißheit in der Moderne*. Hamburg: Hamburger Edition.

Bonß, W. (2000) 'Was wird aus der Erwerbsgesellschaft?', in Beck, U. and Bonß, W. (eds.), *Die Zukunft von Arbeit und Demokratie*. Frankfurt am Main: Suhrkamp.

Bovenkerk, B. (2003) 'Is Smog Democratic? Environmental Justice in the Risk Society', *Melbourne Journal of Politics*, vol. 29, pp. 24–38.

Brannen, J. and Nilsen, A. (2005) 'Individualization, Choice and Structure: A Discussion of Current Trends in Sociological Analysis', *Sociological Review*, vol. 53, no. 3, pp. 412–428.

Bronner, S. E. (1995) 'Ecology, Politics and Risk: The Social Theory of Ulrich Beck', *Capitalism, Nature, Socialism: A Journal of Socialist Ecology*, vol. 6, no. 1, pp. 67–86.

Calhoun, C. (2010) 'Beck, Asia and Second Modernity', *British Journal of Sociology*, vol. 61, no. 3, pp. 597–619.

Campbell, S. and Currie, G. (2006) 'Against Beck: In Defence of Risk Analysis', *Philosophy of the Social Sciences*, vol. 36, no. 2, pp. 149–172.

Caplan, P. (2000) *Risk Revisited*. London: Pluto Press.

Castells, M. (1996) *The Rise of the Network Society*. Oxford: Blackwell.

Chernilo, D. (2006) 'Social Theory's Methodological Nationalism: Myth and Reality', *European Journal of Social Theory*, vol. 9, no. 1, pp. 5–22.

Chernobyl Forum: 2003–2005 (2006) 'Chernobyl's Legacy: Health, Environmental and Socio-Economic Impacts and Recommendations to the Governments of Belarus, the Russian Federation and Ukraine', second revised version, http://www.iaea.org/Publications/Booklets/Chernobyl/chernobyl.pdf

Cottle, S. (1998) 'Ulrich Beck, Risk Society and the Media', *European Journal of Communications*, vol. 13, no. 1, pp. 5–32.

Culpitt, I. (1999) *Social Policy and Risk*. London: Sage.

Dawson, M. (2010) 'Bauman, Beck, Giddens and Our Understanding of Politics in Late Modernity', *Journal of Power*, vol. 3., no. 2, pp. 189–207.

Dickens, P. (1996) *Reconstructing Nature: Alienation, Emancipation and the Division of Labour*. London: Routledge.

Dingwall, R. (1999) '"Risk Society": The Cult of Theory and the Millennium?', *Social Policy & Administration*, vol. 33, no. 4, pp. 474–491.

DMI (2003) 'Solpåvirkning', Danmarks Meteorologiske Institut, http://www.dmi.dk/dmi/index/viden/solpaavirkning.htm

DMI (2009) 'Drivhuseffekten', Danmarks Meteorologiske Institut, http://www.dmi.dk/dmi/index/klima/drivhuseffekten_2008.htm

Douglas, M. and Wildavsky, A. (1982) *Risk and Culture*. Berkeley: University of California Press.

Dovring, F. and Dovring, K. (1971) *The Optional Society*. The Hague: Martinus Nijhoff.

Dryzek, J. (1995) 'Toward an Ecological Modernity', *Contemporary Sociology: A Journal of Reviews*, vol. 28, pp. 231–242.

Dumazedier, J. (1962) *Sociology of Leisure*. Amsterdam: Elsevier.

Durkheim, É. ([1898] 1969) 'Individualism and the Intellectuals', *Political Studies*, vol. 17, pp. 14–30.

Durkheim, É. ([1897] 1970) *Suicide: A Study in Sociology*. London: Routledge.

Durkheim, É. ([1893] 1997) *The Division of Labor in Society*. London: Free Press.

Durkheim, É. ([1893] 2000) *Om den sociale arbejdsdeling*. Copenhagen: Hans Reitzels Forlag.

Easton, D. (1953) *The Political System: An Inquiry into the State of Political Science*. New York: Alfred A. Knopf.

Ebers, N. (1995) *Individualisierung: Georg Simmel, Norbert Elias, Ulrich Beck*. Würzburg: Königshausen & Neumann.

Elias, N. (1970) *Was ist Soziologie?* Munich: Juventa.

Elias, N. (1978) *What Is Sociology?* London: Hutchinson.

Elias, N. (1991) *Die Gesellschaft der Individuen*. Frankfurt am Main: Suhrkamp.

Elias, N. (1991) *The Society of Individuals*. Oxford: Blackwell.

Elliott, A. (2002) 'Beck's Sociology of Risk: A Critical Assessment', *Sociology*, vol. 36, no. 2, pp. 293–315.

Engel, U. and Strasser, H. (1998) 'Notes on the Discipline', *Canadian Journal of Sociology*, vol. 23, no. 1, pp. 91–103.

Ericson, R. V. and Doyle, A. (2004) 'Catastrophe Risk, Insurance and Terrorism', *Economy and Society*, vol. 33, no. 2, pp. 135–173.

Ewald, F. (1991) 'Die Versicherungs-Gesellschaft', in Beck, U. (ed.), *Politik in der Risikogesellschaft*. Frankfurt am Main: Suhrkamp.

Finkelstein, J. (1992) *The American Economy: From the Great Crash to the Third Industrial Revolution*. New York: Harlan Davidson.

Ford, M. (2010) 'What if There's No Fix for High Unemployment?', *CNN Money*, http://money.cnn.com/2010/06/10/news/economy/unemployment_layoffs_structural.fortune/

Furedi, F. (2002) *Culture of Fear: Risk Taking and the Morality of Low Expectation*. London: Continuum.

Galbraith, J. K. (1958) *The Affluent Society*. New York: Houghton Mifflin Company.

Galbraith, J. K. (1967) *The New Industrial State*. Princeton, NJ: Princeton University Press.

Giddens, A. (1990) *The Consequences of Modernity*. Cambridge: Polity Press.

Giddens, A. (1991) *Modernity and Self-identity: Self and Society in the Late Modern Age*. Stanford, CA: Stanford University Press.

Giddens, A. (1994a) 'Living in a Post-Traditional Society', in Beck, U., Giddens, A. and Lash, S., *Reflexive Modernization: Politics, Tradition, and Aesthetics in the Modern Social Order*. Cambridge: Polity Press.

Giddens, A. (1994b) *Beyond Left and Right: the Future of Radical Politics*. Cambridge: Polity Press.

Giddens, A. (1998) 'Risk Society: The Context of British Politics', in Franklin, J. (ed.), *The Politics of Risk Society*. Cambridge: Polity Press.

Gilroy, P. (1993) *The Black Atlantic: Modernity and Double-Consciousness*. Cambridge: Harvard University Press.

Goldblatt, D. (1995) *Social Theory and the Environment*. Cambridge: Polity Press.

Goldthorpe, J. H. (2002) 'Globalisation and Social Class', *West European Politics*, vol. 25, no. 3, pp. 1–28.

Gorz, A. (1983) *Paradisets veje: Kapitalismens dødskamp.* Viborg: Politisk Revy.

Gorz, A. (1989) *Kritik der ökonomischen Vernunft: Sinnfragen am Ende der Arbeitsgesellschaft.* Berlin: Rotbuch Verlag.

Greenwood, J. (1997) *The Third Industrial Revolution: Technology, Productivity, and Income Inequality.* Washington, DC: AEI Press.

Habermas, J. ([1980] 1981) 'Modernity versus Postmodernity', *New German Critique*, vol. 22, pp. 33–45.

Habermas, J. and 18 other authors (2011) 'The EU Needs Leadership to Tackle This Crisis, Not Repeated Doses of Austerity', *The Guardian*, 22 June, http://www.guardian.co.uk/commentisfree/2011/jun/22/eu-leadership-tackle-crisis-austerity

Han, S.-J. and Shim, Y.-H. (2010) 'Redefining Second Modernity for East Asia: A Critical Assessment', *British Journal of Sociology*, vol. 61, no. 3, pp. 465–488.

Hanlon, G. (2010) 'Knowledge, Risk and Beck: Misconceptions of Expertise and Risk', *Critical Perspectives on Accounting*, vol. 10, pp. 211–220.

Hansen, N. G. (1990) 'Individualitetens Metafysik hos Georg Simmel', *Slagmark: Tidsskrift for Idéhistorie*, vol. 15, pp. 26–39.

Hardt, M. and Negri, A. (2000) *Empire.* Cambridge, MA: Harvard University Press.

Hauxner, K. (1999) 'Borgerarbejde under kapitalisme', interview with Ulrich Beck, *Djøfbladet*, no. 39.

Hegel, G. W. F. ([1831] 1976) *Vorlesungen über die Philosophie der Geschichte.* Frankfurt am Main: Suhrkamp.

Held, D., McGrew, A., Goldblatt, D. and Perraton, J. ([1999] 2000) *Global Transformations: Politics, Economy and Culture.* London: Polity Press.

Heng, Y.-K. (2006) 'The "Transformation of War" Debate: Through the Looking Glass of Ulrich Beck's World Risk Society', *International Relations*, vol. 20, no. 1, pp. 69–91.

Hier, S. P. (2008) 'Transformative Democracy in the Age of Second Modernity: Cosmopolitanization, Communicative Agency and the Reflexive Subject', *New Media & Society*, vol. 10, pp. 27–44.

Hinchcliffe, S. (2000) 'Living with Risk: The Unnatural Geography of Environmental Crises', in Hinchcliffe, S. and Woodward, K. (eds.), *The Natural and the Social: Uncertainty, Risk, Change.* London: Routledge.

Hirschman, A. (1970) *Exit, Voice, and Loyalty: Responses to Declines in Firms, Organizations, and States.* Cambridge, MA: Harvard University Press.

Hobbes, T. ([1651] 1985) *Leviathan.* London: Penguin.

Holzer, B. and Sørensen, M. P. (2002) 'Politik i det refleksive moderne: Fra livspolitik til subpolitik', *Slagmark: Tidsskrift for idéhistorie*, vol. 34, pp. 61–78.

Holzer, B. and Sørensen, M. P. (2003) 'Rethinking Subpolitics: Beyond the "Iron Cage" of Modern Politics?', *Theory, Culture & Society*. Special Section on Reflexive Modernization, ed. by Mike Featherstone, vol. 20, no. 2, pp. 79–102.

Hundsbæk, T. (2001) 'Flyselskaber råber på støtte', *Politiken*, 22 September.

The Independent (2009) 'Rise of Short-Time Working: Stuck in a Very Deep Hole . . . and Desperate for Help to Dig Them Out', http://www.independent.co.uk/news/business/analysis-and-features/rise-of-shorttime-working-stuck-in-a-very-deep-hole-and-desperate-for-help-to-dig-them-out-1515313.html

Inglehart, R. (1977) *The Silent Revolution: Changing Values and Political Styles among Western Publics.* Princeton, NJ: Princeton University Press.

Inglis, D. (2009) 'Cosmopolitan Sociology and the Classical Canon: Ferdinand Tönnies and the Emergence of Global Gesellschaft', *British Journal of Sociology*, vol. 60, no. 4, pp. 813–832.

Jacobsen, M. H. (2003) 'Risiko eller frygt? En opsamling på senmoderne sociologiske samtidsdiagnosticeringer og diskurser', *Grus*, vol. 24, no. 68, p. 84–111.

Jarvis, D. S. L. (2007) 'Risk, Globalization and the State: A Critical Appraisal of Ulrich Beck and the World Risk Society Thesis', *Global Society*, vol. 21, no. 1, pp. 23–46.

Jensen, M. and Blok, A. (2008) 'Pesticides in the Risk Society: The View from Everyday Life', *Current Sociology*, vol. 56, no. 5, pp. 757–778.

Kant, I. ([1784] 1991) 'An Answer to the Question: What Is Enlightenment', in Kant, I., *Kant: Political Writings*, ed. H. S. Reiss. Cambridge: Cambridge University Press.

Kaspersen, L. B. (2000) *Anthony Giddens: An Introduction to a Social Theorist*. Oxford: Blackwell.

Kohler, U. (2007) 'Containers, Europeanization and Individualization: Empirical Implications of General Descriptions of Society', in Scherer, S. (ed.), *From Origin to Destination: Trends and Mechanisms in Social Stratification Research*. Frankfurt: Campus Verlag.

Kyung-Sup, C. and Min-Young, S. (2010) 'The Stranded Individualizer under Compressed Modernity: South Korean Women in Individualization without Individualism', *British Journal of Sociology*, vol. 61, no. 3, pp. 539–564.

Lau, C. (1989) 'Risikodiskurse: Gesellschaftliche Auseinandersetzungen um die Definition von Risiken', *Soziale Welt*, vol. 40, pp. 418–436.

Lee, R. L. M. (2008) 'In Search of Second Modernity: Reinterpreting Reflexive Modernization in the Context of Multiple Modernities', *Social Science Information*, vol. 47, no. 55, pp. 55–69.

Luhmann, N. (1990) 'Risiko und Gefahr', *Soziologische Aufklärung*, vol. 5, pp. 137–169.

Lyotard, F. ([1979] 1984) *The Postmodern Condition: A Report on Knowledge*. Minneapolis: University of Minnesota Press.

Mackey, E. (2000) 'Constructing an Endangered Nation: Risk, Race and Rationality in Australia's Native Title Debate', in Lupton, D. (ed.), *Risk and Sociocultural Theory: New Directions and Perspectives*. Cambridge: Cambridge University Press.

Mandeville, B. de ([1705–1733] 1957) *The Fable of the Bees: Private Vices, Public Benefits, vols. 1 and 2*, ed. F. B. Kaye. Oxford: Clarendon Press.

Machlup, F. (1962) *The Production and Distribution of Knowledge in the United States*. Princeton, NJ: Princeton University Press.

Maharaj, S. (2010) '"Small Change of the Universal": Beyond Modernity?', *British Journal of Sociology*, vol. 61, no. 3, pp. 565–578.

Marcuse, H. (1964) *One Dimensional Man: Studies on the Ideology of Advanced Industrial Society*. London: Routledge & Kegan Paul.

Marshall, B. K. (1999) 'Globalisation, Environmental Degradation and Ulrich Beck's Risk Society', *Environmental Values*, vol. 8, pp. 253–275.

Martell, L. (2008) 'Beck's Cosmopolitan Politics', *Contemporary Politics*, vol. 14, no. 2, pp. 129–143.

Martell, L. (2009) 'Global Inequality, Human Rights and Power: A Critique of Ulrich Beck's Cosmopolitanism', *Critical Sociology*, vol. 35, no. 2, pp. 253–272.

Marx, K. and Engels, F. (1848) *Manifesto of the Communist Party*. Moscow: Progress Publishers.

McGuigan, J. (1999) *Modernity and Postmodern Culture*. Buckingham: Open University Press.

McLeod, J. and Yates, L. (2006) *Making Modern Lives: Subjectivity, Schooling, and Social Change*. Albany, NY: State University of New York Press.

McMylor, P. (1996) 'Goods and Bads', *Radical Philosophy*, vol. 77, pp. 52–53.

Merryweather, D. (2003) 'I Will if You Will: Performativity of Risk in the Construction of Youth Identities', paper presented at the BSA Conference, York.

Münch, R. (1991) *Dialektik der Kommunikationsgesellschaft*. Frankfurt am Main: Suhrkamp.

Münch, R. (2002) 'Die "Zweite Moderne": Realität oder Fiktion? Kritische Fragen an die Theorie der "reflexiven" Modernisierung', *Kölner Zeitschrift für Soziologie und Sozialpsychologie*, vol. 54, no. 3, pp. 417–443.

Mythen, G. (2004) *Ulrich Beck. A Critical Introduction to the Risk Society*. London: Pluto Press.

Mythen, G. (2005a) 'Employment, Individualization and Insecurity: Rethinking the Risk Society Perspective', *Sociological Review*, vol. 53, no. 1, pp. 129–149.

Mythen, G. (2005b) 'From "Goods" to "Bads"? Revisiting the Political Economy of Risk', *Sociological Research Online*, vol. 10, no. 3.

Mythen, G. (2007) 'Reappraising the Risk Society Thesis: Telescopic Sight or Myopic Vision?', *Current Sociology*, vol. 55, no. 6, pp. 793–813.

Nassehi, A. (2000) 'Risikogesellschaft', in Kneer, G., Nassehi, N. and Schroer, M. (eds.), *Soziologische Gesellschaftsbegriffe* (2nd edn). Munich: Wilhelm Fink Verlag.

Nugent, S. (2000) 'Good Risk, Bad Risk: Reflexive Modernization and Amazonia', in Caplan, P. (ed.), *Risk Revisited*. London: Pluto Press.

Offe, C. (1984) 'Arbeit als soziologische Schlüsselkategorie?', in Offe, C., *Arbeitsgesellschaft: Strukturprobleme und Zukunftsperspektiven*. Frankfurt am Main: Campus.

Offe, C. (1985) *Disorganized Capitalism: Contemporary Transformations of Work and Politics*. Cambridge: Polity Press.

Offe, C. and Heinze, R. G. (1992) *Beyond Employment: Time, Work and the Informal Economy*. Cambridge: Polity Press.

Outhwaite, W. (2009) 'Canon Formation in Late 20th-Century British Sociology', *Sociology*, vol. 43, pp. 1029–1045.

Parsons, T. (1964) *Social Structure and Personality*. London: Free Press.

Parsons, T. (1980) 'Der Stellenwert des Identitätsbegriffs in der allgemeinen Handlungstheorie', in Döbert, R., Habermas, J. and Winkler, G. N. (eds.), *Die Entwicklung des Ichs*. Königstein: Athenäum.

Popper, K. R. ([1945] 1993) *The Open Society and Its Enemies, vols. I and II* (2nd edn). London: Routledge.

Rambach, A., and Rambach, M. (2011) *Les nouveaux intellos précaires*. Paris: J'ai lu.

Rasborg, K. (2001) 'From Industrial Modernity to Risk Modernity? A Critical Discussion of the Theory of the "Risk Society"', in Carleheden, M. and Jacobsen, M. (ed.), *The Transformation of Modernity: Aspects of the Past, Present and Future of an Era*. Aldershot: Ashgate.

Riesman, D. (1961) *Culture and Social Character*. New York: Free Press of Glencoe.

Rifkin, J. (1995) *The End of Work: The Decline of the Global Labor Force and the Dawn of the Post-Market Era*. New York: G. P. Putnam's Sons.

Sandell, K. and Mulinari, D. (eds.) (2006) *Feministiska interventioner*. Stockholm: Atlas Akademi.

Sartre, J.-P. ([1946] 1975) 'Existentialism Is a Humanism', in Kaufman, W. (ed.), *Existentialism from Dostoyevsky to Sartre*. New York: Penguin Group.

Sassen, S. (1991) *The Global City*. Princeton, NJ: Princeton University Press.

Schroer, M. (2000) *Das Individuum der Gesellschaft*. Frankfurt am Main: Suhrkamp.

Schroer, M. (2001) 'Das gefährdete, das gefährliche und das Risiko-Individuum', *Berliner Journal für Soziologie*, vol. 11, no. 3, pp. 319–336.

Scott, A. (2000) 'Risk Society or Angst Society? Two Views of Risk, Consciousness and Community', in Adam, B., Beck, U. and van Loon, J. (eds.), *The Risk Society and Beyond: Critical Issues for Social Theory.* London: Sage.

Scott, J. (2006) 'Class and Stratification', in Payne, G. (ed.), *Social Divisions.* Basingstoke: Palgrave Macmillan.

Sennett, R. (1998) *The Corrosion of Character: The Personal Consequences of Work in the New Capitalism.* New York: W. W. Norton & Company.

Simmel, G. ([1903] 1950) 'The Metropolis and Mental Life' in *The Sociology of Georg Simmel.* New York: Free Press.

Simmel, G. (1917) *Grundfragen der Soziologi.* Berlin-Leipzig: Göschen.

Simmel, G. ([1900] 1978) *The Philosophy of Money.* London: Routledge and Kegan Paul.

Simmel, G. ([1890] 1989a) 'Über sociale Differenzierung', in Simmel, G., *Aufsätze 1887 bis 1890, Gesamtausgabe Bd. 2*, ed. by H.-J. Dahme. Frankfurt am Main: Suhrkamp.

Simmel, G. ([1900] 1989b) *Die Philosophie des Geldes*, in Frisby, D. P. and Köhnke, K. C. (ed.), *Georg Simmel, Gesamtausgabe Bd. 6.* Frankfurt am Main: Suhrkamp.

Simmel, G. ([1917] 1990) 'Individualismens former', *Slagmark: Tidsskrift for idéhistorie*, vol. 15, pp. 2–10.

Simmel, G. (1998) 'Moden', in Simmel, G., *Hvordan er samfundet muligt? Udvalgte sociologiske skrifter.* Copenhagen: Gyldendal.

Simmel, G. ([1903] 1998a) 'Storbyerne og det åndelige liv', in Simmel, G., *Hvordan er samfundet muligt? Udvalgte sociologiske skrifter.* Copenhagen: Gyldendal.

Simmel, Georg ([1908] 1998) 'Sociologiens problem', in Simmel, G., *Hvordan er samfundet muligt? Udvalgte sociologiske skrifter.* Copenhagen: Gyldendal.

Skeggs, B. (2004) *Class, Self, Culture.* London: Routledge.

Smith, A. ([1776] 1976) *An Inquiry into the Nature and Causes of the Wealth of Nations*, ed. by R. H. Campbell and A. S. Skinner, textual ed. W. B. Todd. Oxford: Clarendon Press.

Smith, M., Law, A., Work, H. and Panay, A. (1997) 'The Reinvention of Politics: Ulrich Beck and Reflexive Modernity', *Environmental Politics*, vol. 8, no. 3, pp. 169–173.

Sørensen, M. P. (2001) 'Den politiske forbruger som subpolitiker', in Fenger-Grøn, C. and Kristensen, J. E. (eds.), *Kritik af den økonomiske fornuft.* Copenhagen: Hans Reitzels Forlag.

Sørensen, M. P. (2002) 'Interview med Ulrich Beck', *Slagmark: Tidsskrift for idéhistorie*, vol. 34, pp. 125–144.

Steele, D. R. (1992) *From Marx to Mises: Post-capitalist Society and the Challenge of Economic Calculation.* La Salle, IL: Open Court.

Stine, H. G. (1975) *The Third Industrial Revolution.* New York: G. P. Putnam's Sons.

Strydom, P. (2002) *Risk, Environment and Modernity.* Buckingham: Open University Press.

Suzuki, M., Ito, M., Ishida, M., Nihei, N. and Maruyama, M. (2010) 'Individualizing Japan: searching for its origin in first modernity', *British Journal of Sociology*, Vol. 61. No.3. p. 513–538.

Thorup, M. and Sørensen, M. P. (2004) 'Inescapably Side by Side: Interview with David Held', http://www.polity.co.uk/global/pdf/sidebyside.pdf

Touraine, A. (1969) *La Société post-industrielle.* Paris: Denoël.

Tulloch, J. and Lupton, D. (2003) *Risk and Everyday Life.* London: Sage.

United Nations (1998) 'Kyoto Protocol to the United Nations Framework Convention on Climate Change', http://unfccc.int/resource/docs/convkp/kpeng.pdf

Wikipedia (2011) 'Precautionary principle', http://en.wikipedia.org/wiki/Precautionary_principle

Wilkinson, I. (2001) *Anxiety in a Risk Society*. London: Routledge.

Woodman, D. (2009) 'The Mysterious Case of the Pervasive Choice Biography: Ulrich Beck, Structure/Agency, and the Middling State of Theory in the Sociology of Youth', *Journal of Youth Studies*, vol. 12, no. 3, pp. 243–256.

Wynne, B. (1996) 'May the Sheep Safely Graze? A Reflexive View of the Expert–Lay Knowledge Divide', in Lash, S., Szerszynski, B. and Wynne, B. (eds.), *Risk Environment and Modernity: Towards a New Ecology*. London: Sage.

Yan, Y. (2010) 'The Chinese Path to Individualization', *British Journal of Sociology*, vol. 61, no. 3 pp. 489–512.

Ziehe, T. (2001) *Modernitets- og ressourceperspektivet: Læring i et hypermoderne samfund*. Aalborg: Sociologisk Laboratorium, Aalborg Universitet.

Zielcke, A. (2011) 'Ein strategisch inszenierter Irrtum', interview with Ulrich Beck, *Süddeutsche Zeitung*, 14 March.

Bibliography of Ulrich Beck

Works in English

1992. *Risk Society: Towards a New Modernity*. London: Sage Publications.

1994. *Reflexive Modernization: Politics, Tradition and Aesthetics in the Modern Social Order*. Oxford: Polity Press. With A. Giddens and S. Lash.

1995. *The Normal Chaos of Love*. Oxford: Polity Press. With Elisabeth Beck-Gernsheim.

1995. *Ecological Politics in an Age of Risk*. Cambridge: Polity Press.

1995. *Ecological Enlightenment: Essays on the Politics of the Risk Society*. Atlantic Highlands, NJ: Humanities Press.

1997. *The Reinvention of Politics: Rethinking Modernity in the Global Social Order*. Cambridge: Polity Press.

1998. *Democracy without Enemies*. Cambridge: Polity Press.

1999. *World Risk Society*. Cambridge: Polity Press.

2000. *The Brave New World of Work*. Malden, MA: Polity Press.

2000. *The Risk Society and Beyond: Critical Issues for Social Theory*. London: Sage. Ed. by Beck, with B. Adam and J. van Loon.

2000. *What Is Globalization?* Malden, MA: Polity Press.

2001. *Individualization: Institutionalized Individualism and Its Social and Political Side Effects*. London: Sage. With Elisabeth Beck-Gernsheim.

2003. *Global America? The Cultural Side Effects of Globalization*. Liverpool: Liverpool University Press. Ed. by Beck, with N. Sznaider and R. Winter.

2003. *Conversations with Ulrich Beck*. Cambridge: Polity Press. With J. Willms.

2005. *Power in the Global Age*. Cambridge: Polity Press.

2006. *The Cosmopolitan Vision*. Cambridge: Polity Press.

2007. *Cosmopolitan Europe*. With E. Grande. Cambridge: Polity Press.

2008. *The Fifty-Year Unknown: The European Union as a Cosmopolitan Narrative*. Schuman Lecture, Maastricht University.

2009. *World at Risk*. Cambridge: Polity Press.

2010. *The God of One's Own*. Cambridge: Polity Press.

Contributions to books and journals in English

1987. 'Beyond Class and Status? Social Inequalities, Societal Processes of Individualization and the Development of New Forms of Association and Identity', in Meja, V. and Stehr, N. (eds.), *Modern German Sociology*. New York: Columbia University Press.

1987. 'The Anthropological Shock: Chernobyl and the Contours of the Risk Society', *Berkeley Journal of Sociology*, vol. 32, pp. 153–165.

1989. 'On the Way to the Industrial Risk-Society? Outline of an Argument', *Thesis-Eleven*, vol. 23., no. 23, pp. 86–104.

1990. 'Risky Businesss: Ecology and Economy', *Risky Business*, vol. 20, no. 1, pp. 51–69.

1992. 'From Industrial Society to the Risk Society: Questions of Survival, Social-Structure and Ecological Enlightenment', in *Theory, Culture & Society: Explorations in Critical Social Science*, vol. 9, no. 1, pp. 97–123.

1992. 'The Side Effects of Modernity & Modernity and Self-Identity', *Theory, Culture and Society: Explorations in Critical Social Science*, vol. 9, no. 2, pp. 163–169.

1992. 'Modern Society as a Risk Society', in Stehr, N. and Ericson, R. V. (ed.), *The Culture and Power of Knowledge: Inquiries into Contemporary Societies*. Berlin: W. de Gruyter.

1992. 'How Modern is Modern Society?', *Theory, Culture & Society: Explorations in Critical Social Science*, vol. 9, no. 2, pp. 163–169.

1994. 'The Naturalistic Fallacy of the Ecological Movement', in Barrett, M. (ed.), *The Polity Reader in Social Theory*. Cambridge: Polity Press.

1994. 'The Debate on the "Individualization Theory" in Today's Sociology in Germany', *Soziologie*, special issue no. 3 (*Sociology in Germany*), pp. 191–200.

1995. 'Freedom for Technology: A Call for a Second Separation of Powers', *Dissent*, vol. 42, no. 4, pp. 503–507.

1996. 'World Risk Society as Cosmopolitan Society? Ecological Questions in a Framework of Manufactured Uncertainties', *Theory, Culture and Society: Explorations in Critical Social Science*, vol. 13, no. 4, pp. 1–32.

1996. 'Individualization and "Precarious Freedoms": Perspectives and Controversies of a Subject-Orientated Sociology', in Heelas, P., Lash, S. and Morris, P. (eds.), *Detraditionalization: Critical Reflections on Authority and Identity at a Time of Uncertainty*. Oxford: Blackwell.

1996. 'How Neighbors Become Jews: The Political Construction of the Stranger in an Age of Reflexive Modernity', *Constellations: An International Journal of Critical and Democratic Theory*, vol. 2, no. 3, pp. 378–396.

1996. 'Environment, Knowledge and Indeterminacy: Beyond Modernist Ecology? Risk Society and the Provident State', in Lash, S., Szerszynski, B. and Wynne, B. (eds.), *Risk, Environment and Modernity: Towards a New Ecology*. London: Sage Publications.

1996. 'Neo-Nationalism or a Europe of Individuals', *Theoria*, vol. 88, pp. 55–68.

1996. 'Beyond Status and Class?', in Holmwood, J. (ed.), *Social Stratification, vol. 2*. Cheltenham: Edward Elgar.

1996. 'Capitalism without Work', *Dissent Magazin*, vol. 52, no. 9, pp. 8–12.

1997. 'Democratization of the Family', *Childhood: A Global Journal of Child Research*, vol. 4, no. 2, pp. 151–168.

1997. 'Capitalism without Work', *Dissent*, vol. 44, no. 1, pp. 51–56.

1997. 'The Social Morals of an Individual Life', *Cultural Values*, vol. 1, no. 1., pp. 118–126

1997. 'Global Risk Politics', in Jacobs, M. (ed.), *Greening the Millennium? The New Politics of the Environment*. Oxford: Blackwell Publishers.

1997. 'A Risky Business', *LSE* [London School of Economics] *Magazine*, vol. 9, no. 2, pp. 4–6.

1997. 'Subpolitics', *Organization & Environment*, vol. 10, no. 1, pp. 52–65.

1997. 'The Sociological Anatomy of Enemy Images: The Military and Democracy after the End of the Cold War', in von Hase, F.-R. and Lehmkuhl, U. (eds.), *Enemy Images in American History*. Oxford: Berghahn Books.

1998. 'Politics of Risk Society', in Franklin, J. (ed.), *The Politics of Risk Society*. Cambridge: Polity Press.

1998. 'The Cosmopolitan Manifesto', *New Statesman*, vol. 127, pp. 28–30.

1999. 'Democracy beyond the Nation-State: A Cosmopolitical Manifesto', *Dissent*, vol. 46, no. 1, pp. 53–55.

1999. 'Individualization and "Precarious Freedoms": Perspectives and Controversies of a Subject-Orientated Sociology', in Elliott, A. (ed.), *The Blackwell Reader in Contemporary Social Theory*. Malden, MA: Blackwell. With E. Beck-Gernsheim.

2000. 'The Cosmopolitan Perspective: Sociology on the Second Age of Modernity', *British Journal of Sociology*, vol. 51, no. 1, pp. 79–106.

2000. 'What is Globalization?', in Held, D. and McGrew, A. (eds.), *The Global Transformations Reader: An Introduction to the Globalization Debate*. Cambridge: Polity Press.

2000. 'Democratization of Democracy: Third Way Policy Needs to Redefine Work', *European Legacy*, vol. 5, no. 2, pp. 177–181.

2000. 'Foreword', in Allan, S., Carter, C. and Adam, B. (eds.), *Environmental Risks and the Media*. London: Routledge.

2000. 'A Global Prospect: Beyond the Work Society', *Global Focus*, vol. 12, no. 1, pp. 79–87.

2000. 'Living Your Own Life in a Runaway World: Individualisation, Globalisation and Politics', in Giddens, A. and Hutton, W. (eds.), *On the Edge: Living with Global Capitalism*. London: Jonathan Cape.

2001. 'The Cosmopolitan Society and Its Enemies', *Politologiske Studier*, vol. 4, no. 2, pp. 82–90. Also found in Tomasi, L. (ed.), *New Horizons in Sociological Theory and Research*. Aldershot: Ashgate.

2001. 'What Is Globalization?', *Journal of International Relations and Development*, vol. 4, no. 3, pp. 274–285.

2001. 'What Is Globalization?', *Acta Sociologica*, vol. 44, no. 1, pp. 81–89.

2001. 'Redefining Power in the Global Age: Eight Theses', *Dissent*, vol. 48, no. 4, pp. 83–90.

2001. 'Global Democracy: The Higher Politics of the Nation-State', *Metapolitica*, vol. 5, no. 18, pp. 66–71.

2001. 'The Fight for a Cosmopolitan Future', *New Statesman*, 11 May, vol. 130, no. 4562, pp. 33–35.

2001. 'The Normal Chaos of Love', in Giddens, A. (ed.), *Sociology: Introductory Readings*. Cambridge: Polity Press. With E. Beck-Gernsheim.

2001. 'Ecological Questions in a Framework of Manufactured Uncertainties', in Seidman, S. and Alexander, J. C. (eds.), *The New Social Theory Reader: Contemporary Debates*. London: Routledge.

2002. 'The Terrorist Threat: World Risk Society Revisited', *Theory, Culture & Society*, vol. 19, no. 4, pp. 39–56.

2002. 'The Silence of Words and Political Dynamics in the World Risk Society', *Logos*, vol. 1, no. 4, pp. 1–18.

2002. 'The Cosmopolitan Society and Its Enemies', *Theory Culture and Society*, vol. 19, no. 1–2, pp. 17–44.

2002. 'Cosmopolitics and Its Enemies', in Ogura, M. and Kajita, T. (eds.), *Globalization and Social Change*. Tokyo: University of Tokyo Press.

2002. 'Terror and Solidarity', in Leonard, M. (ed.), *Re-ordering the World*. London: Foreign Policy Centre.

2002. 'War Is Peace: On Post-National War', *Logos: A Journal of Modern Society and Culture*, vol. 1, no. 4, pp. 1–18.

2003. 'Risk as a Principle of Public Space', *Commentaire*, vol. 25, no. 100, pp. 893–897.

2003. 'The Silence of Words: On Terror and War', *Security Dialogue*, vol. 34, no. 3, pp. 255–267.

2003. 'Rooted Cosmopolitanism: Emerging from a Rivalry of Distinctions', in Beck, U., Sznaider, N. and Winter, R. (eds.), *Global America? The Cultural Side Effects of Globalization*. Liverpool: Liverpool University Press.

2003. 'The Analysis of Global Inequality: From National to Cosmopolitan Perspective', in Kaldor, M., Anheier, H. and Glasius, M. (eds.), *Global Civil Society 2003*. Oxford: Oxford University Press.

2003. 'Families in a Runaway World', in Scott, J., Treas, J. and Richards, M. (eds.), *The Blackwell Companion to Sociology of the Family*. Cambridge: Blackwell. With Elisabeth Beck-Gernsheim.

2003. 'Toward a New Critical Theory with a Cosmopolitan Intent', *Constellations*, vol. 10, no. 4, pp. 453–468.

2003. 'The Theory of Reflexive Modernization: Problematic, Hypotheses and Research Programme', *Theory Culture and Society*, vol. 20, no. 2, pp. 1–34. With W. Bonß and C. Lau.

2003. 'Understanding the Real Europe', *Dissent*, vol. 50, no. 3, pp. 32–38.

2003. 'Cosmopolitan Europe: A Confederation of States, a Federal State or Something Altogether New?', in Stern, S. and Seligmann, E. (eds.), *Desperately Seeking Europe*. London: Archetype Publications.

2003. 'Risk and Power: Why We Need a "Culture of Uncertainty"', *European Business Forum*, vol. 13, p. 27.

2004. 'The Cosmopolitan Turn', in Cane, N. (ed.), *The Future of Social Theory*. London: Continuum.

2004. 'Reinventing Politics and State for the Global Age', *Svobodnaya Mysl'*, vol. 56, no. 7, pp. 3–11.

2004. 'Cosmopolitical Realism: On the Distinction between Cosmopolitanism in Philosophy and the Social Sciences', *Global Networks: A Journal of Transnational Affairs*, vol. 4, no. 2, pp. 131–156.

2004. 'The Thrills of Misery', *Foreign Policy*, vol. 145, pp. 74–76.

2004. 'The Truth of Others: A Cosmopolitan Approach', *Common Knowledge*, vol. 10, no. 3, pp. 430–449.

2005. 'War Is Peace: On Post-National War', *Security Dialogue*, vol. 36, no. 1, pp. 5–26.

2005. 'The Silence of Words and Political Dynamics in the World Risk Society', in Bronner, S. E. (ed.), *Planetary Politics: Human Rights, Terror, and Global Society*. Lanham, MD: Rowman & Littlefield.

2005. 'Second Modernity as a Research Agenda: Theoretical and Empirical Explorations in the "Meta-change" of Modern Society', *British Journal of Sociology*, vol. 56, no. 4, pp. 525–557.

2005. 'How Not to Become a Museum Piece', *British Journal of Sociology*, vol. 56, no. 3, pp. 335–343.

2005. 'Neither Order nor Peace: A Response to Bruno Latour', *Common Knowledge*, vol. 11, no. 1, pp. 1–7.

2005. 'The Thrills of Misery: Review of Frank Schirrmacher's Book *Das Methusalem-Komplott*', *Futuribles*, vol. 306, pp. 41–45.

2005. 'Cosmopolitanization – Now! An Interview with Ulrich Beck', *Global Media and Communication*, vol. 1, no. 3, pp. 247–263. With Terhi Rantanen.

2005. 'Neither Order nor Peace: A Response to Bruno Latour', *Common Knowledge*, vol. 11, no. 1, pp. 1–17.

2005. 'The Cosmopolitan State: Redefining Power in the Global Age', *International Journal of Politics, Culture and Society*, special issue: 'The New Sociological Imagination', vol. 18, no. 3–4, pp. 143–159.

2006. 'Unpacking Cosmopolitanism for the Social Sciences: A Research Agenda', *British Journal of Sociology*, vol. 57, no 1, pp. 1–23. With Natan Sznaider.

2006. 'A Literature on Cosmopolitanism: An Overview', *British Journal of Sociology*, vol. 57, no. 1, pp. 153–164. With Natan Sznaider.

2006. 'Living in the Risk Society: An Interview with Ulrich Beck', *Journalism Studies*, vol. 7, no. 2, pp. 336–347. With Jeffrey Wimmer and Thorsten Quandt.

2006. 'An Empire of Law and Consensus: A Call for a Europe – and Europeans – beyond the Nation-State', *Internationale Politik: Transatlantic Edition*, special issue, pp. 105–111.

2006. 'Living in the World Risk Society' (A Hobhouse Memorial Public Lecture Given on Wednesday 15 February 2006 at the London School of Economics), *Economy and Society*, vol. 35, no. 3, pp. 329–345.

2006. 'European Cosmopolitanism, Cosmopolitan Europe', in Robins, K. (ed.), *The Challenge of Transcultural Diversities: Cultural Policy and Cultural Diversity* (Final Report). Strasbourg: Council of Europe Publishing.

2006. 'Unpacking Cosmopolitanism for the Social Sciences', *British Journal of Sociology*, vol. 57, no. 1, pp. 1–23. With Natan Sznaider.

2006. 'Europe from a Cosmopolitan Perspective', in Delanty, G. (ed.), *Europe and Asia beyond East and West*. London: Routledge. With Gerard Delanty.

2006. 'The Silence of Words and Political Dynamics in the World Risk Society', in Bronner, S. E. and Thompson, M. J. (eds.), *The Logos Reader: Rational Radicalism and the Future of Politics*. Lexington: University Press of Kentucky.

2007. 'Beyond Class and Nation: Reframing Social Inequalities in a Globalizing World', *British Journal of Sociology*, vol. 58, no. 4, pp. 679–705.

2007. 'The Cosmopolitan Condition: Why Methodological Nationalism Fails', *Theory, Culture & Society*, vol. 24, no. 7/8, pp. 286–290.

2007. 'Cosmopolitanism: Europe's Way Out of Crisis', *European Journal of Social Theory*, vol. 10, no. 1, pp. 67–85. With Edgar Grande.

2007. 'Cosmopolitanism: A Critical Theory for the Twenty-First Century', in Ritzer, G. (ed.), *The Blackwell Companion to Globalization*. Malden, MA: Blackwell Publishing.

2007. 'Organizations in World Risk Society', in Pearson, C. M., Roux-Dufort, C. and Clair, J. A. (eds.), *International Handbook of Organizational Crisis Management*. Los Angeles: Sage Publications. With Boris Holzer.

2007. 'Environmental Risks and Public Perceptions', in Pretty, J., Ball, A. S., Benton, T., Guivant, J. S., Lee, D. R., Orr, D., Pfeffer, M. J. and Ward, H. (eds.), *The Sage Handbook of Environment and Society*. Los Angeles: Sage Publications. With Cordula Kropp.

2007. 'Reinventing Europe: A Cosmopolitan Vision', in Rumford, C. (ed.), *Cosmopolitanism and Europe*. Liverpool: Liverpool University Press.

2008. 'A European Antidote to Europe: The European Union as a Cosmopolitan Narrative of Modernity', *Internationale Politik. Global Edition: Confronting Tomorrow's Crises*, vol. 9, no. 4, pp. 46–53.

2008. 'Climate Change and Globalisation Are Reinforcing Global Inequalities: High Time for a New Social Democratic Era', *Globalizations*, vol. 5, no. 1, pp. 78–80.

2008. 'Reframing Power in the Globalized World', *Organization Studies*, vol. 29, no. 5, pp. 793–804.

2008. 'Realistic Cosmopolitanism: How Do Societies Handle Otherness?', in Held, D. and Moore, H. L. (eds.), *Cultural Politics in a Global Age: Uncertainty, Solidarity, and Innovation*. Oxford: One World.

2008. 'Reinventing Europe: A Cosmopolitan Vision', in Hettne, B. (ed.), *Sustainable Development in a Globalized World: Studies in Development, Security and Culture, vol. 1*. Basingstoke: Palgrave Macmillan.

2008. 'Mobility and the Cosmopolitan Perspective', in Canzler, W., Kaufmann, V. and Kesselring, S. (eds.), *Tracing Mobilities*. Aldershot: Ashgate.

2008. 'How Not to Become a Museum Piece', in Romanov, P. and Iarskaia-Smirnova, E. (eds.), *The Public Role of Sociology* (Russian edition). Moscow: Variant, CSPGS.

2009. 'Global Generations and the Trap of Methodological Nationalism: For a Cosmopolitan Turn in the Sociology of Youth and Generation', *European Sociological Review*, vol. 25, no. 1, pp. 25–36. With Elisabeth Beck-Gernsheim.

2009. 'Critical Theory of World Risk Society: A Cosmopolitan Vision', *Constellations*, vol. 16, no. 1, pp. 3–22.

2009. 'Risk Society's "Cosmopolitan Moment"', *New Geographies*, no. 1 'After Zero', pp. 24–35.

2009. 'World Risk Society and Manufactured Uncertainties', *IRIS: European Journal of Philosophy and Public Debate*, vol. 1, pp. 291–299.

2009. 'Cosmopolitanization of Memory: The Politics of Forgiveness and Restitution', in Nowicka, M. and Rovisco, M. (eds.), *Cosmopolitanism in Practice*. Farnham: Ashgate. With Daniel Levy and Natan Sznaider.

2009. 'Risk Society', in Cayley, D. (ed.), *Ideas on the Nature of Science*, Fredericton, NB: Goose Lane Editions.

2010. 'Varieties of Second Modernity: The Cosmopolitan Turn in Social and Political Theory and Research', *British Journal of Sociology*, vol. 61, no. 3, special issue: 'Varieties of Second Modernity: Extra-European and European Experiences and Perspectives', ed. by U. Beck and E. Grande, pp. 409–443. With Edgar Grande.

2010. 'Climate for Change, or How to Create a Green Modernity', *Theory, Culture & Society*, vol. 27, no. 2–3, pp. 254–266.

2010. 'Remapping Social Inequalities in an Age of Climate Change: For a Cosmopolitan Renewal of Sociology', *Global Networks: A Journal of Transnational Affairs*, vol. 10, no. 2, pp. 165–181.

2010. 'Passage to Hope: Marriage, and the Need for a Cosmopolitan Turn in Family Research', *Journal of Family Theory & Review*, vol. 2, no. 4, pp. 401–414. With Elisabeth Beck-Gernsheim.

2010. 'New Cosmopolitanism in the Social Sciences', in Turner, B. S. (ed.), *The Routledge International Handbook of Globalization Studies*. Abingdon: Routledge. With Natan Sznaider.

2010. 'World Risk Society as Cosmopolitan Society: Ecological Questions in a Framework of Manufactured Uncertainties', in Rosa, E. A., Diekmann, A., Dietz, T. and Jaeger, C. C. (eds.), *Human Footprints on the Global Environment: Threats to Sustainability*. Cambridge, MA: MIT Press.

2011. 'Cosmopolitanism as Imagined Communities of Global Risk', in *American Behavioral Scientist*, vol. 55, no. 10, pp. 1346–1361.

2011. 'The Self-Limitation of Modernity: The Theory of Reflexive Taboos', *Theory and Society*, vol. 40, no. 4 pp. 417–436. With Natan Sznaider.

Works in German

1974. *Objektivität und Normativität: Die Theorie-Praxis-Debatte in der modernen deutschen und amerikanischen Soziologie.* Reinbek bei Hamburg: Rowohlt.

1977. *Die soziale Konstitution der Berufe: Materialien zu einer subjektbezogenen Theorie der Berufe.* Frankfurt am Main: Aspekte. Ed. by Beck with M. Brater.

1978. *Berufliche Arbeitsteilungen und soziale Ungleichheit: Eine historisch-gesellschaftliche Theorie der Berufe.* Frankfurt am Main: Campus Verlag. With M. Brater and K. M. Bolte.

1979. *Berufswahl und Berufszuweisung: Ergebnisse einer empirischen Untersuchung zur sozialen Verwandtschaft von Ausbildungsberufen.* Frankfurt am Main: Campus Verlag. With M. Brater and B. Wegener.

1980. *Soziologie der Arbeit und der Berufe: Grundlagen, Problemfelder, Forschungsergebnisse.* Reinbek bei Hamburg: Rowohlt-Taschenbuch Verlag. With M. Brater and H. Daheim.

1980. *Bildungsexpansion und betriebliche Beschäftigungspolitik: Aktuelle Entwicklungstendenzen im Vermittlungszusammenhang von Bildung und Beschäftigung.* Frankfurt: Campus Verlag. Ed. by Beck with Karl H. Hörning and Wilke Thomssen.

1982. *Soziologie und Praxis: Erfahrungen, Konflikte, Perspektiven.* Göttingen: Schwartz. Ed. by Beck.

1986. *Risikogesellschaft: Auf dem Weg in eine andere Moderne.* Frankfurt am Main: Suhrkamp.

1988. *Gegengifte: Die organisierte Unverantwortlichkeit.* Frankfurt am Main: Suhrkamp.

1989. *Weder Sozialtechnologie noch Aufklärung? Analysen zur Verwendung sozialwissenschaftlichen Wissens.* Frankfurt am Main: Suhrkamp. Ed. by Beck with W. Bonß.

1990. *Das ganz normale Chaos der Liebe.* Frankfurt am Main: Suhrkamp. With Elisabeth Beck-Gernsheim.

1991. *Politik in der Risikogesellschaft: Essays und Analysen.* Frankfurt am Main: Suhrkamp. With contributions from O. Lafontaine, T. Schmid, C. Offe and others.

1991. *Sprache und Ethik im technologischen Zeitalter.* Bamberg: Verlag Fränkischer Tag. With H.-G. Gadamer, H. Jonas and W. C. Zimmerli.

1993. *Die Erfindung des Politischen: Zu einer Theorie reflexiver Modernisierung.* Frankfurt am Main: Suhrkamp.

1994. *Riskante Freiheiten: Individualisierung in modernen Gesellschaften.* Frankfurt am Main: Suhrkamp. Ed. by Beck with E. Beck-Gernsheim.

1995. *Eigenes Leben: Ausflüge in die unbekannte Gesellschaft, in der wir leben.* Munich: C. H. Beck. With W. Vossenkuhl and U. E. Ziegler.

1995. *Die feindlose Demokratie: Ausgewählte Aufsätze.* Stuttgart: Philipp Reclam.

1996. *Gespräche zur Zeit: Geführt von Hubert Christian Ehalt mit Ulrich Beck.* Ed. by Katja Sindemann and Toni Badinger. Vienna: WUV-Universitätsverlag.

1996. *Reflexive Modernisierung: Eine Kontroverse.* Frankfurt am Main: Suhrkamp. With A. Giddens and S. Lash.

1997. *Kinder der Freiheit.* Frankfurt am Main: Suhrkamp. Ed. by Beck.

1997. *Individualisierung und Integration: Neue Konfliktlinien und neuer Integrationsmodus?* Opladen: Leske und Budrich. Ed. by Beck with Peter Sopp.

1997. *Weltrisikogesellschaft, Weltöffentlichkeit und globale Subpolitik.* Vienna: Picus-Verlag.

1997. *Was ist Globalisierung? Irrtümer des Globalismus: Antworten auf Globalisierung.* Frankfurt am Main: Suhrkamp. Ed. by Beck.

1997. *Philosophie heute: Gespräche mit Ulrich Beck, Hans-Georg Gadamer, Jürgen Habermas, Hans Jonas, Odo Marquard, Carl-Friedrich von Weizsäcker, Ulrich Wickert u.a.* Frankfurt am Main: Campus Verlag. Ed. by Beck with U. Boehm.

1998. *Politik der Globalisierung.* Frankfurt am Main: Suhrkamp. Ed. by Beck with R. Fellinger.

1998. *Perspektiven der Weltgesellschaft.* Frankfurt am Main: Suhrkamp. Ed. by Beck.

1998. *Das Zeitalter des eigenen Leben: Die Globalisierung der Biographien.* Frankfurt am Main: Suhrkamp Verlag.

1999. *Schöne neue Arbeitswelt – Vision: Weltbürgergesellschaft.* Frankfurt am Main: Campus Verlag.

1999. *Der unscharfe Ort der Politik: Empirische Fallstudien zur Theorie der reflexiven Modernisierung.* Opladen: Leske und Budrich. Ed. by Beck with M. A. Jaher and S. Kesselring.

2000. *Die Zukunft von Arbeit und Demokratie.* Frankfurt am Main: Suhrkamp. Ed. by Beck.

2000. *Freiheit oder Kapitalismus: Gesellschaft neu denken. Ulrich Beck im Gespräch mit Johannes Willms.* Frankfurt am Main: Suhrkamp.

2000. *Ortsbestimmungen der Soziologie: Wie die kommende Generation Gesellschaftswissenschaften betreiben will.* Baden-Baden: Nomos. Ed. by Beck with A. Kieserling.

2001. *Die Modernisierung der Moderne.* Frankfurt am Main: Suhrkamp. Ed. by Beck with W. Bonß.

2002. *Macht und Gegenmacht im globalen Zeitalter: Neue weltpolitische Ökonomie.* Frankfurt am Main: Suhrkamp.

2002. *Das Schweigen der Wörter: Über Terror und Krieg.* Frankfurt am Main: Suhrkamp.

2003. *Globales Amerika. Die kulturellen Folgen der Globalisierung.* Bielefeld: Transcript Verlag. Ed. by Beck with N. Sznaider and R. Winter.

2004. *Der kosmopolitische Blick oder Krieg ist Frieden.* Frankfurt an Main: Suhrkamp.

2004. *Das kosmopolitische Europa: Gesellschaft und Politik in der zweiten Moderne.* Frankfurt am Main: Suhrkamp. With Edgar Grande.

2004. *Entgrenzung und Entscheidung: Was ist neu an der Theorie reflexiver Modernisierung?* Frankfurt am Main: Suhrkamp. Ed. by Beck with C. Lau.

2005. *Was zur Wahl steht. Die Neuvermessung der Ungleichheit unter den Menschen: Soziologische Aufklärung im 21. Jahrhundert.* Frankfurt am Main: Suhrkamp.

2007. *Weltrisikogesellschaft.* Frankfurt am Main: Suhrkamp.

2007. *Generation Global.* Frankfurt am Main: Suhrkamp. Ed. by Beck.

2008. *Der eigene Gott: Von der Friedensfähigkeit und dem Gewaltpotential der Religionen.* Frankfurt am Main: Suhrkamp.

Contributions to books and journals in German

1971. 'Zu einer Theorie der Studentenunruhen in fortgeschrittenen Industriegesellschaft', *Kölner Zeitschrift für Soziologie und Sozialpsychologie*, vol. 23, no. 3, pp. 439–477.

1972. 'Soziologische Normativität', *Kölner Zeitschrift für Soziologie und Sozialpsychologie*, vol. 24, no. 2, pp. 201–231.

1976. 'Beruf, Herrschaft und Identität: Ein subjektbezogener Ansatz zum Verhältnis von Bildung und Produktion' (Part I of 'Die soziale Konstitution der Berufe'), *Soziale Welt*, vol. 27, no. 1, pp. 8–44. With M. Brater and E. Tramsen.

1976. 'Kritik des Berufs' (Part II of 'Die soziale Konstitution der Berufe'), *Soziale Welt*, vol. 27, no. 2, pp. 180–205. With M. Brater and E. Tramsen.

1976. 'Grenzen abstrakter Arbeit: Subjektbezogene Bedingungen der Gebrauchs-wertproduktion und ihre Bedeutung für kritische Berufspraxis', *Leviathan: Zeitschrift für Sozialwissenschaft*, vol. 4, no. 2, pp. 178–215. With M. Brater.

1976. 'Wider den Papier-Horn', *Leviathan: Zeitschrift für Sozialwissenschaft*, vol. 4, no. 3, pp. 402–403. With M. Brater.

1976. 'Bildungsreform und Berufsform. Zur Problematik der berufsorientierten Gliederung des Bildungssystems', *Mitteilungen aus der Arbeitsmarkt- und Berufsforschung*, vol. 9, no. 4, pp. 496–508. With K. M. Bolte and M. Brater.

1977. 'Problemstellungen und Ansatzpunkt einer subjektbezogenen Theorie der Berufe', in Beck, U. and Brater, M. (eds.), *Die soziale Konstitution der Berufe, vol. 1*. Frankfurt am Main: Aspekte. With M. Brater.

1977. 'Berufliche Arbeitsteilung und soziale Ungleichheit: Konzeption eine subjekt-bezogenen Theorie der Berufe', in Beck, U. and Brater, M. (eds.), *Die soziale Konstitution der Berufe, vol. 2*. Frankfurt am Main: Aspekte. With M. Brater.

1977. 'Ist der Erfolg der Bildungsreform Ursache ihres Scheiterns?', in Beck, U. and Brater, M. (eds.), *Die soziale Konstitution der Berufe, vol. 2*. Frankfurt am Main: Aspekte. With M. Brater.

1977. 'Enorme Subjektivität? Eine Replik auf K. Horns Diskussion unseres Aufsatzes "Grenzen abstrakter Arbeit" ', in Beck, U. and Brater, M. (eds.), *Die soziale Konstitution der Berufe, vol. 2*. Frankfurt am Main: Aspekte. With M. Brater.

1977. 'Beruf als Kategorie soziologischer Analyse: Einige Erkenntnisschritte und Problem-perspektiven der neueren Berufssoziologie', in Blaschke, D. (ed.), *Sozial-wissenschaftliche Forschung: Entwicklungen und Praxisorientierungen*. Nürnberg: Verlag der Nuernberger Forschungsvereinigung. With K. M. Bolte and M. Brater.

1978. 'Zur Kritik der Beruflichkeit des Arbeitens', in Duve, F. (ed.), *Technologie und Politik, vol. 10: Die Zukunft der Arbeit 2*. Reinbek bei Hamburg: Rowohlt. With M. Brater.

1978. 'Qualitative Veränderungen der Berufsstruktur als Voraussetzung expansiver Bildungs-politik: Einige bildungs- und arbeitsmarktpolitische Konsequenzen der Berufsform von Arbeitskraft', in Mertens, D. and Kaiser, M. (eds.), *Berufliche Flexibilitätsforschung in der Diskussion* (Contribution to Mitteilungen aus der Arbeitsmarkt- und Berufsforschung, 30 no. 2). Nuremberg: Bundesanstalt für Arbeit. With K. M. Bolte and M. Brater.

1978. 'Berufliche Qualifikationsstrukturen als Medien der Verteilung und Legitimation sozialer Chancen', in Bolte, K. M. (ed.), *Materialien aus der soziologischen Forschung: Verhandlungen des 18. deutschen Soziologentages*. Darmstadt: Luchterhand. With M. Brater.

1978. 'Bildungsexpansion in der Sackgasse? Bildungspolitische Konsequenzen aktueller Theorieansätze zum Verhältnis von Bildung und Beschäftigung', in Matthes, J. (ed.), *Sozialer Wandel in Westeuropa: Verhandlungen des 19. Deutschen Soziologentages*. Frankfurt: Campus Verlag. With M. Brater and K. M. Bolte.

1978. 'Über Klaus Ottomeyer: Ökonomische Zwänge und menschliche Beziehungen: Diskussionsbeiträge von Ulrich Beck, Michael Brater und Hartmut Neuendorff', *Soziologische Revue*, vol. 1, no. 1, pp. 11–25.

1978. 'Beruf, Herrschaft und Identität: Ein subjektbezogener Ansatz zum Verhältnis von Bildung und Produktion', in Beck, U. and Brater, M. (eds.), *Berufliche Arbeitsteilung und soziale Ungleichheit: Eine historisch-gesellschaftliche Theorie der Berufe*. Frankfurt am Main: Campus Verlag.

1978. 'Berufliche Strategien: Zur marktstrategischen Bedeutung und sozialen Dynamik arbeits-teiliger Differenzierungen', in Beck, U. and Brater, M. (eds.), *Berufliche*

Arbeitsteilung und soziale Ungleichheit: Eine historisch-gesellschaftliche Theorie der Berufe. Frankfurt am Main: Campus Verlag.

1978. 'Die berufliche Form gesellschaftlicher Arbeitsteilung: Entstehung und Veränderung der Berufsform von Arbeitskraft unter den Bedingungen einfacher und kapitalistischer Warenproduktion', in Beck, U. and Brater, M. (eds.), *Berufliche Arbeitsteilung und soziale Ungleichheit: Eine historisch-gesellschaftliche Theorie der Berufe*. Frankfurt am Main: Campus Verlag.

1978. 'Grenzen abstrakter Arbeit: Subjektbezogene Bedingungen der Gebrauchswert-produktion und ihre Bedeutung für kritische Berufspraxis', in Beck, U. and Brater, M. (eds.), *Berufliche Arbeitsteilung und soziale Ungleichheit: Eine historisch-gesells-chaftliche Theorie der Berufe*. Frankfurt am Main: Campus Verlag.

1978. 'Kritik des Berufs: Zur Problematik der beruflichen Organisationsform menschliche Arbeitsvermögens', in Beck, U. and Brater, M. (eds.), *Berufliche Arbeitsteilung und soziale Ungleichheit: Eine historisch-gesellschaftliche Theorie der Berufe*. Frankfurt am Main: Campus Verlag.

1979. 'Soziale Grenzen beruflicher Flexibilität: Ergebnisse einer empirischen Untersuchung über Probleme der Berufswahl und Bedingungen knapper Lehrstellen', *Mitteilungen aus der Arbeitsmarkt- und Berufsforschung*, vol. 12, no. 4, pp. 584–593. With M. Brater and B. Wegener.

1980. 'Die Vertreibung aus dem Elfenbeinturm: Anwendung soziologischen Wissens als soziale Konfliktsteuerung', *Soziale Welt*, vol. 31, no. 4, pp. 415–441.

1980. 'Berufskonstruktionen als Medien der Vermittlung von Bildung und Beschäftigung: Untersucht am Beispiel der Entstehung und Schneidung der medizinisch-technischen Dienstleistungsberufe', in Beck, U., Hörning, K. H. and Thomssen, W. (eds.), *Bildungsexpansion und betriebliche Beschäftigungspolitik: Aktuelle Entwicklungstendenzen im Vermittlungs-zusammenhang von Bildung und Beschäftigung. Beiträge zum 19. Deutschen Soziologen-tag, Berlin 1979*. Frankfurt: Campus Verlag. With E. Zeller.

1982. 'Folgeprobleme der Modernisierung und die Stellung der Soziologie in der Praxis', in Beck, U. (ed.), *Soziologie und Praxis: Erfahrungen, Konflikte, Perspektiven*. Göttingen: Schwartz.

1982. 'Die "Verwendungstauglichkeit" sozialwissenschaftlicher Theorien: Das Beispiel der Bildungs- und Arbeitsmarktforschung', in Beck, U. (ed.), *Soziologie und Praxis: Erfahrungen, Konflikte, Perspektiven*. Göttingen: Schwartz. With C. Lau.

1982. 'Vorwort: besonders an die "Praktiker" unter unseren Lesern', in Beck, U. (ed.), *Soziologie und Praxis: Erfahrungen, Konflikte, Perspektiven*. Göttingen: O. Schwartz.

1982. 'Berufe als Organisationsformen menschlichen Arbeitsvermögens', in Littek, W., Rammert,W. and Wachtler, G. (eds.), *Einführung in die Arbeits- und Industriesoziologie*. Frankfurt am Main: Campus Verlag.

1982. 'Soziologie und Praxis: Erfahrungen, Konflikte, Perspektiven', in Beck, U. (ed.), *Soziologie und Praxis: Erfahrungen, Konflikte, Perspektiven*. Göttingen: Schwartz.

1982. 'Das Krisenbewusstsein in der Arbeitsgesellschaft', *Österreichische Zeitschrift für Soziologie*, vol. 7, no. 3–4, pp. 39–49.

1983. 'Identität und Arbeitsmarkt: Ein Diskussionsbeitrag', in Härting, E. and Nuthmann, R. (ed.), *Hochschulexpansion und Arbeitsmarkt: Problemstellungen und Forschungsperspektiven*. Bremen: Institut für Arbeitsmarkt- und Berufsforschung der Bundesanstalt für Arbeit.

1983. 'Jenseits von Stand und Klasse? Soziale Ungleichheiten, gesellschaftliche Individualisierungsprozesse und die Entstehung neuer sozialer Formationen und Identitäten', in Kreckel, R. (ed.), *Soziale Ungleichheiten*. Göttingen: Schwartz.

1983. 'Bildungsforschung und Bildungspolitik: Öffentlichkeit als Adressat sozial-wissenschaftlicher Forschung', *Zeitschrift für Sozialisationsforschung und Erziehungssoziologie*, vol. 3, no. 2, pp. 165–173. With C. Lau.

1983. 'Wer ist der Schönste im ganzen Land? Überlegungen zur Auswahl eines pre-iswürdigen Zeitschriftenaufsatzes', *Soziale Welt*, vol. 34, no. 3, pp. 257–269. With H. Hartmann.

1983. 'Beruf als Kategorie soziologischer Analyse: Einige Erkenntnisschritte und Problem-perspektiven der neueren Berufssoziologie', in Bolte, K. M. and Treutner, E. (eds.), *Subjektorientierte Arbeits- und Berufssoziologie*. Frankfurt am Main: Campus Verlag. With K. M. Bolte and M. Brater.

1984. 'Perspektiven einer kulturellen Evolution der Arbeit', *Mitteilungen aus der Arbeitsmarkt- und Berufsforschung*, vol. 17, no. 1, pp. 52–62.

1984. 'Soziologie und Modernisierung: Zur Ortsbestimmung der Verwendungsforschung', *Soziale Welt*, vol. 35, no. 4, pp. 381–406. With W. Bonß.

1984. 'Wissenschaftlichkeit und Interessen', *Soziologische Revue*, vol. 7, no. 1, pp. 1–5.

1984. 'Jenseits von Stand und Klasse? Soziale Ungleichheiten, gesellschaftliche Individualisierungsprozesse und die Entstehung neuer sozialer Formationen und Identitäten', *Merkur: Deutsche Zeitschrift für europäisches Denken*, vol. 38, no. 5, pp. 485–497.

1985. 'Ausbildung ohne Beschäftigung: zum Funktionswandel des Bildungssystems im Systemwandel der Arbeitsgesellschaft', in Hradil, P. (ed.), *Sozialstruktur im Umbruch: Karl Martin Bolte zum 60. Geburtstag*. Opladen: Leske und Budrich.

1985. '"Du hast keine Chance, aber nutze sie": Zum Verhältnis von Bildung und Beruf', *Merkur: Deutsche Zeitschrift für europäisches Denken*, vol. 39, no. 12, p. 3.

1985. 'Von der Vergänglichkeit der Industriegesellschaft', in Schmid, T. (ed.), *Das pfeif-ende Schwein: Über weitergehende Interessen der Linken*. Berlin: K. Wagenbach.

1985. 'Was will und wozu dient "Verwendungsforschung"? Einleitung zur Ad-hoc-Gruppe des DFG-Schwerpunktprogrammes "Verwendung sozialwissenschaftlicher Ergebnisse"', in Franz, H.-W. (ed.), *22. Deutscher Soziologentag 1984: Sektions- und Ad-hoc Gruppen*. Opladen: Westdt. Verlag.

1986. 'Die Zivilisation des Risikos', *Psychologie Heute*, vol. 13, no. 11, pp. 34–38.

1986. 'Der anthropologische Schock: Tschernobyl und die Konturen der Risikogesellschaft', *Merkur*, vol. 40, no. 8, pp. 653–663.

1986. 'Auf dem Wege in die industrielle Risikogesellschaft? Eine Argumentationsskizze', in Erd, R., Jacobi, O. and Schumm, W. (eds.), *Strukturwandel in der Industriegesellschaft*. Frankfurt am Main: Campus Verlag.

1986. 'Ausbildung ohne Beschäftigung: Zum Funktionswandel des Bildungssystems im Systemwandel der Arbeitsgesellschaft', *Mehrwert, 1986/1986*, no. 27, pp. 1–29.

1987. 'Wie spiesse ich einen Pudding auf?', *PDS (Partei des Demokratischen Sozialismus)*, vol. 4., no. 2–3, pp. 91–101.

1987. 'Auf dem Weg in die industrielle Risikogesellschaft', *Blätter für deutsche und inter-nationale Politik*, vol. 32, no. 2, pp. 139–159.

1987. 'Die Entmündigung der Sinne: Alltag und Politik in der industriellen Risikogesellschaft', *Gewerkschaftliche Monatshefte*, vol. 38, no. 2, pp. 66–76.

1987. 'Entmündigung der Sinne: Egalisierung von Gefahren. Zur sozialen Dynamik hoch-industrieller Risiken', *Universitas: Zeitschrift für Wissenschaft, Kunst und Litteratur*, vol. 42, no. 6, pp. 525–536.

1987. 'Die Zukunft der Familie', *Psychologie heute*, vol. 14, no. 11, pp. 44–49.

1987. 'Leben in der Risikogesellschaft', *Gegenwartskunde Gesellschaft Staat Erziehung*, vol. 36, no. 2, pp. 159–170.

1987. 'Vom Nutzen der Soziologie', *Universitas: Zeitschrift für Wissenschaft, Kunst und Litteratur*, vol. 43, nos. 1–2, pp. 66–70.

1988. 'Die Zukunft der Familie', *Kontext*, vol. 14, p. 76.

1988. 'Wir Fatalisten: Im Labyrinth der Risikogesellschaft', in Schmid, T. (ed.), *Entstaatlichung: Neue Perspektiven auf das Gemeinwesen*. Berlin: K. Wagenbach.

1988. 'Jenseits von Sozialtechnologie und Aufklärung', in Reyher, L. and Kühl, J. (eds.), *Resonanzen, Arbeitsmarkt und Beruf – Forschung und Politik: Festschrift für Dieter Mertens*. Nuremberg: Institut für Arbeitsmarkt- und Berufsforschung der Bundesanstalt für Arbeit.

1988. 'Die Selbstwiderlegung der Bürokratie: Über Gefahrenverwaltung und Verwaltungsgefährdung', *Merkur: Deutsche Zeitschrift für europäisches Denken*, vol. 42, no. 8, pp. 629–646.

1988. 'Risikogesellschaft: Auf dem Weg in eine andere Moderne', *Soziologische Revue*, vol. 11, no. 1, pp. 1–12.

1988. 'Der Berufsbegriff als Instrument soziologischer Analyse', in Bolte, K. M. (ed.), *Mensch, Arbeit und Betrieb: Beiträge zur Berufs- und Arbeitskräfteforschung*. Weinheim: Acta Humaniora. With K. M. Bolte and M. Brater.

1988. 'Wissenschaft und Sicherheit', in Appel, R. von, Hummel, D. and Hippe, W. (eds.), *Die Neue Sicherheit: Vom Notstand zur Sozialen Kontrolle*. Cologne: Kölner Volksblatt Verlag-Gesellschaft.

1989. 'Auf dem zivilisatorischem Vulkan', *Forum Wissenschaft*, vol. 5, no. 6D, pp. 76–81.

1989. 'Zum Wandel im Verhältnis von Sozialwissenschaft und Praxis', *Arbeit und Sozialpolitik*, vol. 42, no. 2, pp. 2–8. With W. Bonß.

1989. 'Verwendungsforschung: Umsetzung wissenschaftlichen Wissens', in Flick, U., von Kardorff, E., Keuppo, H., von Rosential, L. and Wolff, S. (eds.), *Handbuch Qualitative Sozialforschung: Grundlagen, Konzepte, Methoden und Anwendungen*. Munich: Psychologie Verlags Union. With W. Bonß.

1989. 'Wie streiche ich mein Stachelschwein? Zur Verwendung von Sozialwissenschaft in Praxis und Politik', *Basler Magazin*, vol. 29. With W. Bonß.

1989. 'Zum Strukturwandel von Sozialwissenschaft und Praxis: Ergebnisse und Perspektiven der Verwendungsforschung', *Soziale Welt*, vol. 40, no. 1–2, pp. 196–214. With W. Bonß.

1989. 'Risikogesellschaft: Die neue Qualität technischer Risiken und der soziologische Beitrag zur Risikodiskussion', in Schmidt, M. (ed.), *Leben in der Risikogesellschaft: der Umgang mit modernen Zivilisationsrisiken*. Karlsruhe: C. F. Muller.

1989. 'Jenseits von Frauen- und Männerrolle oder: Die Zukunft der Familie', *Universitas: Zeitschrift für interdisziplinäre Wissenschaft*, vol. 1, pp. 1–9.

1989. 'Definitionsmacht und Grenzen angewandter Sozialwissenschaft: Eine Untersuchung am Beispiel der Bildungs- und Arbeitsmarktforschung', in *Beiträge zur sozialwissenschaftlichen Forschung, vol. 113*. Opladen: Westdt. Verlag. With C. Lau.

1989. 'Verwissenschaftlichung ohne Aufklärung? Zum Strukturwandel von Sozialwissenschaft und Praxis', in Beck, U. and Bonß, W. (eds.), *Weder Sozialtechnologie noch Aufklärung? Analysen zur Verwendung sozialwissenschaftlichen Wissens*. Frankfurt am Main: Suhrkamp.

1989. 'Auf dem Weg in die industrielle Risikogesellschaft', in Landesjugendring Niedersachsen (ed.), *Zukunft der Umwelt als Aufgabe der Gegenwart: Denkanstösse Mensch und Umwelt*. Hanover: Landesjugendring Niedersachsen e.V. Hannover.

1989. 'Risikogesellschaft: Die organisierte Unverantwortlichkeit', *Bulletin SEV/VSE, Bulletin des Schweizerischen Elektrotechnischen Vereins/Bulletin des Verbandes SchweizerischerElektrizitätswerke*, vol. 80, no. 21, pp. 1371–1377.

1990. 'Jenseits von Sicherheit und Kontrolle', in Gröbl-Steinbach, E. (ed.), *Licht und Schatten: Dimensionen von Technik, Energie und Politik*. Vienna: Böhlau.

1990. 'Praxis als Forschung: Wer die Gesellschaft zum Labor macht, öffnet die Wissenschaft für die Mitbestimmung', *Forschungsjournal neue soziale Bewegungen*, vol. 3, no. 1, p. 10–17.

1990. 'Gesellschaft als technisches Labor', *Gewerkschaftliche Monatshefte*, vol. 41, no. 1, pp. 26–33.

1990. 'Engagierte Skepsis: Heinz Hartmann zum 60. Geburtstag', *Soziale Welt*, vol. 41, no. 1, pp. 5–7.

1990. 'Eugenik der Zukunft', in Denger, J. (ed.), *Plädoyer für das Leben mongoloider Kinder: Down-Syndrom und pränatale Diagnostik*. Stuttgart: Verlag Freies Geistesleben.

1990. 'Von Überleben in der Risikogesellschaft', in Schüz, M. (ed.), *Risiko und Wagnis: Die Herausforderung der industriellen Welt, vol. 2*. Pfullingen: Neske, Gerling Akademie.

1990. 'Von der Industriegesellschaft zur Risikogesellschaft: Überlebensfragen, Sozialstruktur und ökologische Aufklärung', in Cremer, W. and Klein, A. (eds.), *Umbrüche in der Industriegesellschaft: Herausforderungen für die politische Bildung, vol. 284*. Bonn: Bundeszentrale für Politische Bildung.

1990. 'Die Welt als Labor: Wer die Gesellschaft zum Labor macht, öffnet die Wissenschaft für die Mitbestimmung', in Arbeitskreis deutscher Bildungsstätten (ed.), *Außerschulische Bildung, Materialien zur politischen Jugend- und Erwachsenenbildung, no. 3*. Bonn: Arbeitskreis deutscher Bildungsstätten.

1990. 'Der ökologische Gesellschaftskonflikt', *Forum Wissenschaft*, vol. 7, no. 3, pp. 4–8.

1990. 'Der ökologische Gesellschaftskonflikt', *WSI-Mitteilungen, Zeitschrift des Wirtschafts- und Sozialwissenschaftlichen Instituts des Deutschen Gewerkschaftsbundes*, vol. 43. no. 12, pp. 750–755.

1990. 'Arbeit und Ökologie: Ein Diskussionsbeitrag', in Lösche, P. (ed.), *Göttinger Sozialwissenschaften heute: Fragestellungen, Methoden, Inhalte*. Göttingen: Vandenhoeck & Ruprecht.

1990. 'Die organisierte Unverantwortlichkeit', in Schaeffer, R. (ed.), *Ist die technisch-wissenschaftliche Zukunft demokratisch beherrschbar? Beiträge zum Kongress der Heinrich Böll-Stiftung*.

1990. 'Auf dem Weg in eine andere Moderne', *Forschung Frankfurt*, vol. 3, pp. 41–42.

1990. 'Die irdische Religion der Liebe', *Frankfurter Allgemeine Magazin*, 12 April, pp. 52–70.

1990. 'Anforderungen an gewerkschaftliche Technologiepolitik aus der Perspektive der Risikogesellschaft', *WSI Mitteilungen, Zeitschrift des Wirtschafts- und Sozialwissenschaftlichen Instituts des Deutschen Gewerkschaftsbundes*, vol. 43, no. 12.

1990. 'Risikogesellschaft: Überlebensfragen, Sozialstruktur und ökologische Aufklärung', in Bund für Umwelt und Naturschutz Deutschland e.V. (ed.), *Projekt GLOBUS 2*. Karlsruhe: FZKA.

1990. 'Der Konflikt der zwei Modernen', in Wissenschaftszentrum Nordrhein-Westfalen, KulturWissenschaftliches Institut (ed.), *Das Gründungsjahr*. Yearly report. Essen.

1990. 'Jenseits von Frauen- und Männerrolle oder: Die Zukunft der Familie', in Sloterdijk, P. (ed.), *Vor der Jahrtausendwende: Berichte zur Lage der Zukunft*. Frankfurt am Main: Suhrkamp.

1991. 'Der Konflikt der zwei Modernen', in Zapf, W. (ed.), *Die Modernisierung moderner Gesellschaften*. Frankfurt am Main: Campus Verlag.

1991. 'Der Konflikt der zwei Modernen', *Kölner Zeitschrift für Soziologie und Sozialpsychologie*, vol. 43, no. 1, pp. 193–202.

1991. 'Chancen einer Zwischenpolitik. Beobachtungen zum Strukturwandel der Opposition: Ein Gespräch zwischen Ulrich Beck und Frank Deppe', *Blätter für deutsche und internationale Politik*, vol. 36, no. 4, pp. 402–424.

1991. 'Die Soziologie und die ökologische Frage', *Berliner Journal für Soziologie*, vol. 1, no. 3, pp. 331–341.

1991. 'Opposition in Deutschland', in Giesen, B. and Leggewie, C. (eds.), *Experiment Vereinigung: Ein sozialer Großversuch*. Berlin: Rotbuch Verlag.

1991. 'Politik in der Risikogesellschaft', in Schabedoth, H. J. (ed.), *Gestalten und Verwalten: Aktive Mitbestimmung bei Arbeit und Technik*. Cologne: Bund Verlag.

1991. 'Umweltpolitik in der Risikogesellschaft', *Zeitschrift für angewandte Umweltforschung*, vol. 4, no. 2, pp. 117–122.

1991. 'Die Grünen in der Weltrisikogesellschaft', in Fücks, R. (ed.), *Sind die Grünen noch zu retten?* Reinbek bei Hamburg: Rowohlt.

1991. 'Die Frage nach der anderen Moderne', *Deutsche Zeitschrift für Philosophie*, vol. 39, no. 12, pp. 1297–1308.

1991. 'Jenseits von Frauen- und Männerrolle – oder: Die Zukunft der Familie', *Universitas, Zeitschrift für Wissenschaft, Kunst und Litteratur*, vol. 46, no. 1, pp. 1–9.

1992. 'Der Konflikt der zwei Modernen: Vom ökologischen und sozialen Umbau der Risikogesellschaft', in Gängler, H. and Rauschenbach, T. (ed.), *Soziale Arbeit und Erziehung in der Risikogesellschaft*. Neuwied, Berlin: Luchterhand.

1992. 'Die vertraute Katastrophe', in Hoesch-AG (ed.), *Unsere Welt ist die Erde*. Dortmund: Hoesch-AG.

1992. 'Subpolitik: Der Machtzerfall der Institutionen', *Internationale katholische Zeitschrift 'Communio'*, vol. 21, no. 5, pp. 438–453.

1992. 'Die Renaissance des Politischen', *Gewerkschaftliche Monatshefte*, vol. 10, no. 43, pp. 596–607.

1992. 'Der feindlose Staat: Militär und Demokratie nach dem Ende des Kalten Krieges', in Unseld, S. (ed.), *Politik ohne Projekt? Nachdenken über Deutschland*. Frankfurt am Main: Suhrkamp. Also published in Schäfer, B. (ed.), *Lebensverhältnisse und soziale Konflikte im neuen Europa*. Frankfurt am Main: Campus Verlag.

1992. 'Risikogesellschaft', in *Brockhaus Enzyklopädie* (19th edn). Mannheim: F. A. Brockhaus.

1993. 'Risikogesellschaft und Vorsorgestaat: Zwischenbilanz einer Diskussion', in Ewald, F. (ed.), *Der Vorsorgestaat*. Frankfurt am Main: Suhrkamp.

1993. 'Abschied von der Abstraktionsidylle', *Politische Ökologie*, vol. 31, pp. 20–24.

1993. 'Subpolitik: Der Machtzerfall der Institutionen', in Hohl, J. and Reisbeck, G. (ed.), *Individuum, Lebenswelt, Gesellschaft*. Munich: Profil Verlag.

1993. 'Von der Industriegesellschaft zur Risikogesellschaft', in Göhner, R. (ed.), *Die Gesellschaft für morgen*. Munich: R. Pieper & Co.

1993. 'Nicht Autonomie, sondern Bastelbiographie. Anmerkungen zur Individualisierungsdiskussion am Beispiel des Aufsatzes von Günter Burkart', *Zeitschrift für Soziologie*, vol. 22, no. 3, pp. 178–187. With E. Beck-Gernsheim.

1993. 'Von einer kritischen Theorie der Gesellschaft zu einer Theorie gesellschaftlicher Selbstkritik', *Sozialwissenschaftliche Literatur Rundschau*, vol. 16, no. 26, pp. 38–53.

1993. 'Was ihr wollt', in Kaever, K. (ed.), *Abschied vom 20. Jahrhundert: Ein Lesebuch*. Munich: C. H. Beck.

1993. 'Die Zukunft der Familie', in Niedergesäss, B. and Werner-Rosen, K. (ed.), *Wohin mit unseren Kleinsten: Kinder unter drei Jahren zwischen Familie und öffentlicher Erziehung*. Hamburg: Dagmar Dreves Verlag.

1993. 'Risiko, Risikogesellschaft', in Enderle, G. (ed.), *Lexikon der Wirtschaftsethik*. Freiburg im Breisgau: Herder.

1993. 'Vom Verschwinden der Solidarität', in von Berenberg, H. and Wagenbach, K. (ed.), *Kopfnuss: Essays über Kultur und Politik*. Berlin: Verlag Klaus Wagenbach.

1993. 'Fragen und Dimensionen sozialwissenschaftlicher Risikoanalyse', in Huber, J. and Thurn, G. (ed.) *Wissenschaftsmilieus: Wissenschaftskontroversen und soziokulturelle Konflikte*. Berlin: Rainer Bohn Verlag.

1993. 'Auflösung der Gesellschaft? Theorie gesellschaftlicher Individualisierung revisited', in Lenzen, D. (ed.), *Verbindungen: Vorträge anlässlich der Ehrenpromotion von Klaus Mollenhauer an der FU Berlin am 15.1.1993*. Weinheim: Deutscher Studien Verlag.

1993. 'Ökologischer Machiavellismus? Wie die ökologische zur politischen Frage wird', in Altner, G., Mettler-Meibom, B., Simonis, U. E. and von Weizsäcker, E. V. (eds.), *Jahrbuch Ökologie 1994*. Munich: C. H. Beck.

1993. 'Die Industriegesellschaft: Jenseits von Verantwortung?', in Heller, G. (ed.), *Grundkurs Philosophie*. Munich: Bayerischer Schulbuchverlag.

1993. 'Zurück in die Zukunft', *Der Spiegel*, vol. 47, no. 47, pp. 56–61.

1993. 'Politische Wissenstheorie der Risikogesellschaft', in Bechmann, G. (ed.), *Risiko und Gesellschaft: Grundlagen und Ergebnisse interdisciplinärer Risikoforschung*. Opladen: Westdeutsche Verlag.

1993. 'Bindungsverlust und Zukunftsangst: Leben in der Risikogesellschaft', in *Gegenwartskunde.Zeitschrift für Gesellschaft, Statt und Erziehung*, vol. 42, no. 4, pp. 463–468.

1993. 'Replik', *Gegenwartskunde*, vol. 42, no. 4, pp. 475–478.

1994. 'Kleine Anleitung zum ökologischen Machiavellismus auf dem Weg in die ökologische Demokratie', in von Arnim, G. (ed.), *Politiklust*. Munich: Knaur.

1994. 'Vom Verschwinden der Solidarität: Individualisierung der Gesellschaft heißt Verschärfung sozialer Ungleichheit', in Warnfried, D. (ed.), *Perspektiven für Deutschland*. Munich: Knaur.

1994. 'Bindungsverlust und Zukunftsangst: Leben in der Risikogesellschaft', in Hartwich, H.-W. (ed.), *Bindungsverlust und Zukunftsangst: Leben in der Risikogesellschaft*. Opladen: Leske und Budrich.

1994. 'Replik', in Hartwich, H.-W. (ed.), *Bindungsverlust und Zukunftsangst: Leben in der Risikogesellschaft*. Opladen: Leske und Budrich.

1994. 'Schlussworte', in Hartwich, H.-W. (ed.), *Bindungsverlust und Zukunftsangst: Leben in der Risikogesellschaft*. Opladen: Leske und Budrich.

1994. 'Reflexive Modernisierung: Bemerkungen zu einer Diskussion', in Noller, Peter *et al.* (ed.), *Stadt – Welt: Über die Globalisierung städtischer Milieus*. Frankfurt: Campus Verlag.

1994. 'Freiheit für die Technik! Plädoyer für eine zweite Gewaltenteilung', in Fricke, E. (ed.), *Jahrbuch Arbeit und Technik 1994*. Bonn: Verlag J. H.W. Dietz Nachf. Also in Tinnefeld, M.-T., Philipps, L. and Weis, K. (eds.), *Institutionen und Einzelne im Zeitalter der Informationstechnik*. Munich: Oldenbourg.

1994. 'Angst vor der Freiheit', *Der Spiegel*, no. 38, pp. 248–250.

1994. 'Renaissance des Politischen: Oder Widersprüche des Konservatismus', in Leggewie, C. (ed.), *Wozu Politikwissenschaft? Über das Neue in der Politik*. Darmstadt: Wissenschaftliche Buchgesellschaft.

1994. 'Nationale Gegenmodernisierung: Zur Soziologie von Feindbildern nach dem Ende des Ost-West-Konflikts', *Mittelweg 36, Zeitschrift des Hamburger Instituts für Sozialforschung*, vol. 3, no. 4, pp. 11–23.

1994. 'Grüner Machiavellismus', in von Berenberg, H. and Wagenbach, K. (ed.), *Kopfnuss 2: Essays über Kultur und Politik*. Berlin: Verlag Klaus Wagenbach.

1994. '"Die Ökologie ist ein neues Sinnsystem": Ein Gespräch mit Ulrich Beck', *Psychologie Heute*, vol. 21, no. 10, pp. 31–33.

1994. 'Vom Veralten sozialwissenschaftlicher Begriffe: Grundzüge einer Theorie reflexiver Modernisierung', in Görg, C. (ed.), *Gesellschaft im Übergang: Perspektiven kritischer Soziologie*. Darmstadt: Wissenschaftliche Buchhaltung.

1994. 'Auch der Westen verschwindet . . .', in Kohler, G. and Meyer, M. (ed.), *Die Folgen von 1989*. Munich: Carl Hanser.

1994. 'Leben in der Risikogesellschaft', in Pluskwa, M. and Matzen, J. (ed.), *Lernen in und an der Risikogesellschaft: Analysen – Orientierungen – Vermittlungswege*. Bederkesa: Ev. Heimvolkshochschule.

1994. 'Eine andere Moderne', in *Evangelische Kommentare, Monatsschrift zum Zeitgeschehen in Kirche und Gesellschaft*, vol. 4, pp. 222–226.

1994. 'Eine Prise Machiavellismus für die fade Ökologie', *Natur*, vol. 4, pp. 106–108.

1994. 'Biedermänner und Brandstifter', in Bade, K. J. (ed.), *Aktuell-Kontrovers 1994: Ausländer, Aussiedler, Asyl in der Bundesrepublik Deutschland*. Hanover: Landeszentrale für Politische Bildung.

1994. 'Hin und wieder ins Wasser blicken', in Unseld, S. (ed.), *Der Verleger und seine Autoren*. Frankfurt am Main: Suhrkamp.

1994. 'Erwiderungen', in *Mittelweg*, vol. 36, no. 3, pp. 37–42.

1995. 'Vom Verschwinden der Solidarität', in Keupp, H. (ed.), *Lust an der Erkenntnis: Der Mensch als Soziales Wesen: Sozialpsychologisches Denken im 20. Jahrhundert*. Zurich: Piper-Verlag.

1995. 'Befreiung von der Technik: Befreiung der Technik?', *Monatsmagazin für neue Politik*, vol. 1, no. 5, pp. 26–28.

1995. 'Jenseits des Versicherbaren', *Schweizerische Technische Zeitschrift*, vol. 92, no. 4, pp. 17–20.

1995. 'Zur politischen Dynamik globaler Gefahren', *Natur*, vol. 12, pp. 52–53.

1995. 'Wie aus Nachbarn Juden werden: Zur politischen Konstruktion des Fremden in der reflexiven Moderne', in Miller, M. and Soeffner, H. G. (ed.), *Modernisierung und Barbarei*. Frankfurt am Main: Suhrkamp.

1995. 'Eigenes Leben, eigener Tod', in Beck, R. (ed.), *Der Tod*. Munich: C. H. Beck.

1995. 'Die "Individualisierungsdebatte"', in Schäfers, B. (ed.), *Soziologie in Deutschland*. Opladen: Leske und Budrich.

1995. 'Das Fünf-Minuten-vor-Zwölf-Gefühl: Utopie der Selbstbegrenzung', in von Berenberg, H. and Wagenbach, K. (ed.), *Kopfnuss 3: Essays über Kultur und Politik*. Berlin: K. Wagenbach.

1995. 'In Sprachruinen: Die Trümmerlandschaft der Ost-West-Ordnung', in Henkel, G. (ed.), *Les Beaux Restes: Bilder der Vergänglichkeit*. Munich: Münchner Stadtmuseum.

1995. 'Politisierung des Risikos: Zur Technik- und Technokratiekritik in der reflexiven Moderne', *Politische Ökologie*, vol. 13, special issue no. 7, pp. 56–62.

1995. 'Utopie der Selbstbegrenzung: Gedanken zur Zukunftsfähigkeit und Zukunftsgestaltung', *Ästhetik und Kommunikation*, vol. 24, no. 89, pp. 27–30.

1995. 'Weltrisikogesellschaft: Zur politischen Dynamik globaler Gefahren', *Internationale Politik*, vol. 50, no. 8, pp. 13–20.

1995. 'Vier-Sterne-Soziologie', *Kölner Zeitschrift für Soziologie und Sozialpsychologie*, vol. 47, no. 1, pp. 196–197.

1995. 'Individualisierung im Sozialismus? Zum "System-Missverständnis" im deutsch–deutschen Dialog', in Bögenhold, D. (ed.), *Soziale Welt und Soziologische Praxis: Soziologie als Beruf und Programm – Festschrift für Heinz Hartmann zum 65. Geburtstag.* Göttingen: O. Schwartz & Co.

1995. 'Risiko Stadt: Architektur in der reflexiven Moderne', in Schwarz, U. (ed.), *Risiko Stadt? Perspektiven der Urbanität.* Hamburg: Junius.

1996. 'Die Angst vor der Freiheit', in Bayerischer Städtetag (ed.), *Stadtvisionen.* Munich: Bayerischer Städtetag.

1996. 'Weltrisikogesellschaft, Weltöffentlichkeit und globale Subpolitik: Ökologische Fragen im Bezugsrahmen fabrizierter Unsicherheiten', *Kölner Zeitschrift für Soziologie und Sozialpsychologie*, vol. 36, special issue: 'Umweltsoziologie', pp. 119–147.

1996. 'Die Subpolitik der Globalisierung: Die neue Macht der multinationalen Unternehmen', *Gewerkschaftliche Monatshefte*, vol. 47, no. 11–12, pp. 673–680.

1996. 'Was hält hochindividualisierte Gesellschaften zusammen?', *Mittelweg 36*, vol. 5, no. 1, pp. 33–48.

1996. 'Das "eigene Leben" in die eigene Hand Nehmen', *Pädagogik*, vol. 48, no. 7–8, pp. 40–47.

1996. 'Weltbürgergesellschaft: Individuelle Akteure und die Zukunftfähigkeit der modernen Gesellschaft', in Fricke, E. (ed.), *Jahrbuch Arbeit und Technik 1996: Zukunft der Industriegesellschaft.* Bonn: Dietz Verlag.

1996. 'Demokratisierung der Familie', in Buba, H. P. and Schneider, N. F. (ed.), *Familie: Zwischen gesellschaftlicher Prägung und individuellem Design.* Opladen: Westdeutscher Verlag.

1996. 'Politisierung des Risikos: Zur Technik- und Technokratiekritik in der reflexiven Moderne', in Königswieser, H. and Maas, J. (ed.), *Risiko-Dialog: Zukunft ohne Harmonieformel.* Cologne: Deutscher Instituts-Verlag.

1996. 'Kapitalismus ohne Arbeit', *Der Spiegel*, no. 20, pp. 140–146.

1996. 'Der clevere Bürger: Bemerkungen zu Anthony Giddens' Konzeption "reflexiver Modernisierung"', *Soziologische Revue: Besprechungen neuer Literatur*, vol. 19, no. 1, pp. 3–28.

1996. 'Die Gesellschaft wird politischer', *Das Baugerüst*, no. 3, pp. 28–32.

1996. 'Arbeit und Solidarität in der Globalisierungsfalle', *Gewerkschaftliche Monatshefte*, vol. 47, no. 11–12, pp. 673–800.

1996. 'Technikethik als Risikoethik: Ansatze einer sozialethischen Risikobeurteilungen', *Jahrbuch für christliche Sozialwissenschaften*, vol. 37, pp. 29–50.

1996. 'Das Fünf-Minuten-vor-Zwölf-Gefühl oder die Utopie der Selbstbegrenzung', in Thierse, W. (ed.), *Ist die Politik noch zu retten? Standpunkte am Ende des 20. Jahrhunderts.* Berlin: Aufbau-Verlag.

1996. 'Kapitalismus ohne Arbeit', in Stiftung Mitarbeiter, Bundesarbeitsgemeinschaft Freiwilligenagenten (ed.), *Zukunftfähige Gesellschaft: Demokratische Entscheidungen für eine dauerhaft tragfähige Gesellschaft.* Bonn: Stiftung Mitarbeiter, Bundesarbeitsgemeinschaft Freiwilligenagenten.

1997. 'Natur als Utopie', in Wang, A. (ed.), *Gedanken zur Zeit, Rundfunkessays 1949–1997.* Frankfurt am Main: Fischer Taschenbuch Verlag.

1997. 'Missverstehen als Fortschritt: Europäische Intellektuelle im Zeitalter der Globalisierung', in Kufeld, K. (ed.), *Zukunft gestalten: Reden und Beiträge zum Ernst-Bloch-Preis 1997*. Mössingen-Talheim: Talheimer Verlag.

1997. 'Die Eröffnung des Welthorizontes: Zur Soziologie der Globalisierung', *Soziale Welt, Zeitschrift für Sozialwissenschaftliche Forschung und Praxis*, vol. 48, no. 1, pp. 3–17.

1997. 'Was hält moderne, individualisierte Gesellschaften zusammen? Politische Freiheit als Sinnquelle der Moderne', in Voss, G. and Pongratz, H. (ed.), *Subjektorientierte Soziologie: Karl Martin Bolte zum siebzigsten Geburtstag*. Opladen: Leske + Budrich.

1997. 'Risikopolitik', *Soziologische Revue*, vol. 20, no. 4, pp. 467–469.

1997. 'Weltrisikogesellschaft, ökologische Krise und Technologiepolitik', *Politische Bildung: Beiträge zur Wissenschaftlichen Grundlegung und zur Unterrichtspraxis*, vol. 30, no. 2, pp. 55–77. Also in Massing, P. (ed.), *Gesellschaft neu verstehen: Aktuelle Gesellschaftstheorien und Zeitdiagnosen*. Schwalbach am Taunus: Wochenschau-Verlag.

1997. 'Wieviel Moderne verträgt die Demokratie? Politische Bildung in einer unsicheren Welt', *Widerspruch: Beiträge zur sozialistischen Politik*, vol. 17, no. 33, pp. 103–115. Also in *Forum Politikunterricht*, vol. 10, no. 2, pp. 16–33.

1997. 'Die vertraute Katastrophe: Das unkalkulierbare Risiko wird zur Gewohnheit', in Liebert, W. and Schmithals, F. (eds.), *Tschernobyl und kein Ende? Argumente für den Ausstieg: Szenarien für Alternativen*. Münster: Agenda Verlag.

1997. 'Die Subpolitik der Globalisierung', *Raum & Zeit*, vol. 16, no. 88, pp. 31–35.

1997. 'Kapitalismus ohne Arbeit', *Bankspiegel*, vol. 2, no. 162, pp. 6–10.

1997. 'Für eine neue Moderne', *Socialmanagement*, vol. 7, no. 4, pp. 32–33.

1997. 'Die uneindeutige Sozialstruktur: Was heisst Armut, was Reichtum in der "Selbst-Kultur"', in Beck, U. and Sopp, P. (eds.), *Individualisierung und Integration Neue Konfliktlinien und neuer Integrationsmodus?*. Opladen: Leske und Budrich.

1997. 'Aufbruch in die Zweite Moderne', in Bissinger, M. (ed.), *Stimmen gegen den Stillstand*. Hamburg: Hoffmann und Campe.

1997. 'Zukunft der Arbeit: Arbeit der Zukunft', *Kulturchronik*, vol. 15, no. 2, pp. 49–51.

1997. 'Von der Risiko- zur Möglichkeitsgesellschaft: Telepolis-Gespräch mit dem Soziologen Ulrich Beck', *Telepolis: Die Zeitschrift der Netzkultur*, no. 1, pp. 93–107.

1997. 'Subjektorientierte Berufstheorie', in Arnold, R. (ed.), *Ausgewählte Theorien zur beruflichen Bildung*. Baltmannsweiler: Schneider Verlag, Hohengehren. With M. Brater and H.-J. Daheim.

1997. 'Wie wird Lachen zwischen den Kulturen möglich?', *Lettre International*, vol. 39, no. 4, p. 7.

1997. 'Erwerbsarbeit durch Bürgerarbeit ergänzen', in Kommission für Zukunftsfragen der Freistaaten Bayern und Sachsen (ed.), *Arbeitslosigkeit in Deutschland: Entwicklung, Ursache und Maßnahmen. Part III*, Bonn: Bayerische Staatsregierung.

1997. 'Dem Kapitalismus geht die Arbeit aus: Das Ende der Vollbeschäftigung und öffentliche Arbeit', *Vorwärts: Brennpunkt*, July/August, p. 12. With G. Schröder.

1998. 'Die Seele der Demokratie', *Gewerkschaftliche Monatshefte*, vol. 49, no. 6–7, pp. 330–335.

1998. 'Gesamtkunstwerk Ich', in von Dülmer, R. (ed.), *Erfindung des Menschen, Schöpfungsträume und Körperbilder 1500–2000*. Vienna: Böhlau Verlag.

1998. 'Ein kosmopolitisches Manifest für die postnationale Gesellschaft', *WFM (World Federalist Movement) News*, vol. 11, no. 4, pp. 5–7.

1998. 'Europa als Antwort auf die Globalisierung', in Jörges, H.-U. (ed.), *Der Kampf um den Euro: Wie riskant ist die Währungsunion?* Hamburg: Hoffmann und Campe.

1998. 'Soziologische Aspekte: Demokratisierung der Familie', in Palentien, C. and Hurrelmann, K. (eds.), *Jugend und Politik: ein Handbuch für Forschung, Lehre und Praxis*. Neuwied: H. Luchterhand.

1998. 'Abschied von der Arbeit', in Hammerschmidt, U. and Kleditzsche, T. (eds.), *Im Gespräch: Menschen – Meinungen – Interviews, vol. 2*. Chemnitzer: Chemnitzer Verlag.

1998. 'Neubestimmung der Arbeit: Die Zukunft der Arbeit (auch) in München', in Münchner Agenda 21 (ed.), *Zukunftsfähiges München: Ein gemeinsames Projekt Müncher Bürgerinnen und Bürger*. Munich: Ökom Verlag.

1998. 'Die Politik der Technik: Weltrisikogesellschaft und ökologische Krise', in Rammert, W. (ed.), *Technik und Sozialtheorie*. Frankfurt am Main: Campus.

1998. 'Die Sozialmoral des eigenen Lebens', in Lüschen, G. (ed.), *Das Moralische in der Soziologie*. Wiesbaden: Westdeutscher Verlag.

1998. 'Wie wird Demokratie im Zeitalter der Globalisierung möglich? Eine Einleitung', in Beck, U. (ed.), *Politik der Globalisierung*. Frankfurt am Main: Suhrkamp.

1998. 'Vorwort', in von Pries, L. (ed.), *Betrieblicher Wandel in der Risikogesellschaft: empirische Befunde und konzeptionelle Überlegungen*. Munich: Hampp.

1998. 'Thesen für eine umfassende Bildungsreform', in Dieckmann, H. and Schachtsiek, B. (eds.), *Lernkonzepte im Wandel: die Zukunft der Bildung*. Stuttgart: Klett-Cotta.

1998. 'Freiwillig, aber nicht umsonst', *Politische Ökologie (Zeitschrift für Theorie, Praxis, Diskussion und Dokumentation Ökologischer Politik)*, vol. 54, pp. 61–64.

1998. 'Das Demokratie-Dilemma im Zeitalter der Globalisierung', *Aus Politik und Zeitgeschichte*, B38, 11 September, pp. 3–11. (Special section of the newspaper *Das Parlament*).

1998. 'Wider das Lamento über den Werteverfall', A*viso, Zeitschrift für Wissenschaft und Kunst in Bayern*, vol. 2, pp. 11–14.

1998. 'Stadtpolitik neu erfinden'; 'Die Region ist das Besondere'; 'Botengänger eines tief-ergehenden Wandels'; 'Wir leben längst in einer Weltgesellschaft'; and 'Wer ist reich, was ist arm?', in Eisenschink, N. (ed.), *So gesehen . . . Dulsberg: Seine Menschen, seine Gebäude*. Hamburg: Dölling und Galitz.

1998. 'Globalisierung als Herausforderung', *Telepolis: Die Zeitschrift der Netzkultur*, no. 4–5, pp. 17–35.

1999. 'Die Zukunft der Arbeit oder die politische Ökonomie der Unsicherheit', *Berliner Journal für Soziologie*, vol. 9, no. 4, pp. 467–478.

1999. 'Die Arbeitsgesellschaft als Risikogesellschaft', *Gewerkschaftliche Monatshefte*, vol. 50, no. 7–8, pp. 414–418.

1999. 'Denk ich an Deutschland . . .', in Hoffmeister, B. and Naumann, U. (eds.), *Was die Republik bewegte*. Reinbeck: Rowohlt.

1999. 'Das Modell der Bürgerarbeit', *Politische Studien: Zweimonatsschrift für Politik und Zeitgeschehen*, vol. 50, no. 366, pp. 119–131.

1999. 'Die Risikogesellschaft: "Auf dem Weg in eine andere Moderne"', in Pongs, A. (ed.), *In welcher Gesellschaft leben wir eigentlich? Gesellschaftskonzepte im Vergleich*. Munich: Dilemma-Verlag.

1999. 'Identitätsprobleme bei einer neuen Kultur des Genusses', in Behringer, W. (ed.), *Europa: Ein historisches Lesebuch*. Munich: C. H. Beck.

1999. 'Globalisierung als Unterscheidungsmerkmal der Zweiten Moderne', *Soziale Welt*, vol. 50, no. 13, pp. 535–549.

1999. 'Über den postnationalen Krieg', *Blätter für deutsche und internationale Politik*, vol. 44, no. 8, pp. 984–990.

1999. 'Ortsbestimmungen der Soziologie: Wie die kommende Generation Gesellschaftswissenschaften betreiben will', *Soziale Welt: Zeitschrift für sozialwissenschaftliche Forschung und Praxis*, vol. 50, no. 4, pp. 343–349.

1999. 'Diese ewige Jammerede', in von Glaser, H. (ed.), *Die Mauer fiel, die Mauer steht: Ein Lesebuch*. Munich: Deutsche Verlag.

1999. 'Wie wir in Zukunft arbeiten werden', in von Bonin, K. and Gidion, A. (ed.), *Deutscher evangelischer Kirchentag, Stuttgart, 1999: Dokumente*. Gütersloh: Gütersloher Verlagshaus.

1999. 'Globalisierung', in Schneider, W. (ed.), *Hundert Wörter des Jahrhunderts*. Frankfurt am Main: Suhrkamp.

1999. 'Transnationale Bürgergesellschaft oder: Wie wird politisches Handeln im Zeitalter der Globalisierung möglich?', in Sekretariat für Zukunftforschung und Gesellschaft für Zukunftsgestaltung (ed.), *Zukünfte 27, Zukunftprojekt B*. Gelsenkirchen: Sekretariat für Zukunftforschung und Gesellschaft für Zukunftsgestaltung.

1999. 'Fremde: Ambivalenz als Existenz', in Schubert, V. (ed.), *Fremde: Migration und Asyl*. St Ottilien: EOS Verlag.

1999. 'Weltbürger aller Länder vereinigt euch! Thesen für ein kosmopolitisches Manifest', in Kuschel, K. J., Pinzani, A. and Zillinger, M. (eds.), *Ein Ethos für eine Welt? Globalisierung als ethische Herausforderung*. Frankfurt am Main: Campus.

2000. 'Die Reflexivität der Zweiten Moderne', in Schönherr-Mann, H.-M. (ed.), *Ethik des Denkens*. Munich: Fink Verlag.

2000. 'Zur politischen Dynamik von Risikokonflikten (Risikogesellschaft)', in Lamnek, P. and Tinnefeld, M.-T. (ed.), *Zeit und kommunikative Rechtskultur in Europa*. Baden-Baden: Nomos.

2000. 'Über den postnationalen Krieg', in Merkel, R. (ed.), *Das Kosovo-Krieg und das Völkerrecht*. Frankfurt am Main: Suhrkamp.

2001. 'Theorie reflexiver Modernisierung: Fragestellungen, Hypothesen, Forschungsprogramme', in Beck, U., Lau, C. and Bonß, W. (eds.), *Die Modernisierung der Moderne*. Frankfurt am Main: Suhrkamp. With C. Lau and W. Bonß.

2001. 'Nebenfolgen als Problem soziologischer Theoriebildung', in Beck, U., Lau, C. and Bonß, W. (ed.), *Die Modernisierung der Moderne*. Frankfurt am Main: Suhrkamp. With B. Holzer and A. Kieserling.

2001. 'Gewusstes Nicht-Wissen und seine rechtlichen und politischen Folgen: Das Beispiel der Humangenetik', in Beck, U., Lau, C. and Bonß, W. (eds.), *Die Modernisierung der Moderne*. Frankfurt am Main: Suhrkamp. With P. May.

2001. 'Das Zeitalter des "eigenen Lebens"', *Das Parlament: Aus Politik und Zeitgeschichte*, 13 July, pp. 3–6.

2001. 'Der häßliche Bürger', in Brosziewski, A., Eberle, T. S. and Maeder, C. (eds.), *Moderne*. Konstanz: UVK Verlagsgesellschaft.

2001. 'Mehr Zivilcourage bitte: Ein Vorschlag an die Adresse Gerhard Schröders', in Fiebig, J. (ed.), *Abschied vom Egokult: Die neue soziale Offenheit*. Krummwisch, Kiel: Königsfurt Verlag.

2002. 'Das Zeitalter des "eigenen Lebens"', *dvb-forum*, no. 1, pp. 48–52.

2003. 'Kosmopolitische Globalisierung: Die schöpferische Selbstzerstörung der Weltordnung', *Internationale Politik*, vol. 58, no. 7, pp. 9–13.

2003. 'Weltrisikogesellschaft revisited: Die terroristische Bedrohung', in Hitzler, R. and Reichertz, J. (eds.), *Irritierte Ordnung: Die gesellschaftliche Verarbeitung von Terror*. Konstanz: UVK Verlagsgesellschaft.

2004. 'Entgrenzung erzwingt Entscheidung: Was ist neu an der Theorie reflexiver Modernisierung?', in Beck, U. and Lau, C. (eds.), *Entgrenzung und Entscheidung: Was ist neu an der Theorie reflexiver Modernisierung?* Frankfurt am Main: Suhrkamp. With W. Bonß and C. Lau.

2004. 'Reflexivität und Reflexion', in Beck, U. and Lau, C. (eds.), *Entgrenzung und Entscheidung: Was ist neu an der Theorie reflexiver Modernisierung?* Frankfurt am Main: Suhrkamp. With B. Holzer.

2004. 'Wie global ist die Weltrisikogesellschaft?', in Beck, U. and Lau, C. (eds.), *Entgrenzung und Entscheidung: Was ist neu an der Theorie reflexiver Modernisierung?* Frankfurt am Main: Suhrkamp. With B. Holzer.

2004. 'Erinnerung und Vergebung in der Zweiten Moderne', in Beck, U. and Lau, C. (eds.), *Entgrenzung und Entscheidung: Was ist neu an der Theorie reflexiver Modernisierung?* Frankfurt am Main: Suhrkamp. With D. Levy and N. Sznaider.

2005. 'Theorie und Empirie reflexiver Modernisierung: Von der Notwendigkeit und den Schwierigkeiten, einen historischen Gesellschaftswandel innerhalb der Moderne zu beobachten und zu begreifen', *Soziale Welt: Zeitschrift für Socialwissenschaftliche Forschung und Praxis*, vol. 56, no. 2–3, pp. 107–135.

2005. 'Das kosmopolitische Empire: Ein Plädoyer für ein Europa jenseits des Nationalstaates', *Internationale Politik: Europa neu denken!*, vol. 60, no. 7, pp. 6–12.

2005. 'Empire Europa: Politische Herrschaft jenseits von Bundesstaat und Staatenbund', *Zeitschrift für Politik*, vol. 52, no. 4, pp. 397–420. With E. Grande.

2005. 'Europas letzte Chance: Kosmopolitismus von unten', *Blätter für deutsche und internationale Politik*, vol. 9, pp. 1083–1097. With E. Grande.

2005. 'Europäisierung: Soziologie für das 21. Jahrhundert', *Aus Politik und Zeitgeschichte*, no. 34–35, pp. 3–11.

2007. 'Tragische Individualisierung', *Blätter für deutsche und internationale Politik*, vol. 5, 577–584.

2007. 'Weltreligionen, Weltkonflikte', *Die Religionen der Welt: Ein Almanach zur Eröffnung des Verlags der Weltreligionen*. Frankfurt am Main/Leipzig: Verlag der Weltreligionen im Insel Verlag.

2007. 'Generation global und die Falle des methodologischen Nationalismus: Für eine kosmopolitische Wende in der Jugend- und Generationssoziologie', in Villányi, D., Witte, M. D. and Sander, U. (eds.), *Globale Jugend und Jugendkulturen: Aufwachsen im Zeitalter der Globalisierung*. Weinheim: Juventa Verlag. With E. Beck-Gernsheim.

2007. 'Das wahre Europa verstehen: Eine kosmopolitische Vision', in Baasner, F. and Klett, M. (eds.), *Europa. Die Zukunft einer Idee.* Darmstadt: WGB (Wissenschaftliche Buchgesellschaft).

2007. 'Warum Europa?', in Schulte-Noelle, H. and Thoss. M. M. (eds.), *Abendland Unter: Reden über Europa*. Kreuzlingen: Diederichs.

2007. 'Die offene Stadt: Architektur in der reflexiven Moderne', in Baum, D. (ed.), *Die Stadt in der Sozialen Arbeit: Ein Handbuch für soziale und planende Berufe*. Wiesbaden: VS Verlag für Sozialwissenschaften.

2007. 'Und jetzt, Herr Beck?', in Geiselberger, H. (eds.), *Und jetzt? Politik, Protest und Propaganda*. Frankfurt am Main: Suhrkamp.

2007. 'Leben in der Weltrisikogesellschaft', in Beck, U. (ed.), *Generation Global: Ein Crashkurs*. Frankfurt am Main: Suhrkamp.

2007. 'Bevölkerungsentwicklung im kosmopolitischen Blick', in Beck, U. (ed.), *Generation Global: Ein Crashkurs.* Frankfurt am Main: Suhrkamp.

2007. 'Generation Global', in Beck, U. (ed.), *Generation Global: Ein Crashkurs.* Frankfurt am Main: Suhrkamp. With E. Beck-Gernsheim.

2008. 'Jenseits von Klasse und Nation: Individualisierung und Transnationalisierung sozialer Ungleichheiten', *Soziale Welt*, vol. 59, no. 4, pp. 301–325.

2008. 'Die 50-jährige Unbekannte: Europa ist kein Staat, keine Nation, keine Organisation. Um es zu verstehen brauchen wir neue Begriffe', *Internationale Politik: Die Ohnmacht der Mächtigen. Zukunftsmodelle für eine multipolare Welt*, vol. 63, no. 7–8, pp. 64–77.

2008. 'Risikogesellschaft und die Transnationalisierung sozialer Ungleichheiten', in Berger, P. A. and Weiß, A. (eds.), *Transnationalisierung sozialer Ungleichheit*. Wiesbaden: VS Verlag für Sozialwissenschaften.

2008. 'Familie', in Gosepath, S., Hinsch, W. and Rössler, B. (eds.), *Handbuch der Politischen Philosophie und Sozialphilosophie, vol. 1*. Berlin: de Gruyter. With E. Beck-Gernsheim.

2009. 'Das kosmopolitische Europa: Realität und Utopie', in Thoss, M. M. and Weiß, C. (eds.), *Das Ende der Gewissheiten: Reden über Europa*. Munich: Diederichs Verlag.

2009. 'Jenseits von Stand und Klasse? Soziale Ungleichheiten, gesellschaftliche Individualisierungsprozesse und die Entstehung neuer sozialer Formationen und Identitäten', in Solga, H., Powell, J. and Berger, P. A. (eds.), *Soziale Ungleichheit: Klassische Texte zur Sozialstrukturanalyse*. Frankfurt: Campus Verlag.

2009. 'Gott ist gefährlich. So human Religion auch scheinen mag: Sie birgt stets einen totalitären Kern. Fünf Thesen', in Kemper, P., Mentzer, A. and Sonnenschein, U. (eds.), *Wozu Gott? Religion zwischen Fundamentalismus und Fortschritt*. Frankfurt am Main: Verlag der Weltreligionen im Insel Verlag.

2010. 'Klima des Wandels oder Wie wird die grüne Moderne möglich?', in Welzer, H., Soeffner, H.-G. and Giesecke, D. (eds.), *KlimaKulturen: Soziale Wirklichkeiten im Klimawandel*. Frankfurt am Main: Campus Verlag.

2010. 'Jenseits des methodologischen Nationalismus. Außereuropäische und europäische Variationen der Zweiten Moderne', *Soziale Welt*, vol. 61, no. 3–4, special issue: 'Variationen der Zweiten Moderne', pp. 187–216. With E. Grande.

2011. 'Kooperieren oder scheitern: Die Existenzkrise der Europäischen Union', *Blätter für deutsche und Internationale Politik*, vol. 56, no. 2, pp. 41–53.

Index